Before, During and After the Falklands War:
Part II

Richard Stevens

Before, During and
After the Falklands War: Part II

Richard Stevens

ISBN 978-1-909660-79-3

A CIP catalogue record for this book
is available from the British Library.
Published 2017 Tricorn Books
131 High Street, Portsmouth, PO1 2HW

Printed & bound in the UK

I would like to dedicate this book to Toni for the computer expertise and stress counselling and to Caris and Liam to remind them of their heritage.

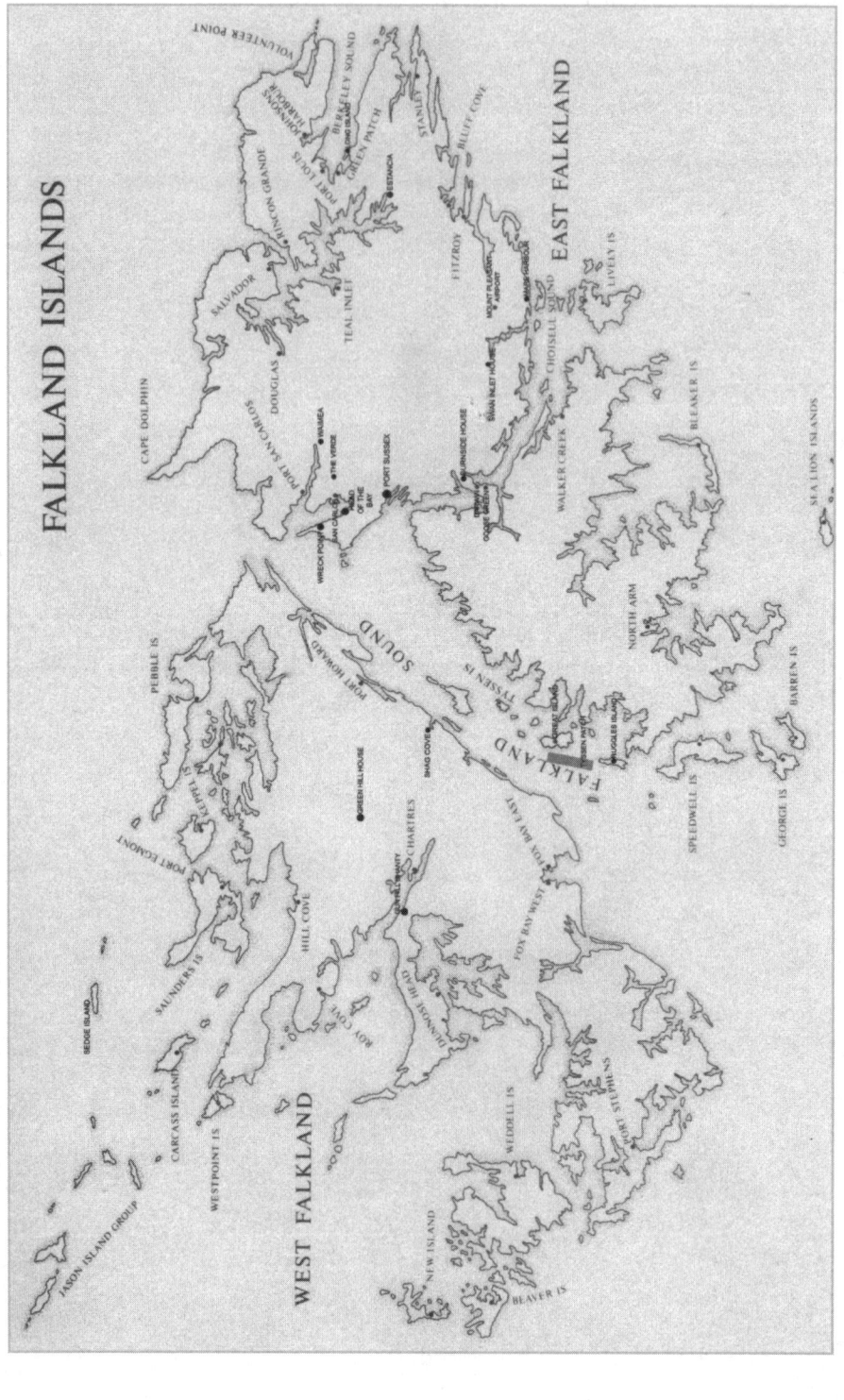

FALKLAND ISLANDS

Contents

INTRODUCTION

I was born in Plymouth and brought up in a small village in Kent. I was educated at a small village primary school in Cobham and then moved to a secondary modern in Longfield.

I didn't know what I wanted to do when I left full time education.

My father had commuted to London all the time we lived in Luddesdown (Kent) but I didn't fancy spending hours of my life doing the same.

I wanted to do something exciting so I worked for Kimberly-Clark to earn enough money to do a professional diving course. I did six weeks of boot camp at Fort Bovisand in Plymouth where ex-military divers bullied us through explosives, cutting with Kerry cable, (flexible thermic lance) underwater welding, a 50-metre dive and much more. I was too young however to work for any reputable firms in the North Sea oil industry.

I then worked on farms with a friend doing anything that was legal for money. We managed to rent a 60-acre field and grew barley but because we were so young, no bank would loan us the money for seed or fertilizer. A farm that we did work for loaned us the seed and fertilizer and we paid for it by working. This led to us working on farms all day and trying to do our land at night. I did a few nights ploughing in a cables tractor. There didn't seem to be a happy ending in sight.

Somehow I ended up working for Securicor, which offered me a career, a dog at some locations and promotion opportunities. When a job was brought to my attention about working 8,000 miles away in the Falkland Islands, I couldn't get my application off quickly enough.

I hand wrote all the adventures that I have had living in the Falkland Islands a few years ago. I then took a while to type them out and even longer unravelling some of the overlapping themes. I have tried to compile a light-hearted but informative narrative covering 40 years of living in the Falkland Islands

Hopefully readers will realise what an amazing place the Falkland Islands is to live in, with huge personal freedom, very special and approachable wildlife and plenty of adventures and excitement, including raising children, to be had.

1. SPLITTING UP THE FARMS

Port Sussex

In 1976 an economic study of the Falklands recommended certain land reforms which encouraged the sale of large farms owned by absentee landlords. These farms would be subdivided into family-sized units, which people hoped would create strong local ownership and also help develop agriculture performance and diversification. The first farm to be subdivided was Green Patch with Roy Cove being in the process of sub-division when the war began. This government-led process carried on through the 1980s, splitting up many of the big farms.

In 1984, two years after the Falklands War, San Carlos farm was split up into eight pieces. Pat and Isobel Short with their daughter Michelle and son Derek got two pieces, as the eighth piece wasn't big enough to make into a separate farm. They called their farm Blue Beach, named after the landing site used by the British forces when removing the Argentine military. Ron and Iris Dickson, with their sons Steven and Keith, got section one, which they named Kingsford Valley Farm after the camp at the top of Head of the Bay Creek. Gerald and Dene Dickson, with their son Charles, got The Wreck and Gerald and Carrie Findlay, with Margo, Bruce, Andrew and Billy, got the Head of The Bay which they named Maryfield (which I think was after Gerald's mother). Robin and Mandy Goodwin, with their daughter Joann, bought the Verde which they renamed Greenfield. Robin and Mandy were living on Great Island, working their time out on a share farm agreement that they had with some of the Falkland Islands Company (FIC) islands in the Falkland Sound. Last of all came Geoff and Marilyn Butler, with their four children Ian Geoff Junior, Callum, Christine and Sarah, and they got Third Corral. We, of course, got Port Sussex.

The sale was a protracted affair, dragging on for months. We immediately wrote to express our interest in Port Sussex and soon received a letter of support from Colin Smith, the owner, giving us the first refusal. Over time a list grew of interested people who were placed on a list of priorities ranging from first to third choice. Not everyone got their first choice, although all those that were working at San Carlos at the time of the sale got theirs. Some people dropped out because it was taking so long to finalise the sale and so others had the chance to move up the list of choices, or even join the queue to own property.

When San Carlos was sold, the arrangement was that you or your representative had to work the first season after the sale in a cooperative or forfeit the wool money for that season. Rob's father and mother, Doug and Rose, stood in for Rob and Mandy.

The co-op was more than all of the farmers working together. It also owned the club, the old store, the transit shed at the shore end of the jetty that held wool bales for collection by coastal shipping, and paddocks so that all farms could use the shearing shed to shear sheep. There were also tractors and trailers and other bits and pieces.

The house at Port Sussex was the greatest asset in our farm sale apart from the stock. It was a large four-bedroomed dwelling built from kit form in 1959. The sheds standing to the east of the house weren't so generous, being small and pokey. It was one building divided into three.

We all got different building assets in the San Carlos settlement as well. Then all the stores and provisions were split equally between the seven new farm owners. There was cement, wood, nails, glass, tin, fencing, spades, crow bars, groceries, all the way down to cigarette papers.

Our only building asset in San Carlos was the bull shed. This was a geriatric shed, which was rather tall, but otherwise undistinguishable. It wasn't a big job to take the building down, apart from the fact that Toni managed to kneel on a rusty nail and had to go to the military doctor at Kellys Garden, and have a tetanus injection in her rear. The real work started when we began carting it home along with all the other seventh share of the stores and things. The farm sheep were divided in percentage terms as per the size of the property, but the horses and cattle were shared equally seven ways.

All these stores were one of the biggest bonuses of the farm sale. If you were one of the five farms living outside the settlement or planning to be, there was plenty to cart home to your homestead and without roads for most of us, there was at least one mountain in the way. Three of the farm owners that lived outside the settlement also had houses in the settlement. The Butlers had two. The green-roofed house next to the hall and the south side of the double house. They only had a shanty on their property unlike all the other homesteads which had houses, although they were in differing states of repair. Rob and Mandy had the other end of the double house and Gerald and Dene (Doreen) had the cookhouse and galley.

The Butlers had very little out at their farm and, when they decided to move out to their section, they chose a new location away from the Third Corral site where the shanty was positioned, and set up a settlement in a valley close to the San Carlos River which they named Waimea. They didn't remove any of their houses, but in the first couple of years bought the hall from the co-op to make into a shearing shed. Once the army camp closed down they took Portacabins out to the farm to make into their home.

As a cooperative we chose Pat to organise the farm work because he had been the manager of San Carlos. So during that season we worked for him as if we worked at San Carlos. It was a difficult position because Ron and Gerald Dickson had worked at San Carlos under different management and so they might have found fault in Pat's leadership. Regardless of this fact I can't remember any mutiny although I am sure it was discussed at times over a few beers.

Sorting out the horses

One of the first things to be sorted out were the horses, which made practical sense because we were going to need some to cover the vast areas to work the farm as a cooperative during the first season. Everyone picked numbers out of a hat and we were lucky enough to get the first choice. Because Toni had a private troop coming from Rincon we were able to be fairly indulgent and chose a lovely palomino filly, which we went on to call Andino. Toni had been eying up this young animal and so we thought why not?

After each round of choosing horses we went back to the hat and drew out another number and the whole process was repeated until the horses were all allocated to their new owners.

This all went on in the pens behind the shearing shed which were historically used to sort the thousands of sheep that San Carlos ran when it was one big farm. Most of the new farmers and their families, plus the horses, stood in the large square pen to carry out the choosing and sorting.

Toni and I knew nothing about the horses and put our trust in Pat, Ron and Gerald Dickson who gave us a few pointers on horses that were fit to ride and, more crucially, information about the ones that were not. These folk had first-hand knowledge of San Carlos horses and many years of experience with horses generally. Gerald Findlay had worked at San Carlos for a few years but he had been a handyman so not involved with stock to any degree. Andy, Gerald's teenage son, had been a novice shepherd. Doug Goodwin was a seasoned farm worker, and then there was Geoff Butler who was a stockman from New Zealand but with no direct knowledge of the horses he was picking, which made them and us a little bit in the dark when it came to the selection process.

It soon became apparent how people were making their selection and there was also some harmless banter going on. Young Andy was going around telling people that they shouldn't choose this animal or that one because of one reason or another and then the Findlay's would choose it. Pat and Ron didn't seem to take any notice and it became clear that the Findlay's were buying many of the old campaigners that were some of the tamest but equally some of the oldest as well.

There was no doubt that Geoff knew his stuff when it came to horses, but I think his expertise wasn't that helpful in this Falkland Island setting. We were picking horses in the spring, which is one of the hardest parts of the year for any animal that lives in the Falklands. Few if any horses that are being worked regularly are fat or shiny examples at that time of year.

Geoff started picking the big, well-conditioned animals with glossy coats that stood out from the others. I knew from my experience that these were the horses that people did not ride because they were usually outlaws that were unreliable. Many a horse can buck on a frosty morning, or do a few pig roots leaving the corral at the start of the day, and the odd spill was tolerated but the bastard that dumped you and or hurt you, wasn't worth riding. A couple of the more experienced hands did try and tell Geoff but he held to his beliefs and ended up with the best-looking horses of all the troops.

At the end of the day we all had horses that we could ride with some troops better than others. We got the palomino's mother, Quickstep, and two tame horses, Oxo and Quaker. We got some young untamed horses and unusable individuals with Dolphin being a prime example of the latter. Dolphin, the poor old chap, had probably given good service in the past but he was just skin and bone.

All the horses were named with a letter of the alphabet, so that Happy was born in 1963 along with all the other horses whose names began with H. The two Qs, Quaker and Quickstep, were both born in 1972. Dolphin, born in 1959, would have been 25 years old, which was a ripe old age for a farm horse.

It was seen as highly amusing that one of the horses that we had acquired, and described as tame and reliable, had bucked Pat off as the gang had been leaving the corral one morning. Even horses that are deemed tame can have an off day or get a fright when things start flapping. Oxo was very tame and had been used by at least one person to check the insulators on the old single wire telephone line that used to go from place to place on the East and West Falklands. It was only really tame horses that would tolerate this job because it meant riding up to the pole and then standing on the horse's back to reach the insulator at the top. Oxo would also allow people to shoot from his back, another thing that many horses would not.

Getting our horses the five miles home didn't happen without some excitement. Toni rode Oxo and Andy Findlay accompanied her on one of his horses. I was the back-up in the vehicle. They had problems with two of the older horses, Dolphin and Kiwi, and had to leave them on the Findlay's land. The rest drove home ok. Toni and I had to go back for the others.

Plan A was for Toni to lead them from our good old stalwart Copernicus. He was bomb proof, strong as an ox and we could tie the leading rein of the horses being lead to the cinch if need be. I was to ride Mister Softee, who wasn't as bomb proof, but he was good to turn either way and he was also fast if we needed it. I would open the gates to make a non-stop trip a possibility. (In 1984 there weren't many gates or fences between Maryfield and Sussex.) Toni was leading Dolphin, and Gerald had tied Kiwi's leading rein around Dolphin's neck so there was a short length between them and she was led along too.

Things went fairly well until we arrived at the foot of the mountain, but by that time we had worked out that Kiwi was a cantankerous mare that hadn't been handled very much. Kiwi was a *manada* or brood mare, which in those days in the Falklands says it all because the best mares were usually kept in a shepherd's troop for work. The lazy, ill-natured, less than perfect animals were put to the stallion. This mare had distinctive markings that made her eyes look as if she wore black eye shadow surrounding both eyes. It gave her a moody expression and she didn't disappoint. She also had a black line that came out of her mane and ran down the length and centre of her back, running along the spine and into the tail.

There was plenty of detritus laying everywhere from the 1982 war, such as 45-gallon drums and jerry cans, sheets of tin and plastic, trenches and rock shelters, and the hills around San Carlos were laced with thin black communications wire and thicker green stuff.

Up the mountain we rode, with me placing myself at forty-five degrees to Toni behind the horses being led, trying to keep them going and also on to Copernicus so that Toni wasn't dragging them.

Suddenly Dolphin and Kiwi got caught in some black wire and as quick as a flash started to panic. In no time they had turned Toni so that there was a horse either side of her and they were careering down the mountain pulling the leading rein between the two horses over her back and nearly sweeping her over the front of her horse. The rein was singing tight pinning her to her horse, but somehow, at speed, she managed to wriggle under it. I was amazed that Toni managed to stay on but didn't have time to congratulate her on her horsemanship and I went galloping after the runaways.

For two geriatrics they didn't hang about, and nor did I as I tried to catch them up and grab hold of their head collar, but it was impossible so I tried to head them off. It was a spur of the moment thing but if I had had time to think I would never have been so foolish because they could only have gone back as far as the last gate. Softee was a sure-footed animal and so, fortunately, I didn't go cartwheeling down the mountain.

It was exhilarating stuff and better and more purposeful than any ride at Alton Towers. I managed to turn them back up the mountain and head them in the direction of their new home, but it was not to be and by this stage Kiwi was really worked up. As we came back to where Toni was, the bitch managed to slip her head collar and as she was a lot stronger than Dolphin, they separated and so we reluctantly called it a day.

Kiwi never made it home and we gifted her to Andy Findlay who had high hopes of a foal or two from her. Dolphin did come home but his teeth were finished and therefore so was he. He would never be fat and healthy again so we put him down.

We hadn't been at the farm very long before Heather rode all the family horses one hundred miles from Rincon Grande to Sussex with Fay Alazia and Dene Dickson, riding via Teal Inlet, Douglas Station and the Verde. To me it was impressive stuff but it was not that long ago that people would ride into Stanley from some of these far-flung settlements or equally ride back home from Stanley. Heather had quite a troop for us. Some that she led from another mount and others that followed. I should imagine she would have ridden Nicky Nanny and Silver Blaze the most, with perhaps good old Bluey getting the odd burst. The other horses of ours in the party would have been Copernicus, Mister Softee, Atesh, Malachite and T'Soulaiky.

Heather came all that way without a hitch only for Nicky Nanny to stumble and fall at the bottom of the mountain with only a flat and our mutton paddock to go. I think she was quite surprised to find herself sitting in the soft white grass.

Taming Quicksilver and riding Noble

When gathering sheep as a co-op was imminent, the horses were kept on the settlement green in San Carlos and we would get out of the house by half five to catch our nags and gear them up to leave by six. Half an hour sounds like a long time to catch and gear up, but even though most of the animals were tame there was an occasional blip like a horse not wanting to be caught which one had to account for.

It was the considered opinion of those that knew the horses of San Carlos that Geoff had got his hands full. Geoff never seemed to be fazed and as people busied about doing this and that Geoff could be found civilising his troop.

He had one mare that had a reputation of being more than wild and closer to being mad. I saw Geoff on several occasions outside, between the green-roofed house and the old hall in the settlement, taming Quicksilver, the grey mare. One day he had a blanket on the end of a rope and stick and he would lift the blanket on this contraption to get the horse used to sudden surprises. He would do it from the ground and then from the horse's back with a leg tied up and he would do this time and time again. At first she would go ballistic and then a little better until eventually she didn't seem to be frightened by a blanket.

Geoff would then gear up the mare and head out to test the quality of his work. Back would come the mare minus Geoff who would walk back a while later. He spent many hours on this one mare and there is no doubt that she was much, much better, but Geoff could never get her to be consistently reliable. Geoff himself confided in me that the defining moment for him, when he knew it wasn't worth continuing, was out in the carthorse paddock when the mare bolted towards the beach bank and then fired him off down a 20-foot bank, onto the beach. Like all of us he couldn't afford to get hurt and it was obvious that if he carried on it was only a matter of time.

Geoff was a great guy for a chat and his experiences with Quicksilver hadn't made him nervous at all when it came to dealing with horses. He was a really relaxed rider and would often have an abundance of slack in his reins as he rode along. Geoff had a big black horse called Noble, which was probably the tamest animal in his possession. It was 90 per cent tame and reliable but whenever he went through Burnt Camp his one desire seemed to be to plant Geoff.

The first time it happened we were off to gather at the Wreck. We were all together – probably about nine riders – having just left San Carlos, chatting about different things as we approached the double iron gates across the creek from the Head of the Bay house. Suddenly Noble cut into it. Buck, buck, buck, root. By the time Geoff had pulled in all the slack in his reins he was going over Noble's shoulder into the grass.

Childish though it may seem, the rest of us were whooping and shouting encouragement for Geoff to hang on and making a meal of this small amount of excitement.

Noble did this three times that I can remember and in the same place each time. Even though the gang were ready for Noble's antics and the thought of some sport, Geoff, on the other hand, never seemed to be ready, sitting as relaxed as can be, with miles of reins, chatting to a fellow gatherer. He always ended up in the grass. Once again Geoff went back to the blanket on the string and stick in an attempt to make him more user-friendly but it might have been easier just to ride a different path or be ready to hold the brute's head up at the one area of the whole farm where his discipline vanished.

Riding Simon

It is true to say that many farm horses had been 'livened up' by young shepherds looking for some sport. One of the tricks to get even the most docile animal to buck was to stick the thumbs into its neck. In this enlightened era such behaviour is unacceptable, but back then it was just having a bit of fun. Then there were the pranks that riders would play on one another, like riding up to another mount and flicking your whip between its back legs. This kind of stuff happened probably more with a younger shepherd gang but even older more experienced men weren't above carrying out a few practical jokes. Not surprisingly, a number of farm mounts had experienced this type of thing, and certainly with our farm horses they were very weary about a friendly pat thinking it was a prelude to some thumbing. Toni and I often gave our horses a congratulatory pat at the end of a long day's work but in the early days you would feel the farm horses tensing up.

On that first trip Jock (Gerald Findlay) was also having problems with some of his horses. He had picked a big brute of a horse, similar to Geoff's Noble, called Simon, also a large black animal. Jock wasn't really a shepherd and he was not getting on well with Simon. We picked the Findlays, Jock and Andy up as we passed on the way to the Wreck and poor old Jock looked red in the face and a little bit uncomfortable on his mount. Leaving the corral Simon did a pig root and in Jock's own words 'he was coming up as I was coming doon.' He didn't get much sympathy, just the usual ribald humour about his nether regions.

Poppy was another mare in Geoff's troop and she was a smaller, lighter animal than Noble. She had a thick shiny coat and was in reasonable condition. Poppy seemed to have been given a bad name because she was fine when we were riding out together to gather the camp next to a neighbouring farm called Port San Carlos.

Gathering on the horses

We were gathering quite large areas, and so you would arrive in the camp that we needed to gather, Pat would give out the instructions to where people would be and then we would all fan out to our start positions and then move forward, trying to keep in line with the people on either side. On some of the bigger camps you may not see your neighbouring shepherd for some time and the trick was to try and anticipate the speed of the other gatherers. Inexperienced shepherds often wonder if they are in the right place and sometimes got 'miss mothered', ending up miles ahead or left miles behind.

On this particular gather with Geoff and Poppy, we all went to our stations and I didn't see Geoff at all from then until we arrived at the finish. Geoff and Poppy were there all right but the horse gear was in pieces. Poppy for some reason had started bucking and managed to get Geoff off and then continued to buck with the gear, which slid back over her rump where she kicked it until it was off and by this time it was badly damaged.

We were going out daily at this time and a few of the older hands were heard to doubt Geoff's participation for the following day, considering the state his gear was in. I wasn't that experienced but I couldn't see how Geoff could carry on. Not the next day anyway.

Next day before six everyone stared in awe to see Geoff gearing up his horse ready for the day's gather. Geoff must have spent the whole night fixing his gear and the whole lot was peppered with pop rivets, which put this leather jigsaw back into one piece.

One of the worst places to gather at San Carlos was Rodeo Mountain. It was a long ride from the settlement and then we had to wait on the mountain as others moved round into position to start the gather. Bozo, who had been a pet, had become competent in gathering. He was a loyal member of the family although untrustworthy to everyone else.

We were waiting to start the gather and we had all adjusted our gear. I had mine on a dark grey mare called Nicky Nanny. She was an old mare that belonged to Heather and I had bought her along because she was meant to be good in the soft. I was leading Mister Softee who Toni used to race in Stanley.

I was sitting on my haunches in front of the horses while Bozo my dog was sniffing around at some good smell by them. Softee, who wasn't renowned for his pleasant nature, booted him. Bozo ran to me for some kind of protection and Mister Softee leant forward and bit him in the middle of the back. Life was tough back then.

This piece of camp was soft and it must have taken the skills of experienced horsemen over the years to gather it without bogging their animals. The side of the mountain and some area by the river were the only firm pieces. The rest was just mile upon mile of swamp and soft peat bank. Pat came and showed me a route which meant keeping to the edges of the peat banks where it was a little drier and even there leading the horses without a rider they were sinking up to their knees in places. Pat would appear again and point out to me the next stage of this quagmire. In this area there were many wild feral cattle in large herds roaming around, but it was the odd bad-tempered solitary bulls that had to be given a wide berth because if you got too close they would charge. These cattle had their own network of tracks, some which you could use and others that you could not. Experience dictated which was which and I was certainly not in the enlightened number.

Feral cattle

There were hundreds of these feral cattle when we went to Port Sussex in 1984. If you went up onto our mountain and looked east over The Flats and up towards Rabbit Mountain you would see several large groups of dark-coloured cattle grazing in herds. Many other herds would be in the Rodeo and Third Corral Mountain area and No Man's Land in the mountains. These cattle occasionally went into the Snipe Camp, which borders our land but we never saw any on Sussex ground.

As the new farmers started to manage the far-flung areas more intensively the cattle were deemed to be a nuisance, by competing for grass and were shot sometimes for dog meat and occasionally for beef. One businessman used to shoot them and then sell the beef to customers in Stanley. Some enterprising farmers managed to round some up and tame them down controlling them with electric fences.

By 2000 if you went to the top of Sussex Mountain you would no longer see those large groups of cattle grazing in big circles. In fact, it was rare to see any although I am sure, even now, odd ones probably do exist.

There was going to be a mass cull to finally rid the Falklands of these feral animals organised by the Agricultural Department. Members of the Agricultural Department hired the Islander and flew over No Man's Land and other areas where these cattle were known to be. I think the whole concept of getting rid of these animals was to control unwanted diseases that these animals could pass on to the domestic herds and to help the Falklands conform to the traceability criteria that we need for the European-standard abattoir to operate.

The on-mass event happened but not with the participation of every farmer that had been proposed, probably because of some of the lethal hardware that many farmers have at their disposal. Perhaps the thought of many farmers working through the mountains with heavy calibre weapons, shooting cattle, conjured up visions of a possible incident. Most farmers on the Islands have a high degree of awareness with firearms but that doesn't guarantee absolute safety and with many of our top officials coming in from a more controlled environment I wouldn't be surprised if they didn't want to take the risk. It was a partial success but didn't eradicate the problem, which was what was planned, once and for all.

Gathering
Rodeo Mountain was a big camp in San Carlos terms, but Ron would say that when it was part of San Carlos 1,600 wethers (castrated male sheep) were kept out there and when the gang rounded them up to go in for shearing they were in poor condition and weak. As wethers are hardy animals this says much about the quality of the land.

We spent a night at Third Corral Shanty and had one of these bachelor-type evenings talking about what people had got up to in the San Carlos area over the years. Families used to live at a house at Third Corral, which was a good distance from the settlement for the man to ride into for work in the season. Amazingly, many years ago, a family was quarantined at Third Corral because they had diphtheria and the man had to bury his wife and daughter while the settlement left stores at a certain location.

I think I could have lived out there because of the close proximity to the river, but on your own after burying members of your family must have been pretty tough.

The next day we had to drive the sheep some distance before they were into the next camp on their way back to the settlement to be shorn. Falkland camp is full of natural hazards like holes, swamps and ditches. The sheep were ambling along and had started crossing a ditch but before you could say Hans Christian Anderson, a number had fallen in and they began to smother. I don't know how many we lost, it wasn't one hundred but it was definitely multiples of ten. Everyone was a little tetchy after that but even now I don't think it was anyone's fault – we certainly weren't forcing them along. For me it was an interesting lesson to see how easy it is to lose sheep that way. With a large gang of people we were able to help the sheep, but even then we couldn't help them all. This kind of catastrophe would have been a lot worse for a family farm with only two people to deal with it.

Gathering on horse back was a very sociable activity and as some of the camps were a couple of hours away you could mill around chatting to everyone. On one occasion we rode out from the settlement to gather Cantera Mountain. This was a two-hour trek but when we arrived we were met by some military chaps who told us that they were firing on the range under Mount Usborne and so we were not to proceed. So we had another two hour ride back to base. There were a few growls but although it was a waste of four hours at least the weather was fine.

Occasionally I was allowed to ride Copernicus if Toni wasn't on the gather. He was easy to catch and a willing animal, which was important with the work we were doing. He was Toni's and like all the animals we possess there is a story. Somehow he was a prize in a raffle and the Petterssons won him. He arrived in town in the spring in quite a sorry state, poor and covered in lice. Toni and Heather kept him in town and treated him for lice moving him around the green grass of people's yards while he recovered.

Copernicus rewarded this kindness by being a willing servant to Toni throughout his life.

So I took him on the Flats gather. We left the horses in the enclosure at the Flats Shanty overnight and gathered the camp the next day. In this enclosure there was nothing to aid catching your mount and you just had to corner them. Some folk left the bosal on to make the task easier but with Copernicus you just walked up to him and led him back to your gear.

The Flats was another piece of camp that was treacherous for any greenhorn and I placed myself in that category. It was soft everywhere. Pat gave me my beat and described how to go into the stream at one point to get around a soft area.

Somehow I wasn't that sure and, catastrophes of all catastrophes, I bogged Toni's pride and joy up to the withers. Being such a tame animal he just looked up at me as if I could somehow get him out. I could only think there were a couple of options and one of them was not to go home. So I got the gear off and placed it in front of him and then coaxed him to try and get onto the gear. He still looked up at me as though I had the powers of levitation but after a few flicks with the whip he realised that it was he that had to make the effort. He tried a few times before he eventually made it up onto the gear and on to some terra firma and safety. It was a lucky escape, but there was no escaping the wrath of Mrs Stevens because both horse and gear were smothered in mud. The tidemark high up on Copernicus's back told the story as clearly as any words.

2. LIVING IN CAMP

Geoffrey the cat

Most of the other section holders who lived outside the settlement had houses in San Carlos. The Findlay's at the Head of the Bay, and we didn't. The Findlay's could walk in in an hour. It was twenty minutes on a horse easily, if the tide was out. We were 40 minutes away in a Land Rover during the summer. This meant that we would stay with Pat and Isobel Short along with their children Michelle and Derek when they were home from the hostel. The hostel was where children in camp boarded in Stanley so that they could attend the schools there. Pat and Isobel were extremely generous with their hospitality and always made us feel welcome and at home.

Our cat Geoffrey's new life in camp carried on with the eventful existence he had had in town with one of his biggest adventures unfolding while staying in the settlement.

On the farm, Geoffrey was a most unusual cat and instead of sleeping in a chair all day he took an active interest in the farm activities. He liked to follow us down to the beach where he would even go into the sea up to the top of his legs if we were clamming or the kids were minnowing or catching mullet. We have never had another cat do the same. He would also often go around the calf paddock when Toni bought the cows and calves in to part.

Cow parting should be explained. When cows are milked in the Falklands the calves are kept with their mothers, but separated overnight so that when you milk the cow in the morning you let the calf have one teat (or when they are very young a little more) and you have the rest. There are two parts to the cowshed, the piece that the cows are milked in and the piece where the calves stay. Each time you get a cow into the cowshed to be milked you tie her up and then let her calf out but on a rope. The calf sucks the teats and stimulates the cow to let her milk down. You then tie the calf up and milk three of the four teats before letting them out into the calf paddock where the calf has its share. The cow and calf then have most of the day together feeding until the afternoon when they are taken back to the cowshed, where the cows are parted out on to their pasture and the calves back into their pen and later into their paddock. If the calves stayed with the cow they would drink all the milk. The cow comes back to the cowshed early each morning to be with its calf.

Geoffrey would also spend hours in the garden not only laying in the shade but also checking out what we were doing. He didn't get over his befriending activities that had got him into bother in Stanley.

While we were working as a cooperative at San Carlos, Geoffrey used to come over to the settlement in the Land Rover or in a pillow case on the front of the horse gear and live with us at Pat and Isobel's.

One day he decided to follow some fisher folk that walked over to Curlew Creek, which was miles away. These guys couldn't believe that a cat would walk so far and thought he would eventually turn back. Geoffrey did eventually stop following but by this time he was on the other side of the San Carlos Mountains. The fisher folk came back and told us about this blue cat that had tagged on for their fishing jaunt. Geoffrey didn't come back. Toni went calling night after night. I was eventually drafted in after I had given him ample opportunity to return under his own steam. It appeared that his animal navigation must be faulty. Eventually we accepted that we had lost him.

A good two months later we were gathering on horse back on the mountains to the northwest of the settlement when I heard some load meowing. There in the middle of camp was Geoffrey. I picked him up and he was very light but he was alive and I took him over to Toni. They both rode home on Copernicus, sharing Toni's chocolate which she had bought along for her snack. Apart from a small boil where his tail met his back and being a lot lighter he hadn't come to any harm.

Years later after many mice, rats and small birds Geoffrey's face caved in, as a result of his altercation with the vehicle in Stanley. The poor lad became listless and not himself. Toni took him to the vets hoping that they would make the big decision and suggest that he was put to sleep instead of her suggesting it. Toni knew her cat but wasn't strong enough to call the shots. The vet gave him some tablets and we brought him home. That night, back on the farm, we put him out and never saw him again. He had gone for his last wander.

At the time we didn't know that Geoffrey was missing, but Tabby Cat (the cat Toni had fed in Stanley and we had caught and bought to the farm) for the first time ever followed Toni around the calf paddock as she got the cows and calves in. He hadn't done it before and he didn't do it again. Tabby lived to a ripe old age and died in the hay shed up by the stable.

Water troubles

On one lengthy stay with Pat and Isobel the tap water became slightly interesting, with bits and pieces, including hair, floating in it. As all farm water comes from the ground somewhere, and is untreated, it isn't unheard of for the odd bit of foreign matter to sometimes appear. The odd jumping-jack and a bit of colour after heavy rain were not out of the ordinary. At San Carlos the water for Pat and Isobel's house came down a pipe from a spring hole to a tank, which fed the property. The problem seemed to clear if you let the tap run fully open for a while, but it wasn't long in the gradual on/off of usual use that the problem would return. During the summer of long days gathering, shearing and sorting sheep it was one of those jobs that didn't get its deserved priority although it is probably hindsight that moves it into that criteria. It was a job that must be looked at when a minute or so presented itself and then 'bugger' the water was reduced to a trickle and so it had to be examined.

Pat started on a system of elimination, looking at the pipe joints that were accessible, and worked back to the tank. Pat found the remains of a rat blocking the pipe leading from the tank. The son-of-a-bitch had fallen in and inconsiderately drowned at the pipe end, only for his body to sink strategically down and share an out-of-body-experience with all those frequenting the Big House. His pelvic bone and tail were the only thing that remained and even then most of the hair from his tail had gone. In essence, we had consumed in one way or another 90 per cent of this rodent.

A few years later we had a similar experience at Sussex. We inherited a concrete tank, which fed the house and in turn was fed by a spring above it. This tank was made out of concrete blocks with a cement floor that was porous, so that in the months between May and October it was kept full by a strong flow of water from the spring. In the summer months the flow was pitiful and most of it was lost through the floor and sides. The top of the tank was covered by two sheets of corrugated iron and with the constant checking during the summer months, they had been left slightly apart and out of sheer willfulness a thrush managed to fall into the water and drown. With all the checking we were able to spot it before it started coming down the pipe.

We had awesome problems with water when we first went to Sussex and it was a few years focusing on the sheep side of things before the priority moved to our domestic water supply. The spring hole and tank were barely higher than the header tank in the cupboard in the west large bedroom that fed the hot water cylinder. Pressure at the taps was reasonable but if air got into the pipe from the tank it couldn't be removed by opening the taps and we would have to dig up the join in front of the house and undo it and wait for the air to bubble out before doing it back up. The 200 metres of pipe from the tank on the hill to the house were also on or near the surface of the ground in some places. This meant that the supply to the house would freeze up in the winter. We had a few winters thawing the 200 metres of pipe to restore water to the house. These were the obvious areas that needed attention but when there was a hard frost it was easier to say which bits would be free from ice. We would put the kettles on the stove and go pour the hot water in the areas where the pipe was above the ground. This could go on for days, sometimes becoming clear through our efforts only to be solid the next day. Sometimes we weren't able to get the water flowing and would wait for the pipes to clear when the weather got milder. However, this strategy wasn't foolproof with an extended period of cold weather and we had a jury-rigged system which entailed pumping water from a spring just west of the house up through the end window of the house into the loft and into the water tank in the house.

This spare pipe was what we used to pump water in general and so on one occasion this pipe had frozen water in it where we hadn't drained it after use. It was too bad to try the kettle treatment so I cut a 45-gallon drum in two to make a long bath and then made a frame to sit it in a foot or so off the ground and then built a fire underneath. I filled the half, sitting in the frame, with some scarce water and as it became hot we passed the pipe slowly through the hot bath. Minutes later sausages of ice slid out of the pipe onto the green and made the pipe ready to pump water from the spring by the house up into the header tank.

The frozen pipe was an inconvenience which as long as you could rough it you could carry on but looking after the pump was on another level and it was treated carefully. Not that its demise was life threatening but it was expensive and there wasn't always a replacement readily available to buy. Sometimes you just couldn't buy a suitable water pump because we needed one with a 30-metre head, which is the height the pump will push water to.

When San Carlos was still a big farm the management had recognised some of the water problems at Sussex and had tackled the shortage in the summer by tapping in to a spring hole at the foot of the mountain and running a pipe all the way to the tank that fed the house. This would have been a godsend if it had worked, but the spring hole was only fractionally higher than the ridge behind the house and so it was very unreliable. What would happen was that the water in the spring hole would flow down to the tank but quicker than it could make water and so eventually air would get in. Then because there wasn't enough height to push the air through once the spring had regenerated, the water would stop. Another design fault was that the joints were improvised sleeves made of slightly bigger gauge alkathene, which weren't all airtight. As the water got over the ridge it would drop to the tank creating a strong gravity effect pulling air into the pipeline. The spring was a mile or so from the tank and the pipe was in 100-yard sections and so there were many different joins that had to be pulled apart and the air removed. We did try mechanised solutions like using a stirrup pump and even an electric water pump to force the water in and the air out. We would get the water flowing but I think the record for it running without any fettling was three days.

Another event, which was outside our control, was that although our attrition on the water supply didn't add up to any serious amount of water the spring under the mountain was losing its vigour. Spring holes are notoriously fickle but they usually move or disappear if they are weak. The older folk with San Carlos experience couldn't believe that this big healthy spring could devalue like this but the truth was that it became a fraction of its former self. It certainly wasn't from the water that was taken from it for the house.

The amount of time and effort we wasted on trying to make this system work could have been more wisely invested in carrying water to the house in buckets and would have probably kept us in water for the rest of our time if we had had a tank large enough.

Christmas at Sussex

The first Christmas at Sussex was special. We had been working hard and long hours and so we decided we wouldn't work on Christmas day. I gave Toni a radish as a present because I hadn't had the forethought to buy something during the last visit to town. I think it would have been received better if Toni hadn't been the one to plant it. Of course, we had books and video but there didn't seem to be anything to entertain us sufficiently on Christmas day. We had our lunch and there was a slight pause and then we decided to get up on the roof and carry on painting, a job that we had already started and carried out on suitable days i.e. low wind speed and dry. As I remember, it was a really nice day and we enjoyed doing the task at hand but we did concede to one another that it was a novel way to celebrate the birth of Jesus.

One of the really good bits of advice we were given on farming, but possibly one of the hardest to carry out, was to have a day off each week especially if you are doing hard manual work like fencing. Few people can work flat out for twelve hours a day or more, day after day after day. What seems to happen is that you do the hours but your output goes down. Even knowing all this, it is incredibly hard to take time out when there are all these jobs that need to be tackled. The principle of rest is best demonstrated if you go on holiday and so can't work. You seem to recharge your batteries and your enthusiasm is rekindled and you find new energy to tap into on your return.

Working dogs

Dogs have always been an important part of our farm, although now more people are running their properties without dogs. With the steep-sided valleys and very rough ground we have never considered being without.

At the beginning I had Bozo who Toni had reared from a very young pup with proper puppy milk substitute from the vets and a small pet bottle. His mother Bell was too ill to raise him. He also had to have calcium medicine added to his milk to help his development. He grew into a big strapping dog with plenty of energy. He was the foundation of my working dogs, with his apprenticeship starting at Rincon where he began to chase sheep. At this time, however, he was a long way from being the finished article.

Once we knew that we were going to Sussex it was time to start building up dogs with the hope that we could train them to work the sheep. Even when we were actually there we hadn't finished procuring dogs.

While over working at Fox Bay Toni had got a pup Lassie from Errol Goss at Fox Bay West and Richard Cockwell gave her two old dogs, Pip and Sadie, that he no longer needed because he had moved from farming into running a wool mill.

We then managed to acquire a quality pup from imported stock through other people's generosity. Heather had looked after two purebred border collies, a dog and a bitch, when they came to the Islands for a chap called Dave Dunford who promised her two pups in payment for her kindness. I became the proud owner of the fluffier one of the two and called him Ben.

The following year Pat had a bitch that had rejected her pups after a couple of weeks, and Lassie had had some pups off Bozo of a similar age and we had kept two. So I acquired a pup from Pat and Lassie became a surrogate mother to this pup that I named Bridget. She was a small short-haired bitch with more white than black.

During the first season we had all our sheep to drive back flock by flock, but also occasionally small amounts of dog meat and mutton that were centralised at San Carlos. We got two lots of dog meat and mutton and neither drive was very successful because we were inexperienced and driving sheep of different strengths, with the mutton being strong and robust and wanting to climb the mountain with some vigour and the dog meat being weak and needing a more leisurely pace. Unfortunately, Pip was the only dog at that time that could haul (run to the front of a flock of sheep and bring them back to you) and the poor old sod was past it. Sadie was Pip's shadow and would only work with him. Needless to say that each time we drove these mixed flocks of sheep home we ended up with just the mutton.

Driving the bigger flocks home after they were shared out was more successful and on many occasions Pat would come and help us. We drove the rams home unaided because they are the easiest of all sheep to drive. Ben was just beginning to work, he didn't have the stamina of an older dog but made up for it with his keenness. On the way along the fence between the Old House Paddock and the Head of the Bay, one of the rams, with a large yellow tag, took an exception to Ben and rushed out of the flock and flattened him. I thought well that is that, Ben would keep his distance from now on.

There used to be a gate in the bottom of the fence between The Head of the Bay and us on the north side of the mountain, through which the shepherds of old drove the Sussex sheep in for shearing at San Carlos and back again. This was how we took our sheep home and this was the route the rams took.

Through the gate we went and up the mountain heading for our paddocks. Nearing the head of the mountain, when the sheep were beginning to feel the efforts of climbing, Ben rushed in and singled out the ram that had butted him and gave him a sharp nip. He had waited his chance to get his own back.

In the early days we did nearly as much running as the dogs, but out of our new dogs we didn't have one failure.

Pip was an old boy and he was broken winded and well past his best-before-date, but when a bitch came on heat, you would think he was in his prime and he would howl and howl and whinge. Initially the dog kennels were close to the house and a dog's bark just has me awake quicker than any other noise. Most of the other dogs would stop if you shouted out of the window, but others especially before they had got the message needed a gunshot to stop them barking.

I used to take the training seriously, because the barking disturbed my sleep, and I would lie in bed listening to aimless barking getting crosser and crosser until I would leap out of bed and bellow or fire a shot out of the window. Toni on the other hand didn't find dogs barking the irritant I did and would have slept through a hundred and one dalmatians barking their way down the house green. My leaping out of bed therefore mostly caught her unawares and she would think something catastrophic was happening, like aliens arriving or the house burning down at the very least – then only to find out it was all about dogs barking.

The dogs did respond, all that is apart from Pip when a bitch was on heat. He would not respond to anything delivered via the house and so I would sneak out in the dead of night so that I could fire a rock at his kennel. I thought he was a bit deaf and so couldn't hear me bellowing from the house, apart from the fact that it didn't matter how quietly I sneaked out to deliver my rock, he would remain mute until the springs groaned in the mattress as I eased myself back into bed.

Poor Toni's nerves were becoming shattered and so as there were kennels up at the stable Pip was banished up there when a bitch was on heat.

Eventually for everyone's sake we moved the main kennels down to the shearing shed where they can bark to their hearts' content. Combined with our move to the west end of the house and it is rare now to hear the dogs.

Ben went on to be an amazing dog for driving any group of sheep whether it be a couple, to hundreds, he could cope. Also holding them up in the drafting race was not a problem for Ben.

I read a dog training book of Pat's that showed how to have a stick with some string and then a rag on the end with which you could teach your dog to hold on to a sheep and to let it go. Ben would rush after the rag as I spun it around. I spent hours teaching him these skills, but I have to say working sheep was in him and I just worked on control, i.e. whistling him out, stopping him and getting him to come back and then the holding a sheep when it was being contrary and I couldn't stop it any other way. In the early days we had a Honda 125 and he would leap up onto the petrol tank and sit between my arms with his feet on the handlebars.

Bridget turned out to be a very handy bitch as well but her style was completely different to Ben's. Ben wanted to be the first to the front and would be going so fast at times he would go flying, even cartwheeling. But it very rarely slowed him down and he would run close to the sheep so that they felt his presence. Bridget the Midget was a small black and white bitch and she was wide and would pass sheep at a distance only coming on to the front of the sheep. Her two greatest assets were that she would go out a long way for sheep and that she had unbelievable stamina and seemed tireless.

Bozo, Ben and Bridget gave me an awesome team and combined with Toni's dogs stood us in good stead.

Lassie raised the two pups as well as Bridget who we got from Pat. We had kept one for a neighbour and Toni kept one. I thought the mixture of Bozo and Lassie would be useless and I told Toni that if the pup, that she had named Bell, was any good I would eat my hat. Bell turned into a very good dog especially driving and gathering and Toni, many years later, still reminds me that my judgement was poor and my word is unworthy as I still haven't eaten my hat.

Bozo could never haul but he matured into a great gathering dog chasing sheep away. Down in Shepherds Brook we used to gather the camp in two swipes because it was so big for just the two of us. We would go along the south half heading east chasing the sheep up onto the mountain and then we would come back on the north side bringing all the sheep in front of us. Bozo loved this gather because on the turn he would get behind the sheep and just run up and down behind them driving them towards the gate. Unfortunately for us on one gather, he did his job that well that the sheep were at the west end and tearing down the fence behind us before one of us could get there to stop them. Result was that we had to come back the following day and do it all again.

I am not sure how we got good dogs but one of the contributory factors was that we probably did a lot more sheep work than was really needed due to our inexperience, but our pens were not very sophisticated and so our dogs held the sheep for hours as we processed them through the drafting race. Another thing we sometimes did when we shifted them was to hold the flock and go through them as the dogs kept them in a group. Instead of driving them home to the pens, if there were odds, the dogs would hold them as we ran down the sheep that were not supposed to be there.

After a few years poor old Pip eventually didn't even want to leave his kennel to come for a walk or howl the place down when a bitch was on heat and so it was kinder to put him down and Sadie was unable or unwilling to work without him and so she went the same way.

Lassie was Toni's top bitch and one of the best dogs we have ever had at Sussex. Her style was laid back and she was the complete opposite to Ben. Even when she was young she never seemed to be flat out but she always got to the front and she never left any behind. She was firm and gentle so, even with weakened sheep in the spring, she was the ideal bitch to gather with. Being able to train dogs was one if not our greatest asset and it meant we could handle any of our flocks comfortably.

The one down side of our dogs were that they were all the same age and so would have to be replaced all at once. Lassie's easy style had her still working sheep until she was twelve but Ben who was rip, shit, tear was finished at nine. Bridget the Midget, who got through so much work, was also not a long-lived dog and nor were Bozo or Bell. It must be down to genetics because I had a pup, Bess, from Lassie and Ben and she lived and worked until she was a ripe old age.

Ron's broken leg

We had hoped that I would learn to shear during our co-op year alongside the contract shearers. This would give me some experience before going solo. I did a couple of full days before a spanner was thrown in the works. Ron went and broke his leg so I was needed on the press, which he had been allocated to.

Ron liked a drink and there was always plenty at Kelly's Garden, the military base which was just outside San Carlos. Ron used to frequent the Sergeant's Mess on such a regular basis that he had his own seat. My judgement is that a broken leg was probably a reasonable outcome in a funny sort of way. Coming back from his regular sorties different things had happened to Ron, with the events getting worse. On one trip home in the Land Rover Ron misjudged the bank coming off the beach and flipped it onto its side. On the walk home with some other bods they fell off a small footbridge into a ditch one on top of another.

It seemed inevitable that something worse would happen and eventually Ron broke his leg and not his neck, which was a good thing for all of us but not great for developing my shearing skills.

Keeping in touch

Living in the Falklands on an isolated farm, four miles as the crow flies from your neighbour, puts you in the category of having to look after your own affairs. One of the first things we did was to find a decent length of metal pipe which was strong enough to stand the rigours of the Falklands wind, attach it to the house with our 2-meter aerial/beam at the top. We were now able to speak to many of our neighbours, although Sod's law dictated that some of our nearest neighbours at San Carlos were not that easy, because of the mountain, unless both beams were pointing at each other. Amazing, as it may seem, we could hear Doreen Clark who lived at the west end of Stanley. As a system that is supposedly line of sight it worked remarkable well in the Falklands. We now had comms so we could speak to people.

Living on edge

When we first moved to Port Sussex I think we were possibly a little bit on edge, although I didn't think I was until a couple of episodes demonstrated that we were. It was still only a couple of years after the war and a lot of action had occurred in this area and there were still plenty of British servicemen located around here, including Air Defence Rapier Missile sites in a number of locations in and surrounding San Carlos Waters.

When we gathered the camp behind San Carlos we came up close to one of these missile sites, which was very much active and the machine was moving as if ready to fasten on to a target. I even wondered if we shepherds on horseback could make the machines track us.

In the first couple of years we would be working in the garden to the sound of drones flying out in the Falkland Sound and the whoosh and bang of the rapiers as they practised live firing against the drones. The idea wasn't to destroy the drones every time because it would have started to get rather expensive but they did shoot them down deliberately during these exercises.

So the sights and sounds of war were still with us. We were lying in bed one evening after putting the generator off when there was a child-like scream. Again and again in the middle of nowhere a scream, which sounded very human, rang out. Toni and I looked at each other and, not wanting to be too hasty, I suggested tossing a coin to see who should go and investigate. Together with a torch we crept downstairs and went out through the back door.

Another scream above our heads had us leaping in the air but also swinging the torch beam towards the noise at the same time. Sitting on the 2-meter beam was a barn owl. They are attractive birds of white and gold with flecks of gold in their plumage. This individual seemed to be mesmerised by the light and sat there rolling its head first one way and then the other. We went in mightily relieved that we hadn't bought a haunted house.

In between working in the cooperative, we were trying to paint the house and stop the windows leaking. Toni was working from a box at ground level and I was doing the higher stuff on a ladder. One night I forgot to take the ladder down which was a big mistake.

The sofa used to sit under the kitchen window and this night Toni was at the kitchen table doing book work, I was reading and the cat was sleeping on the sofa. The wind was getting up but we weren't bothered because we had the Rayburn revved up and we were warm inside.

Suddenly the kitchen window smashed in, the cat just about hit the ceiling in fright and Toni and I leapt an equal height. It was a while before we realised it wasn't an Argentine commando raid. As our racing hearts returned to twice their normal rate we realised that the ladder had blown down, and then pivoted on the box which had spun the ladder through the window.

There was a shed built to the southeast of the house, divided into three smaller units. It was a fairly big structure but made conventionally with wooden framing and shiplap cladding. The interior wasn't that big. In the shed closest to the house was a chimney and fire place to sit a big iron basin on to do one's laundry in and was referred to as the wash house. We never used it for this purpose and pulled down the brickwork in the building. I used to use this piece as a workshop. The middle room had been the dairy, where the milk separator would have been housed and milk stored, and the east end was the meat house.

We didn't have a small rifle in those early days but we did have Toni's full bore 7.62 target rifle. It was a bit overkill but if we wanted a goose for us to eat or the cats, that was the gun that we used. Ammunition was not a problem in the 1980s and 1990s and so cost was not an issue.

I was guddling (working but doing nothing in particular) around fixing something in the shed and Toni went off shooting geese for the cats. It wasn't a big deal and I didn't think of accidents or have any sense of foreboding, because Toni had been around guns from an early age like many Islanders and she had been a member of the Rifle Club for years.

I heard Toni come through the gate and walk up the path and stand behind me in the doorway and I carried on with whatever I was doing waiting for her to say something. As she didn't say anything I turned around to ask her how she had got on and got the fright of my life because blood was pouring from a wound half an inch above her right eye and flowing down her face.

I really thought she had somehow shot herself but I couldn't reason how she was still standing.

In fact, Toni had held the gun too close to her aiming eye and the recoil of the gun had rammed the rear sight into her brow. What a swelling she had and the scar remains to this day over thirty years later. She had still managed to shoot a few geese for the cats though.

These issues did help focus the mind on just how vulnerable we were living miles away from anywhere.

3. LIVING AT SUSSEX

Selling off the cattle

Eventually we were working on our own farm, by ourselves.

Between building sheds and pens and erecting fencing we decided to sell off the more belligerent cattle, keeping what we judged to be the animals with the most potential. We did this in a small race with a rundown horse corral at one end, and cow corral at the other. Looking back, I suppose it was ignorance that even made us think we could do the job in such paltry facilities.

Sort them we did, removing the skittery, wild, and anything with a lot of white on their hides because we had been told that these cows don't do very well in Falkland conditions. Laurie Butler, the butcher at the time, offered us £70 for a decent beef, £50 for a fat cow and £35 for the also ran. We arranged to drive them up to Swan Inlet which was halfway to Stanley and the butchery would send out a couple of men to meet us and drive them in to town.

We had never done anything like this and so we sought some advice. Most of the experienced money was on taking dogs because if we didn't the cattle would take to water at the first chance and we wouldn't be able to get them out. We on the other hand always found that dogs made cattle anxious and unsettled so we took a gamble and left them behind.

Like a poorly funded spaghetti western we let the cattle rip and followed them on horseback, Heather, Toni and I.

The cattle were quite contented while they were on our land but once into the FIC (Falkland Islands Company, who used to own all of Lafonia and Fitzroy) ground, where most had never set foot, they became lively and a group of ten or twelve tore off from the main herd doing the William Tell Overture into the distance. I was thinking perhaps we should have taken dogs and off I galloped after them. I managed to turn them back and they joined up into one herd again. With the experience of a number of years I really think those ten or twelve would have come back to the herd in the next few miles but I had no idea as a greenhorn that this would probably happen.

After about six and half miles the cattle settled down and just followed the clay track. If we stopped to tighten gear they would stop about 50 yards ahead and wait for us to get under way again.

On the first day we drove them as far as Burnside and put them in the big corral, east of the house for the night. We stopped with Gerald and Kay Morrison. We had a bit of a problem with the horses because one of our better, tamer mounts, Copernicus, had become lame and I was riding Quaker who was a bit lively and our spare was Mister Softee who could be pretty mean. Heather was riding Nicky Nanny. We didn't think it through when we were picking our spare because we thought that if there was any dashing about to do I would do it and therefore need another energetic mount. Toni would have ridden Softee but when Falkland, a big dark grey horse, was offered to us we leapt at the chance. He was a big animal and Toni did a bit of scrabbling to get on his back. Luckily he was an incredibly tame animal and didn't seem to mind this treatment.

Next day we were back on the track heading towards Swan Inlet. This time they did take off at a gallop but there wasn't anywhere for them to go so we just dawdled along and caught them up as they waited on the top of the next rise. Once we came into their zone they just moved off and stayed so many yards ahead of us most of the way.

We did have a casualty on the next leg just below Laguna Verde when a cow somehow managed to fall into a ditch and no matter how we tried we couldn't get her out. Sadly, we had to dispatch her. It was just one of those things that happens. The cow had obviously become tired and had stumbled into a ditch and even with our help was unable to get out.

On we went taking our time and eventually after a number of hours we arrived at Swan Inlet, and put the 51 animals in the corral there. We were three happy cowpunchers.

We stayed at Swan Inlet over night with the Goose Green shepherd gang who happened to be there as well and then the next morning the butchery boys left with the cows. These chaps had dogs and the cattle came tearing out of the corral with the dogs milling around, and the herd bellowing. The cattle spread in all directions with the dogs and riders in hot pursuit. We stood around as interested bystanders as we saw them come out at the other side of the Swan Inlet River. They were still going at a good lick across the flat heading for the L'Antioja Stream and on to Mount Pleasant. They still hadn't settled as they disappeared from view with cows coming out of the group to chase a dog at intervals.

We found out later that they lost a few going through Mount Pleasant Airport but eventually they got the rest to town. Laurie was good to his word and paid us for every animal that reached Swan Inlet and was handed over to his men.

Tony P. came out of town in his Land Rover to Swan Inlet to collect Heather and take her back home.

We headed home the next day, picking up Copernicus and dropping of Falkland at Burnside and made it home that night. It had been good, exciting and satisfying work and we got some money as a bonus.

Tractor troubles

When we set off to build fences right at the beginning, we used the co-op County and the big red trailer to get the material on site. We loaded a lot of fencing into the trailer. A large pile of battens, stakes, straining posts and wire. Then off we went to the fence line.

Once again, as we travelled through Sussex with a heavily leaden tractor and trailer, the tide was to play a part in our lives, and finding it full we decided to drive up Hells Kitchen Valley and try to get up one of the smaller valleys that cut into the main one. Just as we thought we were coming to the top the County bogged to the guts. We tried the obvious first but to no avail. There was nothing for it but to start unloading the trailer and carry it piece by piece to the top of the hill. Then it was back to this large tractor and how the frig to get the sod out of the hole. We have heard of other people chaining posts to the back wheels of tractors in desperation and so this is what we did. The tractor moved ahead, but then the posts were jammed under the wheels. We fought the chains undone and the posts out and did it again. Bit by bit, over a full day, we got the tractor out and up to the top of the hill plus reloaded the fencing as well. Soaked to the skin, covered in mud and slightly jaded we finished one more day in the life of the owners of Port Sussex farm.

Building infrastructure

In that first year, apart from the makeshift shearing shed, we put up ten miles of fencing which included a paddock called TriStar at the furthest point east for our stud ewes. We built this fence the old way with six wires and standards every fifteen yards using the fencing that we got as part of our seventh share of farm materials. We finished building it on the day that the first TriStar landed at Mount Pleasant Airport and so called it TriStar.

We resurrected the old lamb-marking pens about a mile to the north of the house. We included a new drafting race (a narrow passage where sheep can only run up one at a time and you have a gate on each side of the race which you can open to take different sheep out of the flock). This race was fairly new in its design in the Falklands. It had sloping sides rather than being straight up and down. This was supposed to make it harder for the sheep to turn around in the race. We had to build the forcing pen and the holding paddock to support the race and then two bigger paddocks for holding sheep and then an outer paddock to hold the rams and cast sheep.

We built a fence the length of the farm at 500 feet, cutting off the higher land. This ground was for the toughest sheep, the wethers (castrated males). We then built fences to cut the lower land into three sections. We then had the biggest camp on the mountain with the poorer quality feed, and then the land below 500 feet to rotate our young sheep, with the two camps by the creek. The third camp to the east of the creek was for our ewes.

This was an awesome amount of work but we were both as keen as mustard and tore into the work with great enthusiasm. At that time we didn't know it but we had nearly three years before the needs of our children, Caris and Liam, made working and developing the farm a little harder.

We had a fencing caravan, (a co-op asset) which we towed behind the tractor. Not one of those sophisticated holiday things. It was really a box with a pitched roof and windows on runners like a big sledge. Inside, in the far corner, there was a peat stove, which provided heat and the means of cooking and heating water. On the outside at the back of the building was a rack that kept enough peat for a few days' supply. Also on the back was a cupboard-like thing, which was the fly-proof meat safe. Inside there was also a cupboard, for storage, and a single bed, a table and that was it.

Tony and Ailsa, Toni's uncle and aunt lent us their tractor to do this work and we would use this tractor to pull the caravan to a central position near to the fence line and then live from this forward base. We would have to go home every few days to feed the hens and ducks and other animals, and so I could kill meat for us and the dogs, Toni could make bread and do laundry, and we could have a decent bath before returning to the fray once more.

The caravan was cosy. In fact, too hot even on the coldest day with a storm howling outside. Even with the fire banked down with the biggest wettest sod, you would still wake feeling absolutely cooked with your tongue stuck to the roof of your mouth.

We had conscientiously read all the books written by so-called experts about goats and their needs. As a consequence, we couldn't leave poor Tanith, our goat who happened to be pregnant, back at the homestead and so she came fencing with us. She slept in the back of the Land Rover. We parked the Land Rover close to the caravan at night so that we could use the 12-volt battery power for the radio in our humble home.

There was a downside to this arrangement and that was at the first flicker of dawn, at silly o'clock in the morning, Tanith would start kicking the floor of the Land Rover. This was annoying enough but if you went half asleep to let her out, her favourite and most ungrateful trick was to push past you in a very offhand manner and charge through the open door of the caravan, as though she owned the place. She would then scoff anything good or bad that took her fancy therein. By the time one had heaved her out it was pointless going back to bed for those last few minutes. She was a good alarm clock if nothing else.

Going it alone

For a few years after the conflict the military seemed to have an endless supply of fuel and flying hours. Chinooks, Sea Kings, Lynxes, Scouts, Gazelles and Phantoms would be buzzing around nearly continuously. If there was a moments rest, the Falkland Island Air Service was in the act of flying low and inspecting every speck of dust.

So sneaking away for one's daily constitutional could be very tricky at best and close to a public performance at worst. It was disaster if the wind was blowing, which it often did, and the loo roll starts unravelling creating a very visible 'X marks the spot'.

I can't remember many bad times. I can remember some of the foul weather that we endured, working through storms of rain, sleet and snow. We had so much to do to make our farm self-contained and workable in the first year that we would turn our backs into whatever and persevere.

That following February/March at the end of the season, we were totally knackered and washed out but we had managed without any outside help, apart from lamb marking which was more of a social occasion with friends, to fly our farm solo.

It is true to say that we were pretty clueless about some of the stuff when we started, although I had kept my eyes open when I had been travelling around and I had also worked with a few sheep when I worked in Kent but not on this scale.

Although I know that self-praise is no recommendation I don't think we did that badly. In the days of the co-op we used to ride for hours before we got to the start of a gather and the old hands like Gez (Gerald Dickson) and Ron used to talk about how some of us would struggle on their own. They didn't clarify who they were, but I suppose we did feature in there along with at least two others.

I was reasonably sure we would cope and perhaps this could be interpreted as overconfidence or ignorance because we had never trained a dog, chased many sheep or bullock and here we were with 3,000 sheep and 90 bullock, and over 7,000 acres to chase them round in.

Most of the summer months in the year of working as a co-op we were chasing, shearing and sharing out the stock and then, once apportioned, driving them back to our farm. The autumn and winter became the time to cart stuff home and get yourself ready to do your own thing in the following October.

Everyone used the co-operative tractor and trailers to cart their stuff home so everyone had to be patient. One of the tractors was a Ford County with four big wheels, and the other was a Plough Master, which has half-sized driving wheels at the front. There were also two big trailers with wide balloon-like tyres for these tractors to tow.

There was also another small, two-wheeled Fordson Major tractor which was really only used for settlement work. It was old but was the only vehicle that I had ever seen with an inertia starter. You wound the starter up until it stopped and then you released the mechanism which whirred and kicked the starter in and away she would go. It saved on batteries but you had to be reasonably fit to wind it up.

Although both 4x4 tractors had a lot of pulling power one still had to judge what load to put in the trailers. If the load were too heavy you would struggle and possibly fail to get to the top of the mountain and then if you managed to get that far, too much weight could result in you becoming bogged in the peat on top.

Driving the tractors was, and still is, one of Toni's least favourite jobs. She had learned to drive in the co-op County when we were fencing TriStar, when I said to her she needed to drive while I threw the fencing out the back of the trailer. She was not keen, but as I pointed out there was no one else to do it, she gamely gave it a go. These tractors were old and basic and the brakes and clutches were very heavy to push down and nothing like the modern tractors of today that are as sophisticated as a car to drive.

Toni and I did a number of these winter runs skidding and fighting our way up and over the mountain. There were two choices of track. One that went straight up behind the Head of the Bay House and the other was the main track that climbed up to the midway point of the mountain and then headed east, gently angling up and over towards the Gin Rock gate and then turning off by the Sussex peat banks towards our farm. Fortunately, at this stage we had the more modern tractor loaned to us by Tony and Ailsa, which Toni drove.

The Head of the Bay track was mostly climbing with room to turn to the left and right but with a steeper part on the last 82 yards. The other track was a less direct route but with a gentler climb but had a bottleneck three-quarters of the way up where buffalo ditches converged and where the army BVs had made a mess and in the winter it was difficult to get passed. (In the 1950s a tracked machine called a Buffalo was used to pull a ditching plough, to make drainage ditches in the hope of improving the land. These ditches were referred to as 'buffalo ditches'.)

On one of these runs home Toni and I had chosen the Head of the Bay option and we had made the top of the mountain and were heading east before turning south towards Sussex. Things were going fairly well. I usually led looking back to check on Toni's progress. On this trip I looked back and Toni was jumping around gesticulating in a very animated manner at something ahead. I turned around to see a fighter jet filling the windscreen. They were that low, if I had been standing on the roof I swear that I would have been knocked off.

What a fright. The sight, the noise, I sort of flinched and ducked and ran away on the spot. My reaction had made Toni's day because a broad grin was spread across her face for the remainder of the journey.

Power

To have water and power on tap, which someone else is looking after, is a great asset that we take for granted in Stanley and in most other civilised parts of the world, but I can't see this provision being extended to farms in the Falklands. When I hear people growl about the costs of water and electricity in towns and cities or the absence for whatever reason for an hour or so, I think people just don't know how lucky they are. In our position I would love to pay for others to look after our water and power and pay more for the privilege.

While on the subject of services I will describe the power situation, which was woeful when we first arrived at Sussex.

We had been used to a more modern electrical arrangement whist living in Stanley although it wasn't that flash because of the antiquated wiring. This wiring had been put in years ago which wasn't designed to cope with much, although it did manage our twin tub washing machine. The most entertaining memory for Toni was the earthing arrangement, which incorporated her earthing properties. Whenever Toni touched the cold tap and the twin tub at the same time, she would get an electric shock. We found out subsequently that the house was earthed to the cold water pipes, which somehow wasn't adequate. The wiring was good for lights, TV and video but anything above that would have the fuses going.

We had military guys billeted with us after the war, and they liked wandering around in their shorts and t-shirts to feel at home. The peat Rayburn didn't cut it for warmth outside the kitchen unless you had on, at least, a thick jersey. To maintain the kind of warmth that these chaps expected, in a drafty, non-insulated house, with sash windows, you needed a huge kilowatt effort. All of a sudden our power kept tripping off at an alarming rate, which in a wooden house needed an immediate investigation. It took us a while to track down the fault, which were a couple of electric heaters. The lads had got a plan to overcome the shortcomings of the fuses, which they were intending to replace with bits of nail. Fortunately, we were on hand to prevent the meltdown of the house's wiring and the inevitable fire and destruction of the house itself. The boys scrounged some oil stoves, which in a wooden building brought their own issues but allowed the wiring to carry on with light duties (pun intended).

I digress. Back at the farm the Lister diesel generator set we inherited was good for one and a half kilowatts. This made it good for lights and TV and video, but anything over a kilowatt it would die. The twin tub could oscillate but the spin was way beyond its capability. Anything below a kilowatt it could cope with, like an electric drill or a small angle grinder, but even a modest kettle was mission impossible.

This generating unit wasn't all bad. Its greatest feature was its fuel consumption. It seemed to go forever on the sniff of an oily rag.

Power in the camp was fairly basic before the 24-hour scheme of 1994. Before subdivision, most middle-sized settlements had around ten-to-fifteen kilowatts and outside houses had 1.5s although there was the occasional generator that was bigger. In the settlements there were set times when the engine came on which depended on the time of year but it was usually a few hours in the morning and after dark at night to ten or eleven. Outside houses and especially family farms used their generators sparingly.

The 24-hour set ups consisted of a wind turbine, a large battery and an inverter. The idea is that the wind turbine charges the battery and the inverter converts the 24- or 48-volt DC battery power into 240 AC domestic electricity. The diesel engine is there to charge the battery when the wind fails. We were the first farm to invest in this scheme although Brook and Eileen Hardcastle, the ex-manager and his wife of the Falkland Island Company farms, had a system in before ours.

A farmer called Clive Wilkinson developed this business importing these set ups and installing them on people's farms. We got a 24-volt system and a 2.5-kilowatt wind turbine and off we went. It was a lot of money but the Falkland Islands Development Corporation heavily subsidised the project making it affordable to financially beleaguered farmers.

We were the guinea pigs, so to speak, along with the Hardcastles. Our wind turbine burned out in a northeast gale a few months after it was installed, and so the manufacturers knew the wires coming from the turbine had to be heavier in the Falkland conditions and it was also soon apparent that the 48-volt systems were better.

In my opinion it is one of the best things that came to the farms in the Islands and with it came fuel savings, although it was yet another capital item that needed to be replaced over time. There are consumables like blades and springs on the wind turbines and then modular components that sometimes need replacing like electronic boards in the inverters.

Our first trace inverter and battery lasted just over ten years but it did need expensive spares during this time. The Proven wind turbine is still going but with the coils having been replaced. To replace the inverter and battery cost us £7,000 which at the time was a lot of money to find.

Ten years before the 24-hour option was introduced to the Falkland Islands we were thinking of all our power needs. Shearing, pressing, grinding, welding and, in a quest for marital bliss, hopefully being able to use the twin tub. We decided to invest some of our hard-earned money into a Lister TS1, coupled up to an alternator which was meant to kick out 5KVA at 1,500 revs.

This new engine seemed to take forever to arrive and more so as we battled along with the feeble thing that was pushing everyone's patience, relying on forgiveness for its patheticness and hanging on its one redeeming feature – its fuel economy

But arrive it eventually did and came ashore, brought by the *Monsunen* and its sea truck, where we then struggled to get it into the engine shed.

Our new engine made an instant difference but it was quite modest in terms of covering our power needs and much thought had to be given when using tools or household appliances that used a lot of power. It was already second nature to turn everything off that wasn't needed, but even with the new generator we couldn't use the washing machine and the vacuum cleaner at the same time for instance.

We had been very wise to build the shearing shed close to the house, not only for me to crawl back after a day's shearing but also because it was close to the power house which meant that a minimum amount of power was lost in the cables. To have two shearing motors operating and the press as well had the generator at maximum capacity and everything else would be switched off.

It was the grinder that sharpened the shearing gear that was the biggest drain on the engine. I used to give it a good spin with my hand and then switch it on. Even then the engine would hunt and belch out black smoke as if it had been converted to peat fired. It was the start that would need all the power but once the disk started to gather speed the engine would relax and the smoke would disappear.

Welding was another operation that was harder over a period of time, because if you could keep an arc the engine would be working hard. Again it paid to weld as close to the engine as possible and even then it was extremely difficult to strike an arc. If you have plenty of power there is less of a problem. I found that the best way was to think that you were striking a big match and as it sparked up to hold a small gap. Once you had got an arc the engine would start behaving like an extra in a Thomas the Tank Engine set, pouring out black smoke and showing its displeasure. After you stopped the run of weld the engine would recover ready for the next session.

On a farm, the welder is often called into action to build or repair and I did wonder whether this kind of effort, even abuse, would damage the generator over time. As it was our only source of power, apart from the old engine, I often felt the weight of anxiety as the engine churned out clouds of black smoke. Time however proved that the Lister unit thrived on this heavy use.

The alternator did fail eventually. We did buy another alternator for the engine and now it is a fall-back generator which we have outgrown. In the early 1980s it was a quantum leap in our power provision, but today it isn't enough for all the electrical paraphernalia that we have collected up over the 30 plus years we have been here. It cannot charge the batteries on the 24-hour system unless the charging rate is turned right down.

Apart from the Lister TS1, which came from UK, all our other engines have been secondhand and we have invested in new alternators. The Lister engines are very basic and not in the high-performance bracket. We brought a three-cylindered Lister ST from Port San Carlos when they split up and it wasn't long before the engine started giving us jip. The fuel pump timing is a laborious job to do with each cylinder having its own individual pump timed by adding or removing shims to its base. The gap between the piston and head is measured by putting a piece of soft metal on top of the piston, fitting the head back on and then turning it over the compression stroke and then measuring it. Then once again, to adjust, removing or adding shims to bring it to the manufacturers' specifications. I was working through all these procedures one Sunday afternoon while listening to a Formula One Grand Prix. On the radio I listened to how fuel mixture and timing and many other things were adjusted from the pits as the cars were flying round the circuit. It did occur to me that Lister wasn't in the same league as Ferrari or any of the other top Formula One contenders.

Travelling along the track
There was around 70 miles of track leading to Stanley and we probably travelled there a little bit more than the other farmers in our area.

Once you get to know a track you get an understanding of which pieces are getting soft and need to be avoided although it sometimes worked the other way when you were going through a bottleneck like a pass and you thought, 'I think we will make it just once more' and then one day you don't.

I remember a particular trip in the middle of winter in 1985, following the clay track and not being able to drive out and around all the puddles because it was so slippery and the puddles were full of very thick ice. We would punch our way through these places, sometimes having to back off and charge forward again. This was one of our earlier runs before we had learnt the track because we rarely used the clay track during the winter after the first year. In the summer, it was different and the clay tracks were okay although you still had to avoid the wallows that had been gouged out during the winter.

It was very strange on one of our first runs into town, to come over the hill approaching where they were building Mount Pleasant Airport and see a single decker bus travelling along a dirt road full of construction workers. One didn't see a bus anywhere in the Falklands but to see one in what was the middle of nowhere was even more bizarre.

If you have never done serious off-road, especially in an older vehicle, it can be quite arduous. When you are going on relatively hard ground the engine is running freely and the doors are rattling and you are thrown from side to side. Then you hit some soft and the engine takes the weight and the slack in every moving part is taken up and the vehicle creaks and groans. The engine will labour even in low range as the vehicle sinks right in. The trips that you remember are the ones where it has not gone that well or there has been an unusual event.

When we went in and out of town we would have the back of our Series IIA packed tight with the things that we needed on the farm. We wondered how we could bring more stuff out. We couldn't fit a roof rack easily because it had a soft-top canvas back. Fortunately, for many years the military would sell off their surplus material and so the solution to our carrying capacity was answered when we bought a trailer from one of these cast sales.

Our old Land Rover was a beast of a machine and gave us sterling work getting a diet of the toughest of off-road work loaded to the gunnels. But it wasn't new and it had survived many years in the hands of the military. Most vehicles need constant work and our vehicle, given such a hard life, was no exception. I was constantly replacing chassis and spring bushes and universal joints, springs and shock absorbers, but it was one small screw that wasn't totally vital, that I delayed replacing, that cost us another few grey hairs. At the bottom of the gearstick is a little grub screw, which keeps the gearstick in position. Without it, it twists around all over the place. Somehow this screw had worked loose, fallen out and was lost, making the gear stick sloppy and not lending itself to find a particular gear in a hurry.

We were coming home with our Land Rover and trailer full of stuff and, as the crow flies, less than 6.5 miles from Sussex house. We still had St Bruno's Arroyo and the Sussex Creek to overcome. It was always a soft swampy little valley, with a ditch at the west side, where a bridge sat with a climb straight after, with a multiple choice of tracks. I decided to swing hard left where you had to stay above a spring hole and then with a bit of momentum climb a short, sharp, steepish piece and you were up on the flat again.

So round the swamp we went and then power on, foot to the floor, nearly to the top and the engine dies. I go for a slick gear change into first gear. That retched screw is sorely missed, as we hurtle back down the hill, remembering that the brakes are at their best, and that isn't fantastic, after at least five pumps. The Land Rover and trailer just hammered back down the hill. It's impossible to control at that speed even if it had happened on the flat. We ended up at the bottom with the Land Rover on top of the upturned trailer and Toni freaking out. I calmly got the bumper jack out and began to jack the Land Rover off the trailer. This means jacking it as high as the jack will go and trying to tip the Land Rover sideways and off. Toni was still peeling off strips of my hide as the Land Rover looked as if it would end up on its roof when I suggested that she took the handheld 2-meter set up onto the top of the valley and call her dad, who was staying with us at the time, to say that we are going to be late for supper.

I eventually got the Land Rover off the trailer, but needless to say the trailer was never the same again. The solid steel rod with the round piece on the end that sits in the jaws of the tow hitch was the shape of a goose's neck. The trailer carried on for nearly twenty more years before the chassis gave up, which was nothing to do with the accident.

This was not the only occasion that the missing grub screw caused problems. We had left San Carlos and gone through the double iron gates opposite Head of Bay House. There was a steep clay cutting that the track went down to the beach. I left it a bit late to change gear, as we were already committed when I tried and then could not get the vehicle back into gear. Again virtually non-existent brakes saw us careering down the hill and shooting out into the middle of the creek. I managed to locate a grub screw after this.

The temporary shearing shed and shearing
One of the first jobs we had to undertake on the farm was a temporary shearing shed and after a while we had enough material back at Sussex to start building. My idea was to try and build without cutting any of the main timbers that we had acquired with the farm so that we could reuse them when we built the permanent shed when that day came.

The first job was digging all the holes for the piles, which were going to be the foundations to our shearing shed, and then cutting and putting in all the piles to the same height throughout the building site. The outside walls north and south were the bull stables walls and the sides were made from the bull stables ends and other scraps.

Another great resource at that time were the rubbish dumps at Mount Pleasant Airport and Stanley. As long as you weren't fussy there was plenty of wood. There were sheets of ply, chip board and pieces of wood of all shapes and sizes. It was a great shame that the roads weren't in existence during this period because it would have been worthwhile taking the lorry up weekly at least. There was a song being played on BFBS (British Forces Broadcasting Service) and FIBS (Falkland Islands Broadcasting Station) at the time which went 'We built this city on rock and roll,' and we would be building our shed singing 'We built this shed out of army junk.'

We did build the shearing shed virtually single-handed, although Derek, Toni's brother, gave us a hand to lift the south and north walls up onto the piles. I remember it well because he got his fingers trapped between the wall and one of the piles and made a bit of a fuss complaining about his squashed fingers for weeks.

We had a Donald's wool press on the way but it was still somewhere on the high seas when we were building the shed.

I asked Tony, Toni's uncle, how high the new Donald's presses were because he had seen one working. 'I can definitely put my hand on the top of one,' he said. I thought one would be tall but I didn't know how high so I took Tony's estimate and added a couple of feet. I thought that that would cover it. Well NO. I ended up putting an extension on the roof in one corner where the press was going to be that looked like a ruddy pigeon loft. Was this the only design fault? No. Fortunately, once again, I happened to shear so things evolved slowly but we hadn't allowed room to store the bales under cover. An extension went on the north end of the shed rapido with more wood and tin from our share of the San Carlos material. It worked reasonably well because the press sat on the floor in the shed and you tipped the bales out of the press, onto the ground in the new extension. We still had problems storing all the bales between boat visits and when we tried tarpaulins the wind always managed to blow it off one part or another exposing the bales to the elements. Sometimes we would roll them into the back pens which wasn't that helpful because it just reduced the number of sheep we could hold in the shed, but these were pioneering days.

We built this shed in a matter of weeks and it was okay for about six years, but when we had the contractors they shore so many sheep that the wool would pile up because we couldn't press it into bales fast enough. When the shearers were shearing the ewes, they would be hitting over 300 sheep each and every day. Our temporary shed was adequate but saved us driving our sheep over to San Carlos to share paddocks and the shed and then drive them home again, but only just.

We equipped the first shed with a Euroclip shearing motor, a Heiniger grinder and a Donald's wool press. I also bought a Sunbeam hand piece and we already had a Lister hand piece, once again, courtesy of our seventh share of San Carlos stuff. It wasn't long before we were shearing the first few of the 3,000.

The first sheep you shear in the Falklands are hoggets which people call hogs for short. These sheep are last year's lambs and are about a year old. They are the smallest but also the hardest for the novice shearer. They curl up, bringing their hind legs up and in the way, wriggle and have a lot of wool right down to their hooves. An experienced shearer uses his weight and his non-shearing hand a lot, to prepare the sheep or wool for the next blow-like pushing in the flank to encourage the sheep to straighten its legs.

To watch a good shearer is poetry in motion. It looks so easy. The hand piece is never still, the cutting edge is always full of wool and the sheep seem to move effortlessly from one position to the next as the shearer uses his legs, feet and hands to move it through the positions as the wool just tumbles off. The belly is taken off first and the rousie (roustabout) throws that into the belly bin. They then move on around the crutch and on to the left hind leg, clearing so far up the back. Then it is off with the topknot on top of the head. Then up the neck, clearing one side of the face and shoulder and then into the long blow which clears one side and the sheep is laying right down and the rest of the face is cleared. The sheep is moved back to the sitting position as the other shoulder is cleared and then finishing what is left on the last side and right hind leg. All the time the shearer is using his legs and free hand to position the sheep and readying the wool for the next blow.

This is not the case with the novice who in comparison does short, jerky blows; the sheep goes to each position in slow, uncoordinated moves with many pauses. The sheep isn't comfortable and struggles and kicks more and the shearer is working really hard to get a small amount of sheep shorn.

The latter was my lot. No one was around to motivate me or for me to learn from. Just another sheep whenever I wanted one. I fought every sheep with brute force and plenty of ignorance so as the days went by I got more and more tired and irritable and felt that we would never get them all shorn. We would get up at 5am and turn to at 6am, working through the day to finish at 5pm and then have all the other jobs to do. The first few weeks were murder and we often joked that it was a good job that the shed was so close to the house as I made my way there like a half-shut penknife.

Toni was really good and patient and encouraged me, but it was obvious that she was bored to sobs and showed this by bringing a book to the shed to read between sheep.

Tony P. was also living with us during some of this time and although he had lived all his life in Stanley he knew how to do many of the camp jobs. Tony also had times as he sat patiently by as I chewed the sheep out.

Different people came out and gave me a couple of days and even passing shearers would do a few here and there, but apart from those I shore them all, with Toni sorting and pressing the wool and bringing more sheep into the shed and pens as needed. There were two main low points in my first year and that was when Keith Heathman (another of Toni's uncles) came up and sheared more sheep, 'turning to' after breakfast, than I had in more than a couple of full days. The second was when we heard that in another shearing shed, Patricia Card shore more than me in a day when she took over from her shearer boyfriend who had hurt his hand in a fight. I was ready to throw my hand piece into the creek. But Toni was able to rebuild my shattered ego and give me a reason to carry on. In hindsight she wasn't working with very much but she managed to steady the ship.

The day that last sheep went through the porthole was one of the most memorable. There was a collective sigh of relief and, ignoring the fuss I'd made along the way, a feeling of satisfaction and achievement.

We did have some laughs but also scares from sheep number one, to the last individual.

Scares – we often picked out mutton from the wethers and so we decided to hold one of the sheep back. I shore it and forgot and was letting it go, but Toni grabbed one of its back legs and I also got my free hand onto a leg. It was a big animal, which was already on the way down the chute and its momentum and weight pulled Toni onto my hand piece, which was still going, catching her in the corner of her eye socket. The small scar on her face is testimony to how close we came to a major disaster. In farming, we sometimes think everything is against us but it wasn't that day – we were very, very lucky.

Laughs – we had a window close to the shearing floor made of reinforced plastic. The rams of the day were big swaggering brutes with plenty of attitude. One ram had so much power that he nearly fired me out through this window. He straightened his neck and kicked and I was giving the window a Newcastle kiss. Toni found it hilarious. I only found it amusing, after a number of years and after a few beers, when we are reminiscing.

As I have already mentioned because I was a novice and with all the other work we did that first year on our own I was getting exhausted. As I was getting tired the bigger sheep would know it and give me jip. One day I was going up the long blow when this big wether kicked me in the delicate area. One hand had the shears and the other was pulling his head on to my leg as you do. I had had enough and instinctively head butted this sheep in frustration. The bloody sheep hardly seemed to notice. I saw enough stars to start my own galaxy and never did that again.

Some visitors

In those early days we saw a military patrol every few weeks. We used to invite them in for a cuppa, some drop scones and a chat. I remember one particular patrol told us how hard and tough they were and if there were such a thing in the British Army they would be the Penal Battalion. Fine, they did talk tough and they had been in a few scrapes from the sound of things. These guys wanted to see a sheep shorn. Fair enough, no problem. They then wanted to see a sheep killed. We were always killing sheep for ourselves, dogs, cats and so again we could do that. A couple even wanted to kill a sheep and we thought that with supervision that would be all right. Nothing was too much for the British armed forces.

We got the sheep in and I began to shear them, but two or three of the 'penal' patrol sat it out just in case a sheep was accidently cut in the process. Okay, so there were a few sensitive members of these hard men, it wasn't a problem. At the end of the process I showed them how to cut a sheep's throat and break its neck quickly to prevent suffering. This act whittled the audience down to one who couldn't bring himself to do it, which again was fair enough.

One of the guys came back and asked if he could have an eyeball to dissect. He said he would remove it from the skull himself. Off he went with this gift, a few minutes later there is a cry of agony. Somehow this individual had gone to remove the eye with his penknife and it had snapped shut on his finger and cut it quite badly. Toni is good at patching people up and so took him away and washed his wound and dressed it.

I could have said it could have happened to anyone but the whole episode made me glad that it wasn't the penal battalion that had come down in 1982 to evict the Argentinian invader.

A gift of rams

Derek, Toni's brother has been visiting us ever since we have lived at Sussex and he has brought out loads of different stuff for us over the years.

On one occasion he was bringing full-grown rams out of Stanley. They had arrived in town on the local coastal vessel and so Derek thought he would run them out in the back of his Land Rover.

Heather was the boss of all things animal and camp having lived most of her younger life outside Stanley. So Derek and Heather went and caught these rams, threw them down and put a rope around their necks and hind legs, which immobilises them. Heather was always a little sensitive and wouldn't let the loops be too small and therefore too tight.

Out came Derek with his live cargo and probably a load of other stuff. He travelled along the Mount Pleasant road with no problems and then through the L'Antioja and onto the white grass flats around Swan Inlet. Just west of Swan Inlet, Derek hit a bump and a big ram, that had escaped its rope, was sitting in the front passenger seat looking at him. Seeing the windscreen he thought it was a gap through which to escape and jumped towards it cracking the glass. With one hand, Derek tried to push the ram into the back and prevent it butting him as he kept his eyes on the track and out of the soft. It is a good idea to keep the momentum going through this type of terrain. I wasn't there but I pictured Derek and the ram fighting like actors do in movies when the baddies are trying to wrestle the wheel from the goodies or visa versa. Derek ended up getting bogged, which gave him sufficient time to sort the rams out before setting to with the jack and getting out.

With his cargo of live animals he had removed his planks and bridges and so he improvised by gathering thick lumps of ice from a place where he had broken it up with the Land Rover moments before his bogging.

Derek did arrive a few hours late and with this great tale to tell, but he had won the battle of wills and ordeal by strength.

The good life

We were self-sufficient in many ways. We had cows, we had a kitchen garden, we had hens for eggs and we had peat to burn on the stove. We still had to buy things like fuel for the generator and the Land Rover. We also needed corn for the hens and ducks, flour, sugar and other foods and household goods.

We tried to be self-sufficient with potatoes and other vegetables in the 1980s because not many were imported. Root crops weren't a problem like carrots and swedes and turnips and, if you planted them early enough, parsnips.

I would dig the garden about the same time that I cut peat, usually in October, and then Toni would plant it. Then we would try to keep on top of the weeds. That cooperative year we just couldn't cope and although we harvested enough vegetables the older folk would have despaired at the state that our garden was in.

The secret is to go into the garden every day if you can or as regularly as possible and pull a weed, and thin the crop. You either have to be very skilled at planting the right amount or spend a lot of effort thinning the crop. None of the crops will do as well if they are crammed together. Carrots are very time consuming and as they grow the weeds do as well and hours of weeding them is a painstaking job.

We also had a potato garden over the hill, which was very productive and so we extended it and Derek and Trudi would help us plant and harvest. But gardening in the Falklands can have its down sides and after Christmas, one year, we had a frost. We had done all the work with digging the ground and taking the manure from under the shearing shed over. Planting the seed potatoes and then when they are about a foot high, weeding them and forming up the soil in ridges so that the warmth can get to the tubers. Just when we were talking about the plants being well grown the frost arrived, which sickened the potato crop and it sickened our enthusiasm for the extra garden.

Most years you can get a rewarding return for what is hard work in most people's book, but the odd year when a storm can twist the necks from your brassicas (cabbage, turnips, Brussels sprouts, etc) or a frost that turns a potato crop into potatoes the size of marbles it is very disheartening.

Horses versus communication wire

During the first few years at Sussex we did all the stock work on horseback. It was only just over two years after the war and although there had been a massive clean-up there was still war debris all over the San Carlos area where there had been so much military activity. The curse of all livestock, but especially horses, was the thin black communication wire that seemed to be everywhere. Our horse, Quaker, who was tamed but who had not had many rides from the feel of him, was a sod to get on and would frig around as you tried to mount, rearing up and shying. Once on his back he would be lively and quite flighty. He never really bucked although he did do the odd pig root (small buck) and shy. The poor animal must have caught up or got tangled in this wire that was strewn around because whenever he saw it he would leap backward or shy and get quite agitated. I would try to keep him calm and get him to walk around whatever obstacle it was and carry on. I rode him quite a lot and Toni rode Oxo who was the tamest horse that we got with the farm. Quaker, with a lot of work, got much better to mount and got to be a handy addition to the troop but he never completely got over his fear of wire.

The riding track to San Carlos, on the Sussex side of Sussex Mountain, was hard until nearly at the top of the mountain and then you had to ride over the peat banks, which weren't too soft there. You then went off the top at the San Carlos side and then down and along at an angle, meeting up to a ridge that took you down to the Hard Hill gate. It was pretty straight forward from then on, riding through Kingsford, Burnt Camp and then into the Carthorse Paddock and into the stable there by the shearing shed.

We had quite a few horses once Toni's troop arrived on the scene, and so during that second year we were able to lend Quaker, to Ron and Iris , when they were short of horsepower. This very well-spoken military officer offered to come and get this horse for Ron and so he turned up in a Gazelle helicopter with a set of Ron's horse gear. This guy had obviously ridden before but Quaker could be a handful and probably very unlike some of the cultured animals he was used to. Anyway, we had a steady ride over to the settlement with this chap holding Quaker in, the entire trip saying things like 'steady there' and 'easy boy'. I think it was noteworthy just in the fact that the officers throughout the Falklands used the 'Teeny Weeny' helicopters ('Teeny Weeny' was the nickname given to the Army Air Corp Helicopters) as their personal taxis.

Other gentlemen would also be flown out to the less accessible trout rivers, and then they and their catches would be flown to wherever they were stationed. This kind of excess petered out over those first five years or so until the Scouts and the Gazelles were pulled out.

Trouble with Quaker

Ron's farm was over twenty thousand acres and so was the biggest single section of San Carlos, but it was made up of some pretty marginal ground with aptly named camps such as The Snipe Camp. The Snipe Camp was a king alongside The Flats, which was very soft and swampy. I think Quaker was an asset to Ron but his time at Kingsford Valley Farm wasn't without incident.

Ron was riding well up into his ground, at a place called Cantera Mountain where Quaker got a fright and bucked Ron off. Ron had the habit of wearing army boots without laces and although Ron was long gone, his boots remained in the horses stirrups. I hoped that this episode hadn't ruined their relationship and Ron continued to ride him, bringing him over later in the year to help us lamb mark, something Ron and Iris and their sons Steven and Keith did every year.

The lamb-marking pens are in the middle of the camp so we used to come together at the end of the gather with the ewes and lambs. Ron's beat didn't have any sheep as he came up to the pens so he got off Quaker and lay in the grass. I am not totally sure what happened but Ron was sure that Quaker tried to kick him while he was lying there. As we were packing up, after the lamb marking was finished, Ron came over and said: 'Richard, when Quaker is old and finished just give me a call could you?' 'Why's that Ron?' I asked. 'Because I will come over and cut his bloody throat.' (Quaker returned to Sussex and lived a long and carefree existence.)

Horse taming

In the first few years I bought two four-tonne army lorries in a cast sale in Stanley. They were jalopies but there wasn't much wrong with the Hiab lorry once everything was connected up. I was doing this as Toni and Heather were taming some of the horses that we had got as our seventh share of horses from San Carlos, out at Sussex.

Toni was using a method that she had seen in a book, which didn't involve throwing the horse down or, if everything went according to plan, riding a bucking animal. The idea was to catch the horse and then with the aid of ropes lift its legs off the ground one by one and get the horse used to human contact. Then with one foot off the ground you would stroke the horse all over, working through putting the gear on and then to lying across and then sitting in the gear. It was a slow but complete way of having a tame horse at both ends and in the middle.

It was at this time that a chap called PED entered our lives on a motorbike. He turned up unexpectedly and helpfully told the girls that they were doing it all wrong and that they should do it the Native American way by blowing up their noses. Heather and Toni patiently listened to the unsolicited advice as he went into minute detail of every facet of this training technique.

They couldn't think of a way of politely disengaging and to some degree they were stunned at the audacity of a complete stranger turning up and rubbishing their efforts. It isn't unusual for people to turn up and have a cup of tea and biscuit and they might tell you about a time they tamed horses or had seen horses tamed and that this was good or that was bad or cruel. Although PED had no first-hand experience he had read about his training in a book and felt it his duty to pass the information on.

We had acquired a nanny goat from Giles and Christel soon after we came to Sussex and she was expecting. Tanith had a billy kid, Buck, who was about a year old at the time of the horse taming and he was quite a character. Unbelievably Buck would stand by the horses' back legs munching away on their tails as they were being tamed. It was as if he was deliberately antagonising them. Toni and Heather would try and shoo him away and get quite worried that he would get kicked and launched sky high. For whatever reason, the horses tolerated Buck's nonsense. It was a surprise because among the horses that we acquired were some wild individuals.

During the selection process in the pens at San Carlos one of the horses took off into the shearing shed, which was open to the pens. No one imagined that a horse would run onto wooden gratings inside a big building. This horse had a very strange action, which was like that of a Hackney carriage horse lifting its legs high as it trotted along. He was a lovely looking animal and Toni took a fancy to him, so we picked him on one of our turns.

It wasn't only this trotting action that was different. This animal was totally mad. During the taming process it threw itself down and bit chunks out of the ground, something I had never heard about in all my travels around the Islands and it is one of those stories that people would talk about if they had witnessed it.

Toni got him so that she was able to sit on his back after many, many days of gently does it. It would start with many hours of rubbing the horse with a glove on the end of a stick and then the same with a gloved hand and then finally the hand. Then there would be many hours of putting the gear on and off. Then there would be more hours of putting the gear on and tightening the cinch and slackening it off. Then putting some weight in the stirrup and then off repeating this process until the horse is used to it. Then you lie across the gear like a sack of potatoes and down and back up countless times. Each time a new move is taken the horse may get agitated so you stop and either go back to the step before or gently continue.

Eventually, with Arrow, it was my turn and I would slowly approach the corral. Although Toni and Heather worked the horses up to riding standard I had the dubious pleasure of doing the riding. Just my appearance was enough for him to go bananas. He would roll his eyes and prance about as if he had never seen anyone before. As we are working up to me getting on this wretch, he grabbed the sleeve of my coat, luckily not my arm, and shook it like a dog worrying a rabbit. My Achilles heel was my patience level, which is a fraction of Toni's. I tried to be calm as this big dangerous bastard, who could kick at one end and bite at the other, tore around the corral as though he was possessed by demons.

When you are young you have a feeling of indestructibility, and the life that we led demonstrated that in many ways, but there was a time when you had to make a judgement and decide that discretion was the better part of valour. A serious injury to either of us then, more so than today, would have had serious implications. I decided that I couldn't afford to take the risk and ride him. During the whole time at Sussex this was the only time I lost a campaign but he was bad and I had the feeling with him that he would try to kick you or even bite you if he managed to get you off. Unfortunately, we had to put him down. We were later told that this animal's mother had been mad too, and had been put in the manada as she was impossible to ride, and had apparently drowned herself in a pond.

Another horse called T'Soulaiky (who was actually from Toni's troop and had been handled from a foal) was another kettle of fish. She was as tame as a kitten and didn't need to be restrained as Toni went through the taming exercise – in fact she appeared to enjoy it. You could pet her, rub your hand under her brisket and down her legs, front and back without the slightest reaction. This was how it should be.

Toni sat alongside me on Oxo ready to take me out for T'Soulaiky's first ride into the Head of the Bay ground. The idea was to ride out together so far to get the young horse away and then for the young animal to carry on, on its own. I would ride out to the west and then up the mountain a little way heading east and then cross a ditch and then come back down the boundary fence, through the pass on the track on the high, high tide track where Liam fell in the snow that Farmers' Week, and back to meet up with the other rider.

Much to my astonishment this mare let me get on, get my foot in the other stirrup and feel my weight on her back, but as we moved off she just cut into an awesome series of bucks. Luckily for me she bucked and carried on bucking straight ahead but she put her heart and soul into it and her head and rump seemed to disappear as she bucked and carried on. I sat it out and rather unwisely tempted providence by saying to Toni, 'If that's all she's got there's no problem.'

She was still quite a small animal so I couldn't get my cinch as tight as I liked but I still remained confident that if she bucked straight ahead I would be able to stay on. So we rode up from the stable to the wooden Mutton Paddock gate leading out into the Head of the Bay ground following the Land Rover track heading towards San Carlos. It was all relatively flat apart from a small dip about 100 metres from the gate. To add to the occasion the two goats came on the riding-out party.

T'Soulaiky had learnt from our first encounter and so changed tactics and went tearing down a slight hill bucking and then shot off to one side. This was the undoing of me as the gear came slack and I went flying.

This was to start a long battle of wills that lasted for many years. I could never understand why such a tame animal could be so different once you were on her back and I always thought that it was the next ride that would make her tame and good to ride

She got to a stage where she was 100 per cent tame when you were with another horse but on her own she was always unpredictable. This was not what we needed because in doing our farm work we needed to work together, but at a good distance apart, and we also did a lot of stuff independently.

One of the most memorable trips with T'Soulaiky started from the stable, going solo to the east end of the farm following the horse track out through the horse paddock.

Sussex is mostly deep valleys and ridges and as you leave the stable you head north until you come to the first steep valley and then ride along its length drifting down from the top, when you join it, to the bottom. It then opens out where you go through two passes, through small water courses. This first valley is not the ideal place to ride a horse like T'Soulaiky, so I rekindled my relationship with God as we rode along this piece. Any bucking or sudden movement would have had us both at the bottom in a heap. I'm sure she probably wouldn't have noticed if I rolled on her a couple of times but she wasn't that small for me not to notice if she did the rolling on me. For many horses, if they are going to buck it is often when you first get on. Most after a long day are less likely to want to play up.

After the two small passes you climb out of the valley again up on to the flat and head towards the Horse Paddock gate on the Land Rover track. Everything was plain sailing and we negotiated the gate, which meant getting off and on. The tide was high so I headed for the top pass in Hells Kitchen. I took more sharp intakes of breath as we negotiated the steep descent into Hells Kitchen, which again with any kind of shenanigans would have had me in big trouble. We successfully came down and climbed up the other side on a pathway cut by someone years ago, called the Zs, which zig-zagged up out of Hells Kitchen. This track is quite entertaining on a tame sure-footed animal but on T'Soulaiky it was heart in your mouth stuff. At the top of the Zs I began to relax and enjoy my ride, because for about a mile it is relatively flat before you ride around the beach. There is just a gate to do and no other complication.

I got off and opened the gate, leading T'Soulaiky through. Shut the gate and then, gathering up the reins, got on and all hell let loose. She turned to the south, which is slightly down hill, and bucked like fury with all her might. I leant back, gripping with my knees and trying to pull her head up. Timed to perfection she did two big sideways bucks just before a ridge of rocks, the gear began to go and I was airborne. I saw my glasses going over the fence as I flipped over in mid-air and landed on my back amongst the flat rocks, knocking the air out of my lungs. Yes, it hurt. It hurt a lot. Did I break anything? No, thank goodness, but why I will never know. If I had been seriously hurt it would have been hours before Toni came looking for me and hopefully found me and then, depending on the injury, got appropriate help.

T'Soulaiky was eating grass about 100 feet away in a small valley. Feeling sore all over I walked down to her, straightened the gear and climbed gingerly back on. This was one of many occasions where we battled it out. I won many battles but the ones that I lost are the easiest to remember because they were usually accompanied by some discomfort.

Another memorable event with T'Soulaiky happened at the end of the shearing season. I had ridden down to the pens in Shepherds Brook at the east end of the farm. Toni drove down in the Land Rover. After weaning, the lambs would go everywhere and about 100 a year would get back to where they were born, which was Shepherds Brook. We went down gathered Shepherds Brook, put the sheep through the lamb-marking pen that was down there and took the lambs off and then took them back to where they belonged and few, if any, went back a second time.

On this day we had gathered the sheep into the pens and I put the *manares* (hobbles) on T'Soulaiky while we drafted the sheep. As we worked, the mare slowly but surely moved away from the pens, but we had to crack on because there was a storm brewing which once it broke we wouldn't be able to continue.

At last we had finished and I had 150 sheep to drive back to the Low Pass, but where was the horse? Trying not to curse my decision to bring T'Soulaiky, I set off with my dogs, walking the sheep to their rightful camp as Toni drove off in the vehicle to try and locate the mare.

It wasn't that far, about three miles, and behind sheep it isn't as if you have to walk very fast to keep up. I soon had the sheep through the gate into the Low Pass. Toni, in the meantime, had found the wayward horse and lashed her head to the *manares* with the *cabaresta* (leading rein) to stop her going any further. She then came back picked me up and we went back to collect T'Soulaiky.

By this time the storm was upon us and it was blowing a hoolie, and the rain was lashing down in sheets. On top of this the daylight was all but gone and the lightning was starting. Toni by this time had got a migraine, which usually incapacitates her. So I was riding home cold, wet and miserable, waiting for the inevitable. T'Soulaiky was very tense and jumped at every peel of thunder and flash of lightening. Toni was following at a discreet distance but each time the vehicle lights swept across us the mare was shying hard to one side and hunching up ready to buck. Down into Hells Kitchen on the Land Rover track and it was pitch black, the car lights gently licking us again as she pranced and slipped on some loose stuff on the side of the track. We then waded through the Low Pass and travelled around the beach and then headed up towards the Horse Paddock Gate, riding left as the vehicle track went straight ahead.

I jumped off at the gate and led her through and took the gear off. Toni came through the gate in the Land Rover and I threw the gear in the back. I didn't fancy slipping and sliding into the main valley and then along the side of the other valley to get back to the stable. The horse was in the paddock where she was meant to be and the Land Rover seemed to be a simple option.

One day Toni and a friend were riding horses chasing the bullock home. I decided to ride T'Soulaiky down to meet them. It was like riding a different animal, and although this mare was comfortable to ride, this day she seemed to be totally relaxed. I honestly believed I had cracked it and I said this to Toni, even persuading her to ride her. I took Toni's horse and she took T'Soulaiky chasing cattle. She didn't misbehave at all.

Had I managed to finally sort her out? The next time I slapped my gear on her she bucked like hell. I never gave up trying to enforce my will on T'Soulaiky but I did think perhaps it would have been wiser to throw in the towel at an earlier stage. I never understood why she could be so tame in every other respect and not eventually become a civilised horse to ride.

Kelly's Garden

Kelly's Garden was a military camp which was close to San Carlos settlement and it bought another dimension to the lives of the new farmers as they started their new ventures. There were always officers and men visiting the settlement and vice versa. We enjoyed many a video tape film when we stayed with Pat and Isobel, supplied via our friends at Kelly's. This kind of cooperation didn't always work out.

We had the Land Rover series IIA (2A) that we had bought from the military in a cast sale. It had been fitted with radio suppression equipment which meant that among the other benefits the distributer was waterproof, something it certainly wasn't on a normal petrol Land Rover. This meant you could drive along rutted out clay track ruts, wade creeks, streams and rivers, as long as the water didn't go as high as the air intake of the engine.

This was invaluable when getting home to Sussex, although judgement still had to be used. We have had the water coming into the vehicle a couple of times when we needed to get home in a hurry but that was in the days of the old Land Rover when we knew it had a finite life expectancy. Wading salt water is bad news for the chassis, the wheel bearings and any part where the salt water gets in.

With our ever-increasing knowledge of the track and the big track grip tyres we brought some really big loads out of town in the Land Rover. If we were going in it made sense because freight on the local ship cost money. The coastal vessel only came to new farms like us for wool or when we had sufficient freight to make it worthy of a trip into Sussex Harbour. Someone who had a home in Stanley made this judgement. We didn't expect a trip with a case of beer or a tin of beans and we hardly ever called on their services. We did make a request once, which led to a huge amount of work and inconvenience on our parts.

All this radio suppression kit was really good until you had a problem and then it was a nightmare. It had a huge 80-amp generator to charge the batteries and sitting behind the seats were two big square batteries, probably there to support the radio kit and other electrical stuff that the military police might need. To add to the complication, it was a 24-volt system so nothing from the civilian 12-volt Land Rover could be substituted.

Something went wrong with the charging on the Land Rover and the charging light remained on all the time. Try as I might with my basic circuit tester I could not fathom out what was wrong. Behind the driver's seat there was a waterproof box which had a bird's nest of wires and other electrical components that would have looked at home in an old television or radio set.

I used to put the battery on to a small trickle charger, which worked while I thought about what to do.

Kelly's Garden was fully operational and they had a number of machines supporting the camp including a few Land Rovers and one of the mechanics offered to have a look for me. What could be better I thought than an army mechanic looking at our ex-military Land Rover.

We delivered the Land Rover to the chap at Kelly's, and a few days later we got a message to say that it was fixed. As we came onto the beach at the Head of the Bay there were big track grip marks going here and there, over rocks and out into the squidgy mud and salt water. As our Land Rover was the only vehicle at that time around San Carlos to have the big track grips we knew it was from our vehicle. We sort of thought they must have fixed it and taken it for a spin to a make sure all was well and to try out these big tyres, which were a lot bigger than anything the military had.

I went into Kelly's and handed over a case of beer and started the Land Rover up and yes the charging light went off. It could be a bit of a performance getting out of Kelly's because there wasn't a road to San Carlos and when the tide was in it could be interesting. On this day it would have taken me about 15 minutes. It wasn't that long before I could hear a strange noise coming from the back of the Land Rover and it got louder and more frantic as time went on. There was also a strange smell.

On arriving at San Carlos I traced this noise back to the batteries in the back. These huge batteries were boiling because the mechanic had wired the alternator straight to the batteries missing out the regulator. It was a wasted case of beer but once again I had learnt an important lesson. Eventually, over time, I rounded up all the 12-volt equipment and when I had it all, we converted it.

Occasionally the military camp would throw a social where everyone was invited and these were very good evenings. The liveliest one that we went to was a barbeque where the food was prepared by the Ghurkhas and was very hot if you chose unwisely. There was a lot of drink consumed and things started to get out of hand with the military throwing each other into the sea and we civilians were wondering when we would take a splash. A BVs tracked vehicle was the bar and it was driven into the sea in Clam Valley so that you had to wade out to get a drink. Some guys took their clothes off when they were chucked into the sea only to find that they had been chucked on the fire when they came ashore. One chap lost just one of a pair of expensive trainers. Late in the evening they grabbed the commanding officer and he threatened them with Christmas duties which calmed them for a while. But not that much later, after a few more drinks, he knew he was going in and asked if he could strip because he was wearing his best uniform in which he was attending a court martial the next day. 'Okay,' they said and the officer stripped down to his underwear where upon the group picked him up shoulder high and heaved him into the sea. As he surfaced, spluttering and spitting out water, a squaddie walked up and threw his clothes that he had taken off moments before, into the sea around him. I'm not sure why but the commanding officer was very annoyed.

Kelly's also had a phone that you could use to phone out of the Islands, which was something that was very rare outside Stanley. I presume it was satellite. You could purchase a phone card for a certain number of minutes and during these nights at Kelly's we would try and phone home to UK. As you can imagine some of these calls could be slightly strange with it being in the very early hours of the morning in England and late at night after a few beers in the Falklands. Despite us usually being in a rather inebriated, burbling state, my parents always seemed pleased to hear from us.

It was a sad day when Kelly's closed. The military were so welcoming to the civilian population – they let the people in the settlement borrow video tapes and would invite, on an open basis, people to come and join them at their messes. Their parting shot was to make a deal with us, leaving some of the building assets to people in San Carlos and sell us, and many others on the East Falklands, the rest. This was instead of the military returning the site to its original condition. Frankly I think we all got a bloody good deal. This was good for us at San Carlos and also for a number of other farms that were starting up. We all needed buildings and the military would have had to spend a huge amount in human and money terms to return Kelly's to anything like its original condition.

We got four Portacabins and the generator shed, the latter being a 60x40-foot Packaway shed, which we hoped to take down and rebuild at Sussex as a shearing shed. We also got two 14,000-litre fibreglass water tanks. The Packaway and one of the water tanks were a complicated multi-tractor job to tow them home. However, with the Portacabins we just hitched on to the frames and dragged them up the main track with the gentle slopes and home. The first water tank was put on the big farm sleigh, which was designed for fencing, and pulled up and over the mountain using two tractors.

The Packaway was another proposition and had to be taken down and carted over the mountain in sections. These sections were too big for any of the trailers we had in the area.

Mike McKay had bought a Massey Ferguson in an army sale and he had dished it up and Gerald Findlay was going to buy it from him. He also had a huge trailer, which was being sold on to someone, but we were able to borrow it for the Packaway move on the way to its new owners.

Mike decided to kill two birds with one stone and bring out the tractor for Gerald, dropping off the trailer to us on the way. I knew Mike was in the vicinity and thought perhaps he would leave the trailer out on the main San Carlos track, which wouldn't make much difference to us. Mike had other ideas and pressed on towards the house. The track before the road came in from the west and the direction of Hells Kitchen through a gate into our horse paddock and then after about two hundred yards went down a very steep hill. I happened to see Mike coming up to the hill with the trailer dwarfing the tractor and thinking 'he's not going down there' even though it was obvious that that is exactly what was intended. This hill is so steep that a group of military police left their Land Rovers at the top one time because they thought it was too dangerous to drive down.

The tractor and trailer disappeared from view as they drove down towards the valley floor. A few minutes later the 2-meter set crackled and with a feeling of relief Toni said, 'You're down then?'

'Yes,' said Mike. 'Upside down.'

We tore over there and saw the tractor on its side with beer cans (which Mike was hastily picking up) strewn across and away from the tractor. The police happened to be visiting Sussex and they also viewed the aftermath of this failed descent. Apparently, just as the trailer's weight was fully on it started to push the tractor, so Mike jumped forward pushing the clutch in and squatted between the seat and steering wheel.

We went and got the plough master and pulled the trailer out of the way and the tractor back onto its wheels. Unbelievably, the only lasting damage was that the cab had been pushed about four inches out of square and the back window didn't fill the gap properly anymore.

Problems with the water tank

Giles, Christel and the girls often came out to visit and Giles was always ready to get stuck in to a project, rain, blow or shine

They were out visiting one weekend. On what was a foul, wet day, Giles and I went up above the house and to the northwest of the cowshed and we levelled a piece of ground for the new water tank. It was higher than the old concrete one and more importantly higher than the spring. This finished the concept of gravity-fed water to the house. The gain was that we had better pressure to the house although this didn't cure the air blocking the water line from the tank to the house when we ran out of water. Once we had pumped more we would have to undo the pipe close to the house to let the air out. It did however allow us to put a strong feed into the loft, instead of between the two bedrooms, to support the upgrade to the heating when we introduced a central heating system.

In the early 1990s our next effort was to dig a trench, a spade's width and depth, from the new tank to the house, which is at least 200 metres. This was aimed at stopping the annual freeze that we had suffered each winter from our arrival. It was a hard job, which I was hoping to encourage an army patrol to carry out but it was not to be. In less than 20 metres the first willing soldiers, with their enthusiasm, had broken two spade handles. The job was tough because the soil depth is a couple of inches and then rock-hard clay. It was not a case of jumping the spade in and pulling it back, like digging the garden, because it was far too hard. We had to move to Plan B which was me doing it.

We manoeuvred the tank into its new home and although now every drop was pumped, the pipe was a spade's depth under the ground and so didn't freeze up

We still had a second tank at Kelly's but this tank took some sorting. I am not sure why but the military had filled a number of these tanks with concrete, up to the hole where the pipe was attached to take the water to wherever. I suppose the idea was to be able to clean them with someone being able to sweep them and wash them out. They were sediment tanks by design where the dirt settled in the bottom below the level of the pipe and by adding the concrete the sediment couldn't go anywhere apart from into the water supply.

Unfortunately for me it was an addition that made the tanks weigh over a ton more than normal. I couldn't deal with it, because it was too much work to break up the concrete and get it out of the inspection hole, but I didn't want to break the seal on the tank, which was a third of the way up. I did break the seal however, taking the heavy H iron off that went around at the join, undid all the bolts that kept the sections together and then lifted the bigger top section from the bottom sections and then broke up the concrete before flipping the bottom over with the Hiab and knocking the remaining concrete out. The concrete had been well made and it took a few hours with a sledgehammer to break it all up and shovel it out. Once again the Hiab arm on the lorry – a hydraulic lifting arm – had saved the day. It wouldn't have been impossible to flip it over by pulling it, but there wouldn't have been the same amount of control and there would have been a greater likelihood of damage. We then loaded the top and bottom sections onto the lorry to bring them home one at a time.

We rebuilt the tank in the valley below the spring, down from where the old cement and block tank sat.

We still had the summer supply to sort because even with the improvements there still wouldn't be enough water between October and May to provide for a young family.

We did try and find a spring above the one that the old farm had tapped into. It would only mean an extension to what was already there. It would have possibly given us the gravity supply that we craved. It was not to be. There was nothing of sufficient quality.

In the Mutton Paddock probably half a mile from the house was a spring hole in a swamp on the south side of a valley. I know it was unwise to mess with this spring hole but there weren't many places for it to go. I dug a big hole next to the spring with a JCB that was in the area. It was about ten feet by six by four deep. We then built a frame and tinned it over to keep things out and to stop green algae growing. We then robbed the old pipe that went up to the foot of the mountain with some difficulty because it had been laid under the ground and wasn't strong enough to just rip out. It was easier however than having to pay for new stuff.

We had been at the farm now long enough to realise that nothing is ever easy and with this new supply of water came another problem and that was getting a pump powerful enough, with a 30-metre head that could pump water over the ridge.

We have still had the odd freeze up when the gate valve outside the house has frozen but this is just a case of a kettle of water. The other times have been when a cold southerly has frozen the feed where it comes under the house from the north but travels the width of the building before coming into the house in the bathroom on the south side. There are holes in the foundation to allow air circulation under the house but unfortunately one of them is close to the water feed. Even with a thick coat of insulation we have still occasionally had frozen pipes which I put down to wind chill. The cure for this is to put a short hose on the hot water tap from the bathroom and squirt water onto the frozen alkathene.

This cured most of our problems but our desire for gravity-fed water continued. In the early years of this century we decided to put a pipe up to some strong springs over two miles away to the northeast of the house at nearly 500 feet. A supply of water with no effort, or so we thought, with some money thrown at it. The spring hole was flowing well in the summer – that seemed to be our main concern. So, armed with many lengths of alkathene and a plough to put it in we got it into the ground, plus a supply tank.

After the season we looked at the colour of the water in the supply tank, as we got ready to join the sections of the pipe. The water was the colour of a poor whisky or even cold tea and was completely worthless as water for drinking, washing or anything else perhaps with the exception of the loo and watering the garden. It would be pretty mean even to water the dogs with it. It did look as if the only way forward was with another large investment of alkathene. There is another large spring with crystal clear water but it is the best part of a mile away from the end of the pipe.

I did find a very small spring hole, with good water, which seemed too small to do the job but I optimistically kept my eyes on it during a few summers and it didn't disappear and so we decided to try it as there was nothing to lose but a lot to gain if it was successful.

So Toni and I put a small branch into the pipe that we had already put in the ground about 400 yards back from the end. We worked back to the house putting in the couplings. The water would arrive at each one as we were working on the joins. That is until the valley just outside our Mutton Paddock; from thereon we didn't see the water. We carried on building to the garden and then went in for a coffee. Because of the many steep valleys the pressure of the water had to push the air out of the pipe and although I was sure this would happen I wasn't 100 per cent certain.

We had our drink and came out to finish the job. As we walked up to the garden we could see the water gushing out and we knew that this part of the job was a success.

We put a medium-sized tank up on the hill, giving pressure to work sprinklers in the garden and the automatic watering system in the polytunnel that the tank feeding the house couldn't give. It also delivered water to the shearing shed plus a stand pipe by the dog spans to the east of the house.

As I write, the water has carried on supplying our needs although green weed did block the ball valve and had us tearing up the mountain to see if the spring hole had dried up.

Moving the Portacabins

Rob Goodwin bought quite a few buildings from Kelly's Garden, including some multiple Portacabins like the Sergeants' Mess, which was five together without the internal walls. Rob had to drag them over the mountains behind the settlement and there were places where the mountain was pretty steep. There were a few youngsters floating around, like Adrian Minnell, brother of Mandy Goodwin and Neil 'Knacker' Goodwin, brother to Rob. They threw themselves into this Portacabin moving with great enthusiasm with all the tractor work and excitement. They gave the old San Carlos tractors, that were now the co-op's, a thorough workout, pulling these cabins one by one over the mountain with sheer will and a smidgen of brute force.

These boys also helped Geoff Butler, who was the furthest flung farm of all the section holders. He had some awful terrain to cross and once again it was the determination as much as anything that helped them to prevail. Geoff had bought himself a secondhand Zetor tractor and so there were three tractors involved in moving the stuff to Waimea. The co-op tractors were both looking at 20-years old and they did the lion's share of the work, but the Zetor, although a lot younger, didn't withstand the abuse as well and Geoff found it was breaking in two. Where the engine was bolted to the gearbox a number of the bolts had pulled through and the casing had broken off.

When a cabin got stuck the two 4x4s would back right up to it and then using long heavy-duty ropes they would tear off and jerk the cabin over whatever obstacle there was.

More sophisticated methods of transporting the Portacabins emerged, with people building elaborate trailers that the cabins sat on. They had to be big enough and strong enough for the job but light enough at the same time. These trailers were built low to the ground with a big wheel either side and were dragged over the land behind a tractor. There were some really good ones that were excellent at transporting heavy loads over the soft ground.

One chap, David Clark, tried a different method. He went to Kelly's and took his cabin to pieces, flat packed it and then dragged it out behind a big 4x4 tractor. This was a one-off but this one trip over our land had a disproportionate effect on our lives.

We had spent many hours and effort sorting out the high tide track using scarce resources so that we could drive back to the house, easily, regardless of the tide. The idea was to forego all the trips at high tide of picking our way home over the numerous ditches that riddle our land. On the bridge in Bodie Peak Valley, which was the main obstacle, we used Harrier matting (aluminium matting which was used to make temporary landing strips for the Harrier Jets) which even after the conflict wasn't that easy to come by in our area. This bridge was the king of our bridge efforts and it had three bearers, which was one more than the norm and seemed strong enough to cope with all anticipated traffic.

We hadn't planned on the flat-packed Portacabin, which was basically a big heavy sleigh that was dragged through everything in its path including our crème de la crème bridge.

Travelling home one day we came through the gate on the clay track above Bodie Peak Valley and down to the premier bridge and were confronted by the twisted and mangled remains of same. It wouldn't have taken the tracking skills of Tonto to realise what had happened. The cabin had hooked up on the bridge and the powerful county 4x4 had kept pulling and just demolished the structure. One of the six-foot planks of harrier matting looked as if a giant hand had screwed it into the ground until less than a foot was showing.

Our other bridges came to lesser ends because people would come and dismantle and rob them if they got stuck nearby. It was a minor irritation but if you are stuck you do all you can to get out. The demise of the Bodie Peak Valley Bridge made us realise that we must look at other routes away from the main track to get home.

Tanith the goat

Tanith has already been introduced into part of this history, but like with many things the stories overlap.

We got Tanith, our nanny goat, from Giles and Christel and she came to Sussex in the back of the series IIA (2A). She was a lovely, inquisitive, friendly animal that gave us a lot of pleasure. She was also pregnant and she gave birth to twins at the west end of the house, which is open to the prevailing winds. It was Tanith's first attempt at giving birth and her choice of location seemed a little odd. Sadly, the nanny kid was born dead but the billy kid (Buck) was very robust from birth. Toni took them up to the hay shed and gave Tanith hay and concentrates. They were in there for about a week.

This was at the same time as the military came around to sort out the Hells Kitchen's access which had got severely used with a lot of military traffic, including tracked vehicles. A ship was loaded up at Mare Harbour with a D6 Caterpillar bulldozer and sailed around towing a mexifloat and anchored off Terra Motas. There was a contingent of officers' wives in this party that visited the house from the ship. Toni cooked some drop scones and the ladies cooed and aahed over the new born kid. Toni used this opportunity to get a bit of help from one of the ladies to hold Buck whilst she applied a castration ring.

The mexifloat, which is basically a motorised floating jetty, sailed up the creek and drove onto the beach to the west of the house and off came the D6. The poor old operator was very nervous as he headed to Hells kitchen a few miles away. Without local experience he must have wondered whether he would bog on the beach as he made his way. Although it really needed digging out and then filling in, he made a good job of pushing out a more defined track easing the gradient and pushing material into the soft area close to the creek. Once done he drove back to the mexifloat and headed back to the mother ship.

They invited us back on board the ship and we agreed, thinking it was an informal thing. Whoops! Everyone was in their finery apart from these peasants from Port Sussex Farm. They later invited us to meet up with them all in one of their homes in Stanley where we were able to dress a little better, be clean and smell of soap and deodorant rather than sheep and hard work (sweat). I'd also had a shave. It was a very pleasant evening where we enjoyed a variety of snuffs and very good company.

The goats went on to give us years of entertainment. Some were annoying, such as when they got into the vegetable garden, but mostly amusing.

When we first got Tanith we had her tethered next to a box so she had somewhere to shelter. Regardless of what people say about goats, if they are kept in one place for long unless they are starving they stop eating. I am not sure how it came about but eventually we just let her roam because there was enough shelter around the farm if she needed it.

Buck was a character too. We didn't ever think of eating him so he was always destined to be a pet. He liked human company and used to follow you about if you were working at home. Once he was fully grown he could become a menace when I was repairing the Land Rover. If I was underneath he had a habit of coming over and running his horns, none to carefully, up and down my shins. It didn't matter how much you threatened him from underneath, he would only stop if you came out and chased him off. He would also try and eat your hair, for some strange reason, if given the chance.

Books tell you that goats need shelter but Tanith certainly didn't and went off for a number of months. We thought she had had an accident and was dead but she just reappeared with no apparent ill effects. We think she went looking for a billy but in those days they were few and far between.

The Agricultural Department thought that goats had potential for diversification and could generate extra revenue for farms. The idea went that goats are browsers and that they wouldn't compete with sheep, eating different food. Some goats have valuable fibre and so this was a venture that farmers should consider.

I don't know enough about the fibre to comment but I do know that although sheep and goats' feeding techniques differ they do compete with one another at that crucial time when the green grass is first coming through in the spring. It is only once the grazing pressure is off that the goats start to browse and the sheep remain grazing.

It is unfortunate that this venture wasn't a success but the idea seemed sound enough and that was to get more revenue from your farm's pasture.

Buck and Tanith could be an embarrassment and they often followed us on gathers. On one memorable trip we went down into Hells Kitchen, with Toni and me riding two horses side by side and two goats in front. There was Pat Short who was meeting his niece on the track. He didn't say anything, but I am sure he couldn't believe his eyes when he saw what amounted to a near circus act appearing in Hells Kitchen. We were heading for the far end of our wether ground behind Bodie Peak to start the gather. The goats just wouldn't give up as they got under the feet of our mounts. Even when their tongues were hanging out with exhaustion they still carried on for another few miles. We eventually shook them off not far from the start of the climb up to Bodie Peak as we trotted to get away from them. We looked back to see them both rocking backwards and forwards as they panted away after all that running. It took them three days to return to the farm.

It wasn't only the embarrassment, there were definite down sides to owning goats. Tanith got into the garden on one particular occasion, which was the crime of all crimes, and was munching away on our vegetables when I discovered her. She knew it was forbidden ground and tore off causing more havoc to the garden. Once caught I smacked her only for her to utter this pitiful bleating noise, so I tipped some cold water over her and shoved her out onto the green.

Buck loved it when the army patrols used to come. He would strut round intimidating the young soldiers. During one visit a soldier came to the door to say that the goat was on his ground sheet and wouldn't get off.

The troops would often give him some compo to placate him, but far from buying Buck off it would make him even more of a nuisance. He had no manners at all and unless you were prepared (and most of the soldiers weren't) he would eat the wrapping and everything. This probably wasn't too serious when it was sweet wrappers, but the boil in the bag meals were in heavy-duty plastic. He must have had an incredible constitution because we only felt it was life threatening on one instance.

After one patrol Buck was nowhere to be seen and we speculated that he had followed the section so far along the track in anticipation of some more food. Poor old Tanith was calling out to Buck as her udder got bigger and bigger until Toni had to milk her to relieve the pressure.

Buck hadn't gone away. He appeared on the scene looking awful with his head hanging down and the back of his legs in a terrible mess. He had overdosed on compo and the accompanying packaging and his tummy was a little bit delicate. It was a few days before he was drinking from his mother again and probably the best part of a week before he was himself.

Buck went missing on another occasion and once again Tanith would be pacing to and fro, this way and that looking for him. After a couple of days, we began to look for him in earnest and eventually I found him way in under the floor of the shearing shed. I suspect awkwardness, and attention seeking was the reason why he had gone so far under there but it was probably also to shelter from rain or a cold wind. What surprised us is that he didn't call out even when his mother and we were calling him.

There was very little room but I managed to get up to him with great difficulty, crawling in on my stomach. Did the sod help me in any way? No, he just lay there chewing his cud like Lord Muck waiting to be rescued. I was able to turn him over on to his side with his horns and pull him inch by inch to the edge of the building and let him go.

Buck went on to have a long and eventful life, something poor Tanith didn't enjoy.

As I have already mentioned the goats were always loose and Tanith occasionally went absent without leave. No big deal, we thought, because if she was hungry or became ill she would come home for help.

At Christmas we would go to town for about a week and I would, in that time, occasionally come out and check the dogs and cats, ducks, hens, rabbits and all the other members of the menagerie and run the engine for a few hours for the deep freeze.

We used to do a big mutton run into town in the back of our four tonner in those days once the wethers were shorn. This generated money for something that would otherwise go onto the beach. We could usually get rid of our cull ewes to farms that couldn't maintain their sheep numbers but we had to get rid of sheep each year because we could only carry so many animals on the farm. We would get £12 a carcass, which we thought was good money for a little work.

We had already killed about 100 mutton and Giles and I went out early from town to load up the lorry and cover it with a tarpaulin, do a few feeding jobs and were in and around the farm house for a few hours. The other visit I made was a fleeting trip but I would still have been around for two or three hours to run the generator.

It didn't occur to me to specifically look for Tanith because the goats were free spirits. Sadly, the poor old girl was in trouble and if only she had sung-out or made some noise we could have saved her life. She had got into the Portacabin with all the wool bales and her legs had slipped down between them trapping her. You would think something as agile as a goat would have managed to extricate themselves but the polypropylene that we used in the 1980s was slippery and she couldn't get any purchase.

The hardest thing to accept was that the Portacabin was about twenty feet from the back gate and we would have walked past her time and time again without knowing of her need. Why she didn't help herself a little bit more so we could hear her is beyond me.

The goats were an extravagance on our behalves because they didn't generate revenue and many of our conventional farming friends couldn't see the point in having them. We saw things slightly differently in as much as we had a huge piece of land and why not enjoy goats or any other animal as long as they didn't divert time and effort from the primary industry, wool.

Sheep cull

Before the roads had even thought about coming to Sussex we started running mutton into Stanley around about Christmas time. We would kill in two goes with our biggest kill ever being over 100 carcasses.

It used to be a social thing where Giles, Tony P., Joost Pompert, Douglas Hansen, Charlie Blackley and others would come out and we would kill the sheep. Each person would do certain jobs like legging, which is opening up the skin on the legs, punching which is forcing the skin from the carcass on each side, which gets the skin further off and then sawing the brisket and then finally the sheep is lifted by its hind legs to have the skin taken off and the guts taken out.

Charlie was a lot older than the rest of us, but he was no slouch when it came to legging. Having done it all his life it was like second nature and he had probably whipped many a sheep out of its skin over the years. At one time skins were worth money and so all the culls were skinned on farms.

Today most cull sheep are driven away in a flock to be slaughtered in situ. Some farms, however, kill at the settlement and cart the sheep away in trailers to their designated location. Some of the bigger farms are killing thousands and so the killing on site is the most cost effective way with no double handling or cost of fuel and labour to cart sheep to the required site.

I would give the helpers mutton as payment, which everyone seemed contented with.

The track at Christmas was at its best but 100 mutton were not light and we had to go over a few soft flats by Camilla Creek house, which in reality didn't give us any problems.

Once in town, Toni would go in and start phoning people and I would stay out on the lorry and as the people arrived I would hand down mutton and take the money. Sometimes people didn't have the money but we just made a note of it and I can't remember any defaulters.

Introducing energisers

The insultimber fencing is really at its best when it has an energiser pulsing along it with enough power to stop any animals pushing through. Over time we have learnt a lot but we had to take people's word for stuff at the beginning. Training animals initially is one lesson we learnt but also that during the winter when things are wet it doesn't work very well because the energy earths to ground. It is true to say that the economics of farms makes conventional fencing, with battens, every few feet unaffordable unless you support your farm through other means. Many farmers still put six wires on their boundary fences, but even then they don't put battens as close as farms did in the past, like every few feet.

Our first energisers were powered by 12-volt car batteries. We would need to change the batteries or charge them on a regular basis. If you were delayed and the battery's power went below a certain level the battery was never the same again. It was always the beginning of the end for that battery.

Living and working with electric fences brings a certain excitement and also weariness.

We used to spend hours trying to make the energisers as efficient as possible by improving the earths and in some cases only using the top couple of wires due to heavy vegetation on the lower ones. I hate electricity, so I always made sure that it was off before I got anywhere near it.

Tony P. was out helping me sort a stretch, which I was trying to improve, and we had a system of lights and waves worked out so that I didn't get a shock. One of us got the signals wrong and I got a good belt. I momentarily lost it and went charging down the hill cursing and swearing but Tony P. was half a mile away so I recovered my composure after a hundred yards or so.

Living with electric fences generates situations regardless of how careful you think you are being. Caris, our daughter, and I were walking up to the house when she was just a toddler and she either stumbled or the wind blew her into the electric fence. I waited for the pulse, as I didn't want to receive a shock too, and then quickly pulled her off. She did a bit of a grizzle but I was soon able to convince her that she was okay.

We used to use electricity to stop the calves getting back to their mothers when they were too big to spend the night in the cowshed and had their own paddock. Without electricity a determined calf can push through a fence to get back to its mum and drink the milk. I also, occasionally, used it to educate Buck the goat.

We have always raised chicks in small coops, because if you don't the chances are a cat or gull or something will eat them before they grow very big. The idea is to raise them to at least half to three-quarter size before letting them go free range. When the hen comes on the scene with her chickens you go out with some corn, catch the hen and gather up the chickens, put them in a bucket and then place them all in a coop with food and water.

Our goat Buck would watch us feed the brood each day, and he eventually worked out that all he had to do was swagger over, get his horns in the mesh and tip the coop over which allowed him to eat the food. We in turn had to catch the hen and chicks again. No matter what we did we couldn't stop him doing this, so serious remedies were needed to cure serious crimes. I surrounded a coop with a short piece of wire with an energiser attached. With such a short length of wire the energiser was putting out at full power. Buck swaggered over to pinch the food and got a shock, but he didn't believe the first shock and so went back and pushed hard against the wire to get his reward only to get another shock which knocked him off his feet. Even Buck got the message and didn't eat any more food destined for the chickens.

When Toni milked the cows she would separate the milk (a milk separator is used which utilises centrifugal action to separate the lighter cream from the heavier milk) and then have gallons of separated milk (semi-skimmed), which was spare and so she would tip it into a basin on the green for the goats. Buck and his mother would just drink and drink until it was gone, regardless of how uncomfortable they were, they would stand there with their legs spread and their heads down but with a look of achievement spread across their faces. Even with this amount of milk Buck could still summon the energy and appetite to drink from the orphan lamb feeder bucket, which we hung on the fence for the motherless lambs which were kept as pets.

I decided that I would make a heavy wooden lid to fit in the top of the feeder bucket. Buck would contemptuously flick this out with his horns and then once again drink the milk. I had tried to be humane, I had tried to be nice but it was time for the energiser and this time on a length of wire no more than two feet long. Needless to say it gave Buck a hefty shock and we were then able to see the expensive Lamlac (ewe milk replacement mix) being used for the job that it was intended for.

Things are more sophisticated these days with mains-powered systems, which can power more than 30 or 40 miles, and solar-powered units although none of them are foolproof.

To demonstrate that there is still work to be done before the energisers are perfect Toni was overseas, and I also had to go away so Derek and Trudi said they would look after the farm. One of the things I had to show them was changing the battery on the energiser by the Bodie reseed. Down we went and I climbed into the small fenced-off corner, which stops animals getting to the unit and rubbing on it. Derek and Trudi were on the other side of the fence watching my every move.

This unit is at the corner of the reseed where there is a nice big wet swamp to use as an earth. Unbeknown to me the earth wire had come off the energiser, and so the minute I touched the unit I was the earth. Being so close to the unit I was thrown back, with some force, onto the sopping wet ground. As I was getting up I heard Trudi whisper to Derek, 'I'm not touching that.' In fact, the trick is to wear rubber gloves if it's wet or if in doubt.

4. ADVENTURES ON THE FARM

Bullion the bull

Life on the farm was full of adventures. Not many days, in the early years, went by before something fundamental would occur.

We got a South Devon bull as a wedding present from Diana and Ron Turner from Rincon Grande, along with a couple of nice young Polwarth rams. We called this bull Bullion because he was a rich golden colour. He was a big animal with thick horns that stuck out of his head 180 degrees from one another. He was also incredibly tame. He would swagger in with the rest of the herd and stand chewing his cud. His only weakness was his habit of going wherever he wanted.

He didn't have any earmarks and although he was very distinctive we thought we should put a tag in his ear. The plan was that I would drive him into the cowshed, Toni would throw a loop over his head and then we would tag him. The cowshed was divided into two pieces with wooden rails and a small gate and as I have already described the calves would be in one side and the cows would come into be milked on the other.

Toni was standing in the calf pen and I drove Bullion in. Toni was very nervous as Bullion plodded in as there was only one door out of the cowshed – the one the bull was coming in through. She didn't even have time to throw the loop. Bullion decided he was not going to tolerate this and turned around to leave. But by this time I had all my weight against the door to stop him coming out. The bull sort of jumped at the door knocking me down by the gate post and then fell on his back beside me and pushed me onto the gate post, which moved, thankfully, under this assault.

As I was lying there wondering whether I was still in one piece, the bull got up and walked out through the north side of the cow corral, the wood splintering around his shoulders, and out into the neighbour's farm. I jumped up feeling a little battered and bruised, but still able to function, and ran around Bullion and got him to go back to the corral where he walked in through the hole that he had made in one side and out through the other. Once again there was splintering wood showering around, in all shapes, as he smashed through. I was running after him again but this time he had found a sense of urgency and was going a little quicker.

'Go and get a dog,' I shouted to Toni, as I carried on trying to head him off. Toni ran down to the dogs but instead of letting one of mine off, which would have run up to me, she let her dog go and so she had to run up to the top of the hill to work it on the bull. By the time Toni had run down and then up the slope of the green we are talking 400 yards. I said: 'Go on then' to which she replied, 'Who do you think I am, Zola Budd?' (an infamous, British middle-distance runner of the time). Needless to say the bull went without a tag and carried on feeding wherever he liked.

Ron and Iris asked if they could borrow him to breed with their cows so off I went and drove him over to Kingsford Valley Farm and put him in with these cows, a number of which were in season and ready for the bull. Ron had a big black bullock called Honeyghan, named after a successful boxer of the day, who was obviously the top animal. He came out of the herd to confront Bullion, who contemptuously lifted him off his feet and knocked him over. With Bullion installed amongst a number of girls I went home.

The next day Bullion was back grazing in Cantera his favourite pasture, which wasn't even ours. Despite all those girlfriends and seven fences he couldn't have stayed long before he had headed home. He was a great bull that had thrown some really impressive offspring but we had zero management with him doing whatever he liked, so a few days later I had to put him down. He was a huge beast and his last contribution to the farm was feeding the dogs for weeks and the hens were also able to benefit, picking on his bones.

Cows and their calves

The cows gave us endless work and for many years every cow that we had, went through the cowshed. It was a good way of taming the older cows at the start and taming all the calves for future milking or handling in general. The first few years, even with us taking out the wildest, kept us going with taming down the older animals. We had a routine where I would help at the cowshed every morning until the new cow would walk into the shed and be tied up.

The first job was to find a cow and calf and to bring it home. It is easy to find the cow with a new calf because they have a large udder, and if it is only a few days old she will be feeding some distance from the herd. Finding the calf is a different matter. We have searched for hours and not found a calf. The cow gives you no clues at all, apart from she will be as far away from it as possible. You can keep the cow in overnight, but it won't charge back the next morning and lead you to its calf. She will bimble off, taking a mouthful of grass by the track and then have a mooch in a green valley. Most of us will have given up on the game before she does. Eventually you will catch them together and then you have to get them home, and mother cow can be more than a little touchy if you venture too near her pride and joy especially if you are on foot. Even tame old cows have attacked and injured the unwary.

Once back in the fragile cow corral you have to part mother and baby. The first time is the worst and it usually means lassoing the calf and dragging it, bellowing, into the calf pen. As you can imagine the cow doesn't go a bundle on this kind of treatment being dished out to her calf and again you have to be weary and nimble if she charges you. Of course I am sure there are better, more humane ways of getting the calves away from their mothers but it means getting close and personal and even then, a very young calf, can pack a punch when it kicks.

At first you would be amazed how wild some of these cows were and a lot of them had long pointed horns. They all came back to the cowshed for their calves each morning and most would go into the cowshed because their calves were there. Some, however, had to be dragged in on a lasso inch by inch. It is amazing how strong a cow is when it doesn't want to do something. Toni would be in the cowshed pulling on the end of the lasso with a turn around the tying up ring and I would be outside pushing, trying to avoid the cow kicks. A cow's favourite trick was to go at right angles to the door so that you had to pull it through the wall to get it in. Then it was my job to get hold of its tail and try and rock it around the corner. In close proximity it was a battle that even if we won, which we always did, we didn't come away scot-free. I was occasionally kicked and often smothered in cow muck. Usually one session of this was enough for most cows. Some cows took longer than others but we didn't have many that after a few weeks of being tied up and milked weren't chewing their cud as though they had been born to it. Any that did not tame down were got rid of.

We did have two big bad natured cows that over the course of time found their way to our basic cow-taming establishment. The older of the two walked into the cowshed and instead of turning away when Toni threw the loop over her head she lunged at her and snorted sending a fine mist of snot all over her. Toni nicknamed her 'The Atomiser' because of this skill. The Atomiser played us up for three whole weeks, which was the time only the worst of the worst kept up their nonsense.

Toni's patience and taming ability prevailed but it was a supreme effort because I began to wonder if she would ever calm down. I was just considering an alternative use when she turned the corner and stood there with the best of them. Incredibly after a few years she wouldn't need to have her head tied up although the legs were a must. One, because even the tamest of cows will kick if they have sore teats and two, the tail is also restrained because it is often covered in excrement and it is not very nice to have this slapped in your face or bits of muck shake off into the milk.

The other individual that gave us some serious cardiovascular was a red cow. She seemed to have a problem with her eyes, similar to red eye that sheep get. She obviously couldn't see properly. We got this cow and her calf into the corral and she had been very difficult from the start. Into the shed went the calf and the cow hung around outside which is normal for the first night. Next day she was acting as though Toni and I were aliens and being really weird. We managed to get her in and Toni got a bit of milk from her and then turned them out with the other cows and calves into the calf paddock. The cow went totally mental and ran away from her own calf (that she has been waiting for all night) tearing off over the fence and heading west down towards the Point paddock. Of course, the quad was down by the house so the cow had a good head start plus all along the coast are steep valleys coming from the coast. I eventually caught up with her a couple of miles on with her tail up going for it. It took a lot of persuasion to turn the bitch back towards the place she was meant to be. This cow was grumpy and unlike most cows was prepared to charge the quad. In circumstances like this I push the cow from behind letting the animal feel the power of the quad, which usually persuades them who the real boss is.

I had been renewing the fences around the cowshed that do take some pressure over the years with anxious mothers trying to get back to their calves. This included some posts that had taken some work to put in. It did make the area look good, apart from the corral that is.

The cow was still not that keen to return and I was working hard to keep her going east. At the top of the hill where the fence from Diver's Cove and the Mutton Paddock join, the gate was open to let the cows go out to feed from the cowshed and come back the next morning. This is obviously what this cow was waiting for and at this juncture the cow went flying down the lead deciding to jump the newly built fence coming off from the cowshed. The retched animal was unsuccessful and straddled the fence, falling down with the front legs one side and its back the other, pulling a post up. To say that I was slightly aggrieved is an understatement. I was livid.

I struggled to give this cow the benefit of the doubt but because she had a calf I was prepared to give her another chance. She had this eye issue so we let her go hoping that she would get better in time and she would raise her calf. A couple of weeks later I noticed that she had lost her calf and so the following week she was earning us just over £300 from Fresco the local butcher.

As I have mentioned, I would accompany Toni to the cowshed when the cows first came up with their calves. Cows can be funny creatures and quickly get used to a routine, with any change to this routine unsettling them. For instance, if Toni wore a different coat they would frig around and poo all over the place. Toni had this very tame cow that did not need her legs tying up, but she was used to there just being Toni in the cowshed with her. I went up to ask Toni something one morning when she was milking this cow, and casually leaned on the cowshed door. The cow took exception to this and kicked Toni, hard, on the thigh. Toni leapt off the milking stool and made to come out of the cowshed. I remained in situ and suggested to Toni that in fact the kick had not hurt, it had merely given her a fright. Toni disagreed with this statement, but gamely went back to finish the milking as I, having found out what I came for, toddled off down the green. I did have to concede that perhaps Toni was right, and maybe it had hurt, when I was shown the hoof shaped bruise on her thigh that evening.

Aylwin was Toni's first calf and at that early time our names were going to be alphabetical. Aylwin somehow got distorted to Baby. Baby grew and grew and because he was the first he was therefore a novelty. His mother was kept up until Baby was bigger than she was. Toni had a love–hate relationship with Baby because as he got big and strong he began to know what was best in the cowshed. Toni liked the calves to come straight out and suckle on the calf pen side because it was easier to pull them off and tie them back to the pen. Aylwin liked to go on the offside and then it was a battle to get him back. Aylwin eventually joined the herd as potential beef but whenever it was suggested that the animal that looked down on everything else should be for the chop there was always good reason why not. He was not really big enough! He was too rangy or not quite right. Any excuse for Baby. He was big enough. He still thought he was a calf however and when he came home he would get wedged in the calf pen after walking into the cowshed. I think Aylwin became beef, well after his best-before-date, but to be honest I am not 100 per cent sure. He could have just died from old age. You do have to be mercenary to be a farmer, but equally the day that you don't have a fondness for certain animals is the day to do something else.

When the children lived at home the cows began to get some very exotic names. A year followed a theme and so the Thunderbird puppets had their time. We had Virgil, Brains, Parker and Lady Penelope and then Stingray with Phones and Marina. Children's presenters, Cosmo and Dibs from a children's programme, flowers, fruit, friends and many more.

I wondered whether it is this fact that most cows can be tamed down that man started to have this association with this animal or is it after thousands of years of being one of man's farm animals they have become receptive to being tamed. I suppose it is a combination of the two.

Once the cows have settled down the whole activity becomes therapeutic with the cow standing chewing its cud and the rhythmic swish, swish of the milk squirting into the jug.

Caris started going to the cows in the backpack and then when Caris was a toddler Liam would take his turn in the backpack. Most of the time they stayed with me but they liked going and getting to know the cows and calves and knowing, which belonged to which. They also liked parting the cows in the afternoon running around them when they were big enough and on Toni's back when they were too young.

The cowshed was a bit of a trap, only having one door, although there was a small window in the west wall. Toni felt that after having two children, she no longer expected her bottom to let her dive out through this window. Eventually I did put a second door into the calf pen, but with this addition also came the demise of the milking effort. It was as if the challenge had disappeared.

Military friends.
We became good friends with the Motor Transport Section from Mount Pleasant Airport.

Our new friends would drive up in convoy on Saturday afternoons. They would spend the night with us, taking on many of the farm projects while they were here.

One of these projects was filling up holes on the track to make it a little more user friendly for every traveller.

We would hitch up the tractor and trailer and the team would fill it up with rocks from the beach. Then we would go and tip the rock in an offending hole. It was surprising how many holes took ton after ton, load after load.

They guys were always up for raising spirits by splashing one another by chucking large rocks into the holes full of water. One guy called Matt Dunbar, who was the children's favourite, splashed a few too many of his chums and so they grabbed him and chucked him into a great big puddle. Caris and Liam were outraged, and we had to run them through the sequence of events so that they could understand that Matt had been asking for it.

The memory from all these visits is probably when the tractor and trailer came out of gear and careered off down the steep hill in Hells Kitchen with Paul Hutchinson at the helm. Needless to say the brakes weren't any good. The trailer shed its back and sides and things were looking bad for a few seconds as it picked up speed – fortunately Paul managed to jam it into a slow gear and arrived at the bottom under some kind of control.

We became quite involved with members coming on camping runs, celebrating New Year at Cerritos Corral. It always involved extreme 4x4, from camping at Loch Head to swimming in the Black Tarn we had a representative from MT.

Our trip to Volunteer Point was memorable for a number of reasons. The first was that one chap called John Page had his wife and children visiting from UK. Michelle and kids touched down in the Falklands after an 18-hour flight and it was drop off luggage and straight into a vehicle to bounce another four hours to Volunteers. It was suggested by the other ladies that this was beyond the call of duty.

Next day as people are getting up and making breakfast, John was reading *The Times* that Michelle had bought down and reminded her that he liked his bacon crispy. Without exception the other ladies thought they could have resorted to violence under such provocation.

John was a dapper kind of guy and always wore a cravat. This was nearly his downfall as we were trying to move on to Loch Head. Poor John just couldn't get the bow right however much he tried. As the collectives patience was evaporating Hilary Hutchinson voiced what we were all thinking when she threatened to strangle him with said cravat should he try any further attempts.

Hamish the pig

Pigs in my opinion are nice animals to rear but we got off to a very bad start before we moved to the farm from Stanley, which prevented us rearing them for years at Sussex. Our experience with Hamish the pig in Stanley, when we lived at Rincon Cottage, for me was not a happy one.

Straight after the war there was so much compo, like tinned cheese and Argentinian powdered milk that we bought a pig. Without the pig most of this stuff would have just gone to the dump. There was just no way you could eat all the Argentinian and British food that was in and around Stanley.

I think Hamish came from the Estancia, Tony and Ailsa's farm about 15 miles from Stanley. I built him an enclosure at the top of the yard and I found him a decent wooden box that he could grow into for a house. He was one happy pig. He had all the food that he could eat and a nice warm box to sleep in out of the elements.

Toni did most of the feeding and watering and spoilt him rotten and cared for his every whim.

He liked his compo cheese cut up and floating in the milk, which he liked made with warm water. He would dip his snout up to his eyes in the milk and blow bubbles as he bobbed for the cheese in his trough. To me he epitomised the term 'to eat like a pig'. He became a bit of a celebrity up on Davies Street where children would bring him titbits. I am sure that some people think how dangerous and they would never let their child get close to a pig. The truth is that because he had never been treated roughly and had been handled from a young age he was as gentle as a lamb.

I think he only got one true surprise in his life and that was when Heather was looking after him while we had a weekend in camp. By Hamish's trough was a stick to give his milk and cheese a last stir before it was handed over. As Heather was feeding him he came over to have his daily face scratch and tummy rub, which gave her a fright and so she hit him over the head with his own food stick.

Hamish did well on compo cheese and Argentinian milk and was colossal, but he still liked to rollover and have Toni tickle his tummy. Eventually when Hamish had to charge his house in order to get into it and when he was out he was virtually as tall as the fence, I casually suggested that the time had come to reap the rewards of our labours. After another month of coaxing and persuading, the day arrived and the butchery left a box for me to put him in for his trip up the road. I coaxed him in that night and he was gone the next morning.

No one mentioned the job well done when the cleanly scraped halves of Hamish adorned our kitchen table. I distinctly felt a chilly atmosphere and the hard looks as if I was a mass murderer. It was if we were preparing to eat a member of our close family like a sister or brother or mother or father rather than a pig we had bought to fatten up to eventually eat. We went through the motions of eating Hamish over the following weeks but our hearts weren't in it, pathetic, as it might seem. Pork wasn't abundant in those days in the Falklands and the stuff in the stores was expensive and tasteless.

We did start to raise pigs again but it was many years later. It was made very clear from the beginning, with a clear message to the children, that the pigs were being raised for the freezer. We decided to raise two each time and with the first couple we did debate, with Caris and Liam, the wrongs and rights of raising something to eat, but after that we were able to have fresh pork on the menu without too much aggro.

When it was time to turn them from pigs into meat it always helped if they had got into the garden and wreaked havoc or committed some other crime.

One of these catalysts lives fresh in my memory. Before the roads we probably went into town about once a month to every six weeks to see family and friends. Returning from one such run we could see, standing and sitting around the back gate, an army patrol. As we got closer we also noticed that the pigs had muscled their way out of their enclosure and were in our vegetable garden. The patrol must have thought us crazy as we come to an abrupt halt, offered a cursory greeting, and tore past, demonstrating by our actions and some swearing that the pigs were in the garden and we weren't pleased. We ushered them out and Toni got some food and led them back to their pad. We repaired the place where they had got out of their palace and then all went in for some drop scones and tea.

We found that the pigs would be happy in their enclosure in the summer as long as they had food and water and a bit of shelter from the sun and the wind. They would mooch around grubbing up stuff with their snouts. When the temperatures dropped, they got restless and one has to make sure they can't get their noses under anything because shaped as a wedge it is surprising what they can move and lift. They are quite destructive if they get out, doing a lot of rooting in wet areas around the house and they can do some impressive gorging if they get into the garden. We have used our pigs to clean up the potato garden at times to stop self-sets growing. They have a highly developed sense of smell and work the plot until even the smallest potato has gone.

Electric fencing is probably the best method of controlling pigs because they are unable to use their immense power to break out. It pays to use it within a solid barrier to start with

San Carlos before the War and sub-division.

Port Sussex Farm, our first visit. Note the old phone poles and line going down the green.

Army Air Corp Gazelle on the green at Port Sussex, like the one that bought the horse gear for the Officer. They used to have to check everything before they left to make sure the goats had not chewed anything essential.

Toni on Silver Blaze moving cows, with West Falklands in the background

Silhouette of Port Sussex showing how tall the two meter beam was and the fencing caravan attached to the tractor.

Building the temporary shearing shed, looking up the creek.

Shearing in thorn proof trousers. Pet
sheep tend to get covered in prickles
from the calafate

Loading the sea truck with bales of wool from the back of the trailer.

![MV Monsunen loading wool bales in the harbour at Port Sussex.](image)

MV Monsunen loading wool bales in the harbour at Port Sussex.

Burying the water pipe.

Toni & Heather riding up the Z's.

The lorry coming up the old track out of BBQ Bay in the Horse Paddock.

Coming up the hill out of our High Tide track in Hells Kitchen Valley.

Swan Inlet Bridge winter crossing. Note the two meter halo on the Land Rover.

Pulling Military guys with their light weight out of a hole at St Brunos Arroyo.

Mike's tractor and trailer at the bottom of the steep hill into BBQ Bay.

Taking the Packaway down at Kellys Garden.

Crossing Head Of The Bay Creek with sections of the Packway.

Towing two sections of Packaway up the mountain with three tractors attached.

Bringing the water tank home, coming up the San Carlos side of Sussex Mountains.

Second water tank on the back of the lorry.

The creek in front of the house frozen over.

Waimea

Caris "Helpin" feed Copernicus with Toni.

Toni & Caris feeding the pet lambs Dennis and John.

Toni, Caris & Liam with Geoffrey the cat, returning from milking the cows.

Caris upland goose egging.

Caris & Liam swimming in the creek.

Caris & Liam with the fish they knackered and caught behind the fish wall.

Trainee Gauchos on Aseef and Felicity. Note string stirrups for safety, if you fell off the stirrups came too so no risk of getting caught up and dragged behind the horse.

Police Land Rover bogged in the creek at Hells Kitchen. The lorry is also bogged by this stage and we had had to call in reinforcements with our tractor, Pat Short in his Zetor and Ron Dickson in his County.

Liam & Caris busy in their school room.

because the small pigs can get a shock, which propels them forwards and through the fence. Even after a small amount of time a pig won't wander far from his food source even if he does escape.

Not that many years ago we got some pigs and they got out while we were gathering sheep. We had only had them for about a day and so they didn't know where their food was coming from or where they lived. We got back and there was no sign. I searched the beach and under the shearing shed and Toni looked on the green and under the sheds. Nothing. We were wondering what to do when Toni noticed that the stallion was behaving peculiarly. Knowing that horses aren't fond of pigs she went to investigate with a bucket of food. Always on the lookout for food, they heard Toni calling and rattling the bucket and were led quietly back to their pen where, after a few alterations, it was pig proof for a while.

A pig in the Falklands usually has a good life. They are in small groups with a reasonable area to live their lives. The quality of life is high and usually they are despatched quickly.

Processing a pig is not that straight forward but can be made easier with a little bit of preparation. Scraping a pig is quite a palaver but can be done fairly quickly if the water temperature is right. The idea is to pour hot water onto the bristles on the pig's skin and then scrape them out with a blunt knife. Too cold and nothing happens and too hot the skin gets glazed and the bristles can get set in place. In our situation we found that hot water from the domestic supply was the best but you had to be energetic to get the bristles out before you ran out of water. We have used all kinds of systems including a steam thing for removing wallpaper. It was thorough but slow. The best method I saw at another farm that was set up for doing a number of pigs was a gas-fired hot-water system that supplied water at a specific temperature for as long as you wanted it. One person would apply the water as the other scraped the pig.

Today since the roads were built and the abattoir is in place things are easier but they have a cost. The abattoir does pigs and a better job you would not get, but when you buy a piglet at £90 to £100 it begins to make your pork a luxury item. If you sell any by the time you take in the cost of your time it isn't a money-spinner. We always kept two, keeping one and selling the other but to make any money out of it you would have to discount your time or charge a ridiculous price.

Driving the sheep

Ron and Iris's farm, with a lot of marginal ground, meant poor lambing and high death rates in their young sheep. This made maintaining numbers very difficult. Although the land wasn't much for the more vulnerable sheep it was perfectly good for the tougher wethers that thrived there.

The Falkland Island Company farms, running over 200,000 on the East Island, always had a surplus of sheep which they had to kill each year because there wasn't a market. So Ron would buy several hundred at a time for a couple of quid a head and then he would pay a shepherd to drive them to a small pen in Cantera called Ajax Pen. This was an enclosure that was erected and used by the old meat works that was built and run at Ajax Bay, below

The Wreck house, in the 1950s. Ron would then go over and drive them through our land up and over the Sussex Mountain to the west of Bodie Peak where there was a gate going into the Snipe Camp.

The easiest way, with the least number of gates, was to take them to the Iron Gate overlooking the creek and drive them straight up from there only having one more gate to the west of the Bodie Peak stone run before the one into his land.

These drives could be eventful.

On one occasion Steven, Ron's son, came up to the farm to say that his dad couldn't get the sheep across the creek and would we come down.

Some sheep that are used to water will plough through, even swimming at times, but others that hadn't experienced much water were the most cantankerous and stubborn things out. The sheep that day were the latter and where Shepherds Brook ran into the creek amounted to a few inches of water for about twenty feet at most.

Ron had these sheep pinned up to the edge, but they just refused on mass to put a hoof in the water. We arrived and Bozo rushed along the sides and barked and the other dogs were pushing them. We all had a go at pulling a sheep over to the other side, but in an extreme display of contrariness, instead of running off and drawing the other sheep over, it would run straight back through the water to join the flock. The extra dog power made the difference and eventually they started to go and once you have got them started they follow one another just like… sheep.

I went and helped Ron on other occasions. The most memorable was in the pouring rain on horseback. I don't think the day had started badly but the heavens had opened and we got quite cold, wet and miserable. Ron had come prepared with a bottle of rum and we thought, what better way to keep warm and raise morale than to drink the rum. We also had a big slab of chocolate.

So once the sheep were in the Snipe Camp we sat on the ground by the gate drinking the rum and eating the chocolate with the horses turned back on to the weather patiently waiting for us to ride them home.

It must have been wet because on eventually deciding to go home Copernicus seemed to do a lot of slipping and sliding and I did some theatrical swaying in the saddle to such a degree that I eventually led my mount to the foot of the mountain before I got back on. I am sure it had nothing to do with the copious amount of rum I had consumed.

For a number of years Toni and I used to drive the sheep over for Ron. It was no big deal and driving a flock like that was really good training for your dogs. These sheep were cull-aged wethers, which Goose Green could no longer carry on their ground, but they were still strong robust animals that walked over to their new farm with few dramas. (Cull age means sheep that are usually seven and no longer required and if a farm can't sell them they would carry some for the dogs but the remainder usually had to be killed.)

Shearing the sheep
When we started employing the shearing gang Heather would come out and cook for us

all. Sometimes to make it easier she would cook up a batch of cakes and buns for the early mornings and the smokos (tea breaks). It was a real help to us and gave us a chance to fully focus on the sheep work. It was an added bonus with Toni's pregnancies and then when Caris and Liam came on the scene. Caris and Liam really adored Granny Heather because she would get them doing things.

Toni would find it hard standing all day when she was six months pregnant, when we shore the ewes and particularly when we would stretch the days to get the job done. In the early days, when we had Keith Heathman and then Neil McKay as the gangers, we would get the shearers at weekends when the FIC/FLH farms didn't work. This was okay unless the weather was against us, which would make two days not enough to shear the flock in question. We would then shear extra hours to make up lost time when it was dry. When I shore the sheep Toni wasn't keen to have lights in the shed because she knew it would mean many extended hours but with the shearers it only meant at worst three long days at any one time.

Shearing is a time-consuming occupation. The day is spread out to incorporate some long rest spells, which is designed to maximise the actual eight-hour shearing time. Although we have tried different combinations depending usually on the shearer's preference we now work with a start time of 6am (although we need to rise at 5am to get things prepared for the day) and then shear until breakfast at 8am. A traditional shearer's breakfast is eggs, chops and toast and spread. We then start again at 9am and from thereon in we shear in one-and-a-half hour blocks. So 9am to 10.30am and then a half an hour spell for a drink and biscuits and then 11am to 12.30pm when we then stop for an hour-long lunch break. Then shear again from 13.30pm to 3pm and then rest and drink for half an hour and then the final one-and-a-half hour spell to knock off at 5pm.

Most shearers eat quickly at mealtime and then return to the shed to sharpen and improve their shearing gear. The points of the comb get a lot of attention because they need to be pointed enough to penetrate the dense fine wool but not so sharp that they cut and injure the sheep.

We have, mostly, employed two shearers at a time although occasionally we have allowed a trainee to come up and work on another stand. Two shearers bring a rousie, who is usually female although not exclusively. Their job is to pick the bellies up and take the stained and daggy wool from the fleece before it arrives on the wool table. Once the shearer has finished she will pick up the fleece and throw it onto the table spreading it evenly for the person on the table to remove the neck and any other stained pieces that remain. The rousie has to throw and then be quickly back with their paddle to sweep the second cuts from the floor to allow the shearer to bring his next sheep to a clean shearing area. The rousie also works hard to keep the table area clean by sweeping up all the second pieces that drop through the slats of the table or are distributed far and wide in the throwing process.

The person on the table, which is Toni on our farm, takes off the neck which can be kempy (have coarse fibres) and also have more vegetable matter attached compared to the main fleece. Discoloured wool around the legs also needs to come off. On some bigger farms a person is employed to class the wool but here Toni does the table work and then classes the fleece putting it into bins of different quality. There is A, B and C, with A being the best and C the worst, and then you have double categories AA, BB, CC, and this is where the wool that has a fault, which can be excessive dirt, broken fibre or short staple, is placed.

My job in the shed is to do everything else like baling the wool, filling the catching pens with sheep for the shearers and keeping the shed full from the paddocks close at hand but also bring other flocks back to the farm from areas not so close. It is really important to keep the shed topped up during bad weather to give yourself the best chance of carrying on until the next fine day arrives. You know if it starts to rain how long you've got before you run out of dry sheep. If the weather is too extreme and the sheep chill index is high the shorn sheep are back-filled through the shed, so as the roughies (woolly sheep) are shorn the clippies (shorn sheep) come back through the shed. Eventually, if rough weather continues you have shorn sheep back where the roughies have been right up to the catching pens. Our shed is a chute shed and so the sheep come from the shearer down a slide under the shed but this isn't big enough to hold all the sheep that can be shorn from the pens that hold rough sheep. (Sheep chill index is calculated by the weather forecasters to give farmers an idea of weather conditions and how they may affect newly shorn sheep.)

Today our shed can hold 700 sheep, although we rarely use the pens under the shearing floor. There are ups of having this capacity but also downs. The ups are that you don't stop unless you have a couple of days of rain. The down side is that there is not that much room under the floor so you are on your hands and knees when working these pens and also there is only so long that you can keep sheep in a shed before they start to become weak and get smothered.

When we started shearing for the second season, 1986–87, Toni was pregnant with our first child. All was well at first but she began to believe that she was psychosomatic because every time she would talk to someone about their pregnancy she would get the symptom. She didn't have morning sickness until someone told her about it, or bad headaches which came on after a chat with another lady. It was probably coincidence, but Toni used to get very annoyed that her pregnancy was able to incapacitate her. All these plans that we had had of minimising the disruption with a well-planned pregnancy were becoming unravelled. I was shearing away one day and I could hear all these coughing like noises and said to Toni 'that sheep seems to have a bad cough.' Only for a muted reply from her telling me it was her being sick.

After many years, Heather stopped being as keen to help out on the farm, even when the shearers were coming, although she would still send out cooking which was an enormous help. I uncharitably felt that *Eastenders* and *Coronation Street* had become addictive because she was an avid fan and we didn't have TV at that time, but in hindsight I believe that Heather wasn't in the best of health although she never said as much. Heather did stop coming out and we had to cope without her monumental contribution. Toni would then have to prepare breakfast before 6am and leave the shed ten minutes before breakfast to serve everything up and cook the eggs and toast. I would make sure the catching pens were full and then stand in for Toni doing her job on the table and classing.

At lunchtime Toni would leave twenty minutes early to get lunch sorted. Once again, timing for me was critical because I would have to cram as many sheep into the catching pen at the last minute before Toni left and hope that that would be enough to last twenty minutes. There have been odd times when it hasn't and I have had to jump up onto the shearing floor and through into the pens to quickly replenish the catching pen.

Sky and Bold, the working dogs

Working dogs are a completely different animal to the domestic equivalent and seem to have a sort of pack mentality with a top dog and a top bitch. Time and time again I have witnessed the same pattern in our dogs where there is a dominant dog and/or bitch and along comes the young pretender and with us it has led to some terrible dog fights.

It all came to the end one Farmer's Week when we returned to the farm every couple of days to feed everything. Sky was the dominant dog and Bold was the pretender. Bold had broken his span and in the ensuing excitement another dog called Blake got off as well and they killed Sky.

The worst two protagonists we ever had were two dogs called Sky and Bold. Sky was mine and Bold was Toni's and they hated the sight of each other. I had to be on constant lookout to try and break their fights up before they started, but sometimes this was not possible and they would wade in ripping pieces off each other. It was my job to try and stop them killing each other. If I was on the farm I would lay into them with a bit of alkathene but if we were out on a gather I would wade in usually with my boots. It doesn't sound very nice but it was the only way to stop them and even then you occasionally got bitten. During one fight Sky ripped Bolds mouth and bottom lip so badly it never healed and Bold ripped a big flap of skin from under Sky's eye that was about two inches by three which had to be stitched back on. I was bought up in Kent with two dogs that lived in the house but I had never seen anything like it for ferocity.

For a small family unit losing a working dog leaves a big hole, which doesn't get covered, as it would be on a big unit where there are a few shepherds.

The really galling bit was that Blake, the second dog involved, was in work terms useless, but because he was such a nice-natured, likable animal, full of energy and vitality I kept him as decoration. He wasn't naturally aggressive but something made him take part in this act.

Bold became top dog but already waiting in the wings was Speed. However there was never the pure hatred as there had been with Bold and Sky.

Bold was seven when he died. The poor sod died in harness, actually collapsing at the end of a gather. It had been a really hot day and we had come up the race from the Head of the Bay to gather ewes. We came together and Toni could see that he wasn't looking well but it was at a crucial time with the sheep coming towards and over the fence that Ted always cut. Once the sheep were through the fence we went back for Bold and he wasn't where Toni had left him so I went over this rocky outcrop and headed back on a course I thought Bold would have gone. I eventually found him and he was quite dead. I carried him back to the quads and put him on Toni's bike. It was a long miserable drive home. Bold had been a slow learner and I think most, less sympathetic, people would have shot him, but Toni had faith in him and he had rewarded her with a reasonable standard of work.

Toni had two dogs ready to move into the main team but it was true to say that the Kelpie, Jade, was going to take some controlling and so it turned out. Toni let her rip when we were taking the ewes back to their camp after shearing and did this dog want to work. The only problem was stopping her or getting her to do what Toni wanted and not what she wanted to do. I think in all truth if we had both had a Jade that would have been enough because two such dogs could have done all our sheep work. She wasn't very stylish but Toni was able to get her to run a long way for sheep and depend on her to return with them.

She could do twice the amount of work that a collie could do and after a long day working sheep she would come back, jump off the bike and round up the geese. She was a total workaholic.

Toni also had a huntaway bitch called Sue who was the nicest natured dog I think we have had. I would take her out at first when Toni was getting Jade trained and we would joke about 'our dog' but she was always Toni's.

She would like to do work and then tear back, jump up onto the quad and then peer round and up into Toni's face as if to say 'Did you see what I did?' Or just driving along she would put her paws on Toni's shoulders. She did have a bad habit which was to tear up the side and deliberately collide with a sheep, knocking it flat only to run back to the quad and once again look Toni square in the face as if to say 'Did you see that?' with what could only be described as a grin on her face.

Toni had two excellent dogs to gather and drive with and it was a good job too because when I was on Council I didn't have to worry about most of the sheep work because it just happened automatically.

Both Jade and Sue are coming to the end of their working lives with them both being in their twelfth year. Poor old Jade has had two cruciate ligament operations on her back legs and although wants to work, has to be on light duties for the rest of her natural. Sue has got another ailment, which affects her breathing on a hot day. You wouldn't think either of these dogs were old in canine terms because they are still dedicated to chase until they drop.

Already Egg, a Kelpie-collie cross, is taking Jade's mantle, but there is still work in progress if she is going to be as good as Jade. Sue's replacement, Dee, has just started her apprenticeship and is showing a lot potential but it is still early days.

We have always carried about eight dogs and of course this is a lot to look after and feed, especially today when cast sheep have a value. We are probably too soft and don't kill our old dogs, as some might, and so our pensioners that have given good service are given light duties and a retirement. The apprentices that you hope to move to the top team plus that top team means a number of dogs. We always have a couple of pensioners but as I write we have four in the top team three apprentices and three retirees.

We have had our failures, but only a handful in the years we have worked the farm. My best dog? Well it was Bess whose mum was the dependable Lassie. She was also very reliable, tough and dependable and was still working in her teens but she had become rather deaf and on her last outing she was trying to bring sheep to me but we were actually trying to put them through the gate. I spent about twenty minutes running around the flock after Bess as she stayed diligently at 180 degrees.

Today the farm is split up into small areas, although they are still hundreds of hectares each, and we practise a system of rotation, which helps us manage our grazing assets. We have a wether flock that we move in the three mountain camps and eight camps that we rotate our young sheep around in including the two small ones TriStar and Teds paddock. Each of these flocks is moved once a week and so it gives our dogs every opportunity to become proficient. Since starting writing, we have changed again and now holistically graze our farm.

We have rarely used our dogs on cattle much to the disbelief of the older experienced hands and visiting antipodeans from the Agricultural Department. All I can say is it has worked for us.

On the few occasions we have used them it has been with Toni's milk cows. When you first get a calf up the cow doesn't go away on that first night or not very far and they stay around the cowshed where their calf is. As the days go by the cow leaves the calf for longer and longer foraging far and wide returning to its calf, in our case, later and later. In fact, they would start coming home in the afternoon if they weren't chivvied up.

Once again we looked for advice from the more experienced members of the farming community and that was to chase them home with dogs. It was always pandemonium with the cows chasing the dogs and then they would get the message and trot home.

My two best dogs for driving cattle were Bozo and Ben but they both had varying techniques. Bozo used to cross from right to left and grab a cow's tail and swing by his teeth and sort of flip himself off the other side. Ben would rush in and bite them in the flanks. Both strategies had the cows picking them up. Equally the cows would chase after the dogs, horns going this way and that. I can't remember Bozo ever breaking the skin on the cow's tail, which seems unbelievable but I can remember a well-aimed kick stunning him for a few minutes.

Straight after being chased home with the dogs the cows would be back mooing nice and early in the morning and then over weeks and months their memories would fade and they would slowly get later and later again. Usually a couple of times a year was enough of a reminder.

Getting bogged down

Only the skilled camp drivers would drive out as far as Sussex in the winter when we first came here, but as time went on and the roads got further out, even a novice could make Sussex if they kept their wits about them. Our ground was a different ball game with tides and passes in creeks and really steep tracks and ditches everywhere. So one of our regular weekend activities was to go and pull people out of the many hazards that littered our farmland.

It was incredible how many people were experts at the art of getting un-bogged when you went out to help them, even when you knew they didn't have an iota of a clue about off-road. If I was in a generous mood, I would often humour our armed forces. 'Pull us out uphill mate and then we will be closer to the gate.'

So I would say something like, 'I don't think it will come out that way but I will try.' Usually we would pull them out my way, which was the one of least resistance. Out of a hole backwards if the front was down or in a ditch and down a hill rather than up it unless you had driven into a swamp. It was just common sense really. It also minimised the wear and tear on our Land Rover. A good pull involving a couple of savage jerks was hard on our vehicle.

One night, again in the first few years, Gerald Dickson, Jock Findlay and his two boys had driven up the second valley out of Hells Kitchen because they couldn't get up the hill on the high tide track. It was before we put a small bridge in there but with a couple of decent boards you could get across it. It was winter and everything was cold because the old Land Rover heaters weren't much, or the cabs at keeping what little heat you had inside the vehicle. It was pitch black as well.

So armed with a decent rope we got back down to the Land Rover, which was stuck in the ditch. The front was in and I was the other side of the ditch. I could have gone back and around slithering down into Hells Kitchen and pulled them out backwards, but then we would be both the wrong side of the ditch.

The biggest mistake I made was not going to have a look myself with a torch. Anyway, I gave the Land Rover a gradual but firm pull. Encouragement came from the assembled party. 'Nearly did it.' So I gave a bigger effort, and then an even greater one where you back up to the bogged Land Rover without getting stuck yourself and then charge off to the end of the rope. Bang! I had broken a half shaft. Our old IIA didn't have heavy-duty Salisbury axles. End of attempt, we all walked back to Sussex house.

The next day we went back to the scene of this fiasco, in daylight, to find that the Land Rover that was stuck was up against a flat wall of peat and rock. Even a tractor wouldn't have pulled the vehicle through that. I put it down to experience and made sure I would always survey the site myself, with a torch if necessary, and not rely on the occupants of a vehicle returning from enjoying the social amenities of Stanley.

I would often use the Bedford lorry to pull people out if they weren't up on the mountain. It was great at pulling Land Rovers out with very little effort. The reaction of some of the military, especially as I went to crank up the lorry, was great to observe and some of them would question the suitability of this vehicle. Once again if I wasn't in any hurry I would ask them for the second time where they were and then I would reassure them that I would easily get the lorry there and rescue them.

A group of military posties (postal workers) had decided to go on an excursion on mass and had done reasonably well to get to Bodie Peak Valley, before becoming badly bogged and burning the clutch out of another vehicle trying to recover the bogged Land Rover. So, as the light was fading the dogs started barking and into the farm walked two squaddies and explained their plight. I instructed them to jump in the lorry. 'You'll never get there in that mate.' They were able to offer a few other helpful tips for good measure. I managed to convince them enough for them to get into the lorry and we headed out to the rescue. The track in those days was down to the beach, and then round and up a valley, which could get cut up, and then up an incredibly steep hill towards the horse paddock gate. 'You'll never get up there mate,' one chap was able to say, but we were already on our way. These poor sods looked terrified and they hung on for grim death with their knuckles going white. They hadn't seen anything yet but they looked scared enough at the start.

Then we went down the steep track into Hells Kitchen, which was dry and steep but then we go up the centre ridge out from the creek. It is mostly stone and so you don't slip around but it is narrow in places so that you can see down into both valleys either side. These guys were bricking it with their eyes nearly popping out of their heads, but surely they must have realised that actually living there I should know what I was doing and that I wasn't laying it on for their benefit.

On we went to where the ridge becomes fairly wide and we drove along the top of the valley looking down at where the military guys were bogged. It was an interesting sight with a number of small red tents pitched along the ditch, obviously because they had resigned themselves to spend a night in the open. We got onto the government track and doubled back to where the Land Rover was stuck passing the abandoned Rover, which had the burnt clutch. (A Chinook recovered this vehicle days later.) I drove up to the vehicle, which was well bogged and jumped out and put the rope to the Land Rover and to the front tow hitch on the lorry. It was getting dark and people were milling around marvelling at a lorry turning up in their midst and the two that had gone for help were recounting their trip back in the 4 tonner.

There didn't seem to be anyone even thinking of getting in the Land Rover and driving it out while I pulled. I put the lorry into low 4x4 and slowly drove back pulling the dead weight of the Land Rover out of the ditch. Before the surprised looks on their faces had gone I had jumped out of the lorry, unhooked the rope and said my goodbyes. It was getting dark and although the lorry had lots of pluses the lights were pretty dim so I needed to get going. I do wonder if these guys remember the night they camped in Bodie Peak Valley and had their Land Rover pulled out by an ex-army lorry. Would their mates believe such a tale or would they think it was an exaggerated yarn?

One of the greatest memories of recovery was when some military folk walked into the farm one afternoon. Dick Sawle was here and we were catching up on old times and commiserating with each other because both our wives were in the UK. Toni was having Liam. These four guys hadn't gone that far and had come off the beach at the head of Sussex Creek and followed the old government clay track to the first valley and got stuck. It was a brute of a place in winter and needed a bit of care even in the summer. Coming from the south you come down a steep but hard slope and then you are faced by a number of different alternatives with three ditches converging on to the main one. These guys had just tried to cross the first one and down they went. Being on their own and having nothing like a bumper high lift jack they were stuck and couldn't get out.

Dick and I went over in my Land Rover and put the rope on the military vehicle and gave it a couple of gradual but firm pulls, but it did not budge so I told the driver I would have to give it a jerk.

Unfortunately, the bumper was only held on by one bolt on each side rather than the two which are meant to be there. The result was that the pull bent the bumper into the shape of a banana, but they were out of the ditch.

Back at the farm I advised them that they should try and straighten the bumper without taking it off the vehicle because I knew, from experience, that if you straighten one off the vehicle it is very difficult to line the bolt holes up. I might as well have talked to myself because they took it off and they found out that my prognosis was right. Mind you they had made a wonderful job of straightening it.

All was not lost as they had brought out a bottle of whisky and so after a few eye openers we decided to escort them over to San Carlos, which is where they were heading. Dick took his Land Rover and I drove the army one because it had small tyres.

We popped into Ron and Iris's and shared out the whisky and then Ron thought we might like to try a malt that he had been keeping for a special occasion and so we ended up rather merry. The daylight had gone and the tide was high and the army guys were getting a bit anxious about getting home the next day.

So off we went.

It was blacker than the inside of a cow and the Land Rover lights were not fantastic and so when we got up to the Head of the Bay Creek it was hard to see where the pass above the fish wall was. It was made harder by the tide being very high.

We couldn't sit there forever and so I decided to go for it and, whoops, we got hung up on a big rock. It was very deep, so much so that the back of the Land Rover had enough water in it to play bob an apple, it being up to and over the back tail gate.

Of course, these things always seem to happen in the winter when it is perishing, but there was nothing for it but to wade out to the back and put a rope on the tow hitch of the army Rover. It was cold and as I bent down to put the rope on there wasn't much of me that was above the water. As I put the rope on I heard a sharp exhaling of breath and at that moment the lights of Dick's Land Rover swung on to me and about two feet away was an elephant seal. I'd seen bigger but not that close and not while we were both in the water.

One of the military chaps began to panic, but I was able to reassure him that if we couldn't get off the rock we could go and sleep in the Findlay's shearing shed at worse and that nothing untoward would happen.

Dick's lightweight soon had us off the rocks but even though I felt confident and knew the mountain well I did wonder how eventful it would be going over it in a vehicle that wasn't really equipped for the task.

We got back without another blip and I was pleased that we were home because I was chilled to the marrow and the rather feeble heating in the Land Rover hadn't done a heck of a lot in raising the temperature above that of the outside. There wasn't the wind chill inside the Land Rover though.

Once again I wonder when those boys recount their tale how many of their friends believe them.

5. JOHN ROWLAND

Bodie Peak Valley also had a lot to do with us meeting John Rowland. John had been a Royal Marine and had married a local girl, Charlene, in the 1970s and they had come back to live in the Falklands after the war. John was now a police constable. We were getting ready for the boat, loading wool bales onto trailers so that we could put them on the sea truck, when John and a military policeman called Mark Van Cuylenburg, turned up at the farm. They were on a police patrol to San Carlos, something that was virtually unheard of, and they had come to grief in Bodie Peak Valley. We left the farm in the short-wheel base Land Rover that we got from Toni's Dad.

Today you can get to Bodie Peak in less than ten minutes, but before the roads it took a lot longer especially if the tide was in. Because it was summer it wasn't too arduous to get there and see the Land Rover stuck in the stream. What caught my eye was how neatly it fitted into this particular piece of the stream. It looked as if it had been dropped into the hole. The fit was so neat with the hole being not much bigger than the Land Rover itself. Not wanting a repetition of the half-shaft breaking we spent a little time digging the bank on our side down and putting a slope on it. We hitched on the rope and out came the constabulary's vehicle. So off we headed home but we didn't get very far before we realised that something was amiss, because a serious clunk was coming from the front axle at regular intervals. It sounded very serious. On our return to Sussex I whipped the front diff off and found that a number of teeth had been broken from the crown wheel. Apparently in their enthusiasm to get out they had gone backwards and forwards and had sustained this damage in the process.

I could have fixed it but it was a government vehicle and the government mechanics were able to see themselves clear to come and sort it during the following Sunday, on double time.

Every cloud has a silver lining and, as Sunday was many days away, we had John and Van Cuylenburg as free labour for an equal period. Usually the job of loading wool had Toni and me with our tongues hanging out trying to keep coastal shipping happy but, with two strapping guys, we were in cushty mode and we made the most of it.

During this operation, Van Cuylenburg caught the top of his head on the doorway of the shed. It was such a small incident that hardly anyone else I know would have even mentioned it but this chap was made of more sensitive material and thought that the door frame had scalped him, removing the skin down to the bone. He made such a fuss that Toni threatened to squirt his head with the antiseptic purple spray that we used on sheep cuts in the shearing shed.

We had many more adventures with John over the years and he still enjoys, to this day, his off-road travelling. I think Van Cuylenburg kept in touch with John for a few years before they lost contact. I wonder if he is checking in the mirror to this day to see if Sussex farm scarred his good looks.

Danger Mouse

Another character that came to Sussex was a civilian/military liaison officer, who Toni nicknamed Danger Mouse (DM) after the cartoon character with the voice of David Jason. He was the spitting image in his roll-neck jumper and his posh voice, so not only did he resemble him visually but vocally as well. He became friendly with my parents and ended up coming out to Sussex with them. They had chosen the best time to visit for excitement and adventure because it was the middle of winter.

The tide never seemed to be right during the winter months and so it was with this party. They arrived when it was just possible to sneak around the beach and arrive at the steep track, which was impassable. We went over and led the winter revellers up the valley over our bridge and through our passes that had been fortified with a few loads of rock and then up onto the flat that we were once going to have as our airstrip.

After a few tongue-loosening drinks Danger Mouse pontificated about the failings of mother's driving and how if he had been at the helm he would have demonstrated the value of the Land Rover product combined with army expertise and determination that would overcome any obstacle. Even though we patiently told him that even the best camp drivers found it virtually impossible with the conditions he had witnessed earlier, he was confident that he could achieve what no one else could.

I would have loved to be able to give him a Land Rover and let him have a go just to see him cut down to size but I couldn't afford to see our vehicle rolled, or worse DM getting hurt through his misplaced confidence.

The evening ended on a cultured note with DM knocking his whisky over and he and my mother licking it off the tablecloth. Although we had a big house we had to double up DM and Liam. Half way through the night Liam woke up and did a bit of a grizzle and the liaison officer shouted out at the top of his voice 'BE QUIET.' We were lying in bed thinking the whole house would now be awake, especially Liam, for the rest of the night. Fortune was smiling on us because Liam just turned over and went back to sleep.

Staying with tales of the Falkland Islands DM, a military patrol came through Sussex for the obligatory cuppa and drop scones. They seemed really nice lads and they stayed for a day and a bit giving us a hand on the farm. We chatted and they told us their plans as they headed back in the direction of Mount Pleasant Airport. Their next stop was Camilla Creek, which was a house that was prominent in the push for Goose Green in the Falkland war. There was an old house still there, which was tiny but had once housed the large families of the past.

Anyway a day or so later there was a lot of billowing smoke in the direction of Camilla Creek and 'whoops Chay' the old house is no more.

We happened to meet some of the guys some time later in the NAFFI at Mount Pleasant Airport, as we were making our way to Stanley, and they told us what happened. They had spent a night sheltering behind the house and then in the morning they had burnt their rubbish and warmed up in the lee of the building. On departure they buried their fire in snow and assumed that it was out.

This was a big mistake because as they got going along the track to Goose Green they looked back to see clouds of smoke and realised what had happened.

Not long after this event we were at a party in town held by Robin Bell who was a mate of John Rowland. Danger Mouse was loudly telling a group that the fire was nothing to do with the military and there was no proof etc. Toni told him how this wasn't true because the chaps had told her what had happened and that it was a worthless abandoned property with historical worth only so why was he taking this attitude. DM went on the offensive and was forceful in defending his position. Toni never likes these intense discussions but wasn't going to be browbeaten by DM, and told him she wasn't going to be told such nonsense when she knew differently.

The name Danger Mouse fitted an absolute treat and people called him it without thinking. Rumour had it that after he left the Falklands he forgot himself at a mess night and bit a woman's backside and had to resign his commission. It's a great story but probably not true. There was something I liked about him even though he could be a pompous arse at times.

Douglas Hansen

The next big job was to get ready and take down the Packaway at Kelly's Garden and transport it over the mountain to Sussex.

We had the Hiab hydraulic lifting arm on the lorry with the two main lifting rams and a boom ram for extended reach. On the main ram close to the lorry you could lift nearly three tonnes. If it was lifting with the boom ram fully extended it was a lot less. The lorry was good in the soft but this again happened over the winter and the Hiab was a good weight in its own right. We did manage to get it over to Kelly's Garden without too many problems.

The first job was to strip out all the fittings and stuff that wasn't part of the Packaway itself. There were lights and miles of cables everywhere. There were all the switches and inspection platforms plus miles of copper earthing straps. We were working in the winter so the days were short and the weather was atrocious. Driving over at first light, then trying to get on top of the mountain before it was pitch black coming home, was not always easy. After one day we drove home in nearly a foot of snow, which made it especially tricky. We didn't have a portable generator so we couldn't work late but if we had it would have meant more agro if we got stuck going home.

Different people came to help. John Rowland came a couple of times including the night of the snow and he was also there when Douglas Hansen came out to help. Douglas worked for the studio which was the radio station and the telephone system and was always up ladders working, so who better to help us strip out the lights in the roof of this building. He was going great guns even though he seemed to have the ladder at some weird angles but he was meant to be experienced. The floor of this building was smooth concrete. It kept everything clean but I was worried that Douglas's ladder would slip on it. I did mention it, but Douglas was his own man.

BANG! Down went Douglas. He was on the ground and couldn't get up. I wasn't sure if it was shock or if he had broken something. Douglas said he was okay and would get up presently. 'Come on you old bugger,' says John but I didn't let him help him up. Eventually we took a cautious approach and we helped him to the Land Rover and Toni drove him round to the settlement and spoke to a doctor in town. They decided to send the plane and take him to town to be on the safe side.

It sounds mercenary but we carried on working although we were all surmising what, if anything, Douglas had broken.

In fact, he had broken his leg lengthways up the thigh bone, which required a metal plate to be fitted and was in the hospital for a couple of nights and in plaster for a number of weeks.

I had put Douglas out of action, even if I had warned him about the dangers, so I thought I would do him a favour and every time I went to town I would go up to his peat bank and cut his peat. It didn't take me that long before the peat was cut. Douglas is very particular about certain things and I should have done more research on how he liked his bank cut although I might still have failed to deliver. Douglas cut his bank at an angle to reduce the dry and crumbling peat at the edges of the bank. I just cut my normal way 3, 2, 1 and spread the rest. Douglas didn't mention to me that I wasn't that neat, and there is no denying that. He did mention to others some of my inadequacies as a peat cutter. It would have burnt okay and I am glad I saved him paying someone else to cut it for him and spared that person the attentions of Douglas as he showed them the Hansen regulation cutting technique. I think Douglas got his peat cut by machine from that day on. He probably thought it couldn't be rougher than me.

A Packaway is modular in construction and the one that we had acquired had eight pieces. The plan was to break it down into sections and then put the sections onto a large trailer that we had managed to borrow and then pull it over the mountain with tractors. I had also managed to borrow the KC's big County tractor and Phillip Miller to come and drive it. We had both of the co-op tractors as well, with Ron driving one and a chap called Bill Berntsen to drive the other.

The first job was to lift out the ends and the roller door and put them somewhere out of the way. We then undid the bolts where the walls and the roof join, leaving one in on each side so that the wall could be swung in under the roof. We did this on both sides and then we had one section with the roof with the walls tucked underneath. In this position, we swung the complete section up onto the trailer with the Hiab. On the first run we put two sections on the trailer.

With everything firmly lashed to the trailer we set off to tackle Sussex Mountain. Same old story for many trips in the Falklands as it was when leaving Kelly's. If the tide was out then it was plain sailing if it was in, especially with a long vehicle, it was a bloody nightmare.

Off we went from Kelly's letting the KC tractor do all the work until the foot of the mountain. Just before the first climb we roped up the other two tractors and off we went.

We were starting to climb and we were all looking back to see how easy or hard it was going to be and it looked okay. All of a sudden there was a bang and the main drawbar pin had unbelievably broken in the KC tractor and as that is the direct link to the trailer it was the last thing we wanted. The trailer and two Packaway bits, which amounted to a quarter of the shed, went hurtling down the hill with the big turntable on the trailer turning this way and that. I wanted to look away before the crash but I was mesmerised. I couldn't believe it didn't turn over and smash not only the sections of building but the trailer that didn't even belong to us. If I were a religious person, I would be convinced I had witnessed a small miracle. Someone must have been looking down on us because the trailer just gently jack knifed itself to a standstill about 400 yards away. Even today I have yet to hear of a similar happening where a proper draw bar pin fails so spectacularly.

We collected our wits and drove down, found another pin, and hooked up to the trailer before we started to go back up the mountain. It had been a narrow escape and we all knew it. This time all went well and remarkably nothing else of note happened as we got back to Sussex. There was a down side to the lifting on and off and that was that the lorry with the Hiab had to go backwards and forwards over the mountain.

Our next trip was terrible. We did exactly the same thing but once we were on top of the mountain we just kept on getting bogged. Even with the pulling power of three 4x4s we couldn't keep going. With the turntable we would unhook the tractor, attach a rope and then try and jerk the trailer out of the hole and back onto the surface, but the whole event was pretty precarious with the Packaway on board. Eventually we gave up and I bought the lorry up and lifted one of the pieces off and then carried on to Sussex to lift the other piece off. We left the offloaded one on the mountain while we brought the remaining five sections one by one.

On one of these trips we were all following Phillip before we got to the Hard Hill Gate and Ron noticed that his gloves had fallen out of the tractor. They weren't just any old gloves they were his pride and joy goatskin gloves. We are talking about the loss when Bill piped up, 'Yes, I saw the gloves fall out in the Creek, Ron.'

Ron and I both looked at Bill for a further explanation, which wasn't forthcoming. Like, perhaps, 'I didn't stop to pick them up because so and so' or 'I didn't try and attract your attention' followed by the reason. Ron was not amused but Bill seemed to be tickled that he alone had this vital information, which he hadn't shared. Bill's sense of humour was slightly different to ours on that occasion.

On another occasion Bill was travelling to a military mountain site with Gerald, Ron's brother. It was a rough old track and when they arrived at the top Gerald noticed that the lens to one of his indicators had fallen off. They were wondering where it had gone and how it had managed to shake loose. On the way back down Bill started quietly laughing to himself. 'What's wrong with you,' asked Gerald. 'Well you know that lens we lost coming up? You just ran it over and smashed it.' There was no 'Look out' or 'There it is.' Bill was really happy he was having such a splendid day out but Gerald was not so tickled.

The job carting the shed over continued until it was completed and after many boggings, but with our good humour intact, the job was completed.

Diving without Dave

Nothing ever seems to be easy and, during what was a huge operation for us, I was asked if I could come and dive on a fishing vessel. At that time we had a lot still at Kelly's and the section on the mountain. Dave Eynon was out of the Islands and other divers had gone out but couldn't commit. I said that I would come and dive at £3 a minute, which was what I was paid before the war to dive on fishing vessels. Things had changed slightly with Dave providing a more professional service and the price was calculated for the service being performed. The captain thought I was being greedy but I was in the middle of my own thing, other folk had had a look and decided they couldn't help so it was me or a tow to Montevideo. In a way, I thought I was also covering Dave's business interests because he had developed a diving service to the fishing vessels operating in Falklands waters. All the negotiation was done on the 2-meter set and so was pretty public and an army officer asked if I would like a hand. Phillip Miller worked with Dave Eynon as boatman at the time but had only just started to learn to dive so he had access to Dave's equipment. Again, I reckoned that providing this service would help the fishing industry to realise there was a reliable diving facility in the Falklands as well as making me some money.

I have done a number of these dives but this was the worst mess I had ever seen. There was a huge tangle of net around the propeller with hawsers and rope which then dropped off, trailing down toward the sea floor. The army officer and I started to attack this mess with saws, bolt croppers, knives but it was wound on so tightly it was hard to know where to start once we had cut the tail free. We did a lot of hours consuming all our air before going ashore to put more air in the bottles.

I was a little concerned working in that kind of environment with someone who I didn't know very well. I was relieved to realise that he was competent and cautious, which was just what was needed. We were swimming in amongst the nets and rope that could wrap round the pillar valve on the aqualung bottle or your knife or any protruding piece of gear and ensnare you. Cutting big pieces free, one had to be sure that you weren't attached as a lot of it still had weights connected. The water wasn't deep, about 30 feet, at a guess, but being dragged to the bottom under a quantity of net was an added danger. We did a lot of hours together trying to remove this massive tangle. Eventually the army chap had to go back to Mount Pleasant Airport and take up his day job once more. He earned over £1,200 but reckoned he would have to buy the beers in the mess with it.

Philip became the second diver. He had done a little bit with Dave but I knew it hadn't been much when he didn't know how to clear his ears. We overcame this obstacle and ripped into the remaining net. I came up with a novel idea for the last few feet and that was to put a hook attached to a hawser into the net and have the crew pull it up on the winch which ripped hunks out of the tight netting and made it easier for us to deal with it.

At the end of the job I smelt of oil and looked wrinkled and mottled as you do when you soak in the bath for too long. Dave made £1,500 for the rent of his equipment and I think I made well over £2,000. It was a great injection of cash when we needed it. I bought Toni a brand new Kenwood Chef Major, which is still in use today.

Putting up the Packaway

Back at the ranch we had to build the piles to support the Packaway building, but unlike the wood of the old shed which could be bodged to fit, the steel framed Packaway wasn't so forgiving when it came to accuracy. Neither of us had had any experience of building something this big so it was quite an undertaking. I borrowed, yet again, a theodolite and we messed around with string to get our square. We put one metre square piles in each of the four corners, and a 75cm square where each section joined along the ends and side. The cement was courtesy of the seventh share of the San Carlos stores. The shingle we got from the beach below the house but the sand was a problem. With no roads and the closest sand being at Ponds Rincon, which had a mountain to negotiate, it was a case of using a co-op tractor and trailer and getting enough without getting bogged on the way home.

The piles took some sorting out to be in the right place at the right height but eventually they were all in place ready for the sections to be put up.

To be able to use the Hiab each section had to be swung from one side of the lorry into position. Then the lorry would move to the end and lift one end up, as Toni pulled the wall out at right angles to the roof with rope so that the bolts in the corners would slot into place. Once one side was done the lorry was moved to the other side and again the section was lifted up and the opposite wall was pulled out and bolted into place. As I write this, the print falls easily onto the paper but it was a hard job, especially for Toni doing the pulling. Not only was the pulling hard but also by this time we had a little helper, Caris, who was in a backpack on Toni's back. I would use the Hiab arm to lift and then when Toni had pulled it out I would lower the section thus keeping the holes lined up.

Each section was bolted into place with a number of tapered head bolts in the plate that held the wall and roof at the right angle. Then each section was held to one another by a bolt either side, which went through the corner plates and a single bolt in the eaves. The bolt in the eaves was a bastard to line up and then get close enough for the bolts that we had taken out. It was the height as much as the struggle that made the job so challenging.

Caris was very good, and I suppose she was used to being with us as we worked on the farm, however occasionally we had to let her rip. When loose we had to have eyes in the back of our heads because she loved to climb and explore. I would be putting the bolts in on the corners and Toni would be fetching the podger or some other tool and Caris would be straight up the ladder to get involved. Caris thought this was great sport mainly, I feel, because of the reaction she got from her mum and dad.

It took us a couple of days and during the process a humdinger of a gale came through. We thought it was going to undo all the work we had done, plus wreck the building to boot, because it wasn't properly fastened down or have both ends in for strength. I drove the lorry into the building and put the Hiab arm out through one of the air duct holes and then with big heavy duty cargo straps strapped the other side of the building onto the lorry. It was going to take some gale to shift the shed and the lorry. The plan worked and once the gale had passed the shed was still there.

To put the ends in was a challenge even though we waited for a calm day. A light breeze got up making the last few sections very hard to push into place and bolt them top and bottom. The east end was easier because we didn't have the wind to contend with and the roller door waited for a while.

So the shell was up and now we had to pull the old shed down to use its wood to build the internals for the new.

We followed a New Zealand plan of a raised board and sloping catching pens which was meant to make the sheep face uphill and away from the shearer thus making them easier to catch and drag from the pens.

Helping ourselves

Fortunately for us Mount Pleasant Airport were starting to sell off all the surplus stuff they had left over after building the airport and army camp. The rubbish dump was also getting used in a very productive way. I always popped into the dump on my way to and from Stanley, and if I was driving the lorry it could be very rewarding, but even the Land Rover struggled away from the dump loaded to the gunnels on a regular basis.

For some reason the military began to get a bit tetchy about the rubbish dump and changed from a passive to an aggressive attitude towards people recovering items. One day I was in and got some aluminium planks and large pieces of wood and as I was struggling the last few bits into the truck a military police Land Rover drove past with two policemen in the front.

I pulled out of the dump and two hundred yards further on the police vehicle was sitting at right angles to the road. As I came closer, they motioned to me to pull over. One of the officers was an obnoxious, surly individual that ripped into me for going on to the tip and told me that I had to take everything back. I let him rip into me until he ran out of steam. The other chap looked a bit embarrassed and didn't say anything.

First of all I told them that I wouldn't be taking the stuff back to the tip and as the military were throwing the stuff away I couldn't see the problem with me relocating stuff.

I thought the aggressive chap was going to flip. He went bright red and he screwed up his face and he let me have it. Once more I just looked at him as he was delivering his tirade and patiently waited for him to finish.

I then said that I was prepared to take the stuff back to the dump but here was the deal. Army patrols often came to our farm and we always gave them a friendly welcome, making tea and providing them with cake or biscuits or drop scones and even feeding them main meals. Many people from Mount Pleasant Airport walked into Sussex broken down and bogged at all times of the day and night and we have pulled them out, fixed their vehicles and put them up, including the military police. But I said that if I took the stuff back to the dump that would be the end of our hospitality and we would treat all military personnel coming to our home as he was treating me.

This was far more effective than I could have imagined and he started to be friendly saying he was only doing his job, to which I said that he could do it without being so hostile. He blamed the housing estate for reporting people going on to the dump.

Anyway, we had found common ground and they both became friendly and they were happy for me to continue my journey without going back to the dump. As we now seemed to be all matey matey, I asked them if they would return to the dump with me because there was a large steel plate that I couldn't lift onto the lorry on my own. They were very apologetic in their refusal and at that we both went on our way.

Another more embarrassing time was when I was on the dump with the Hiab lorry and I had seen some goodies down in the bowels of the refuse. I put the legs down and fully extended the arms and the boom. I tied a chain onto the booty and then found that I was low on oil and couldn't pull the boom in. In fact, it wouldn't do anything. So, with the lorry monopolising a good amount of the dump I walked into Mount Pleasant Airport to bum some hydraulic oil.

Collecting wood

Things like army fencing standards, wood, chain, and rope were the main commodities but there were all sorts. On one trip I rescued a number of long lengths of angle iron. These, along with the standards I had also got, were enough to carry all the gratings in the shearing shed and extension. I welded them together in long lengths running the length of the pens on wooden bearers inside the shearing shed. It was a great cause of annoyance that the wood relocated from the dump wasn't any good for gratings and so we had to buy that.

The whole internals of the shed sat on wooden piles. These wooden piles were made from the telephone poles that ran up to the targets at the old Sappers Hill rifle range. After the war, the rifle range was moved because people didn't think it was appropriate anymore for full bore rifle rounds to possibly whistle over the road that ran off towards Pony's Pass. It's an ill wind that blows no one any good and I was given the poles, which I lifted promptly before some other thieving farmer got a sniff.

This wood was very hard and heavy and it was also very strong and rot resistant. I was to find out later that if you needed to cut a small amount off, it was easier to grind it off with an angle grinder than to saw it. I tried to plane one of these piles with the electric planer and it spat the blades out. Lesson learnt.

Collecting the wooden piles was a lorry run and it was one of those loads where you are wondering miles before the off-road stuff whether you should go along a flat or through a pass. The choices weren't vast and none of them guaranteed a successful outcome. This run was remarkably trouble-free although we did sink well down in places.

We had ordered a large amount of wood to come to the farm on the *Monsunen*. The Coastal Shipping Office said they would deliver to Sussex and we had the facilities to lift it out of the sea truck so it was no big deal. The captain of the vessel however thought otherwise and decided to offload it at San Carlos.

It would have been far better to have left it in town or taken it to Goose Green because the mountain between us and San Carlos was a pain. We tried to cart it back over the mountain on our 4x4 four-tonne ex-army Bedford. I ended up getting bogged on the mountain and having to ask Ron Dickson to pull me out with a tractor.

In a way the boat was good because the service was to the door, but coastal shipping had very little flexibility and made it easy for them but difficult for us. We had a neat system where we would reverse a big four-wheel trailer into the sea and have the four-tonne lorry alongside which had a hydraulic lifting arm. It was just like a jetty with a lifting facility with all heavy items like fuel being lifted from the sea truck with no physical work for the crew. I don't think there was another sea truck port with such capacity.

They continued to pick up our wool and deliver fuel which would have been a pain to cart overland at that time. Once the road got to Burnt Side we started to cart our wool and bring our fuel home but that was a number of years in the future.

6. MAKING A LIVING

Wool

Since day one it has always been clear that to make more money with wool as your major source of revenue you have to reduce the micron and increase the weight. The Turners of Rincon gave us two ram hoggets to get the ball rolling with improved genetics; and San Carlos had made a small start with imported Polwarth rams and we had our share of the progeny.

In the late 1980s we took part in the first laparoscopic insemination programme to improve the genetics of our sheep. It was only a handful of sheep but we were delighted when we selected two cracking ram lambs from our five ewes. Of course, farming in the Falklands is hard on animals and there are so many things that can go wrong with any stock, even if it has the most valued of all the traits, which I call the survivability gene, in its make-up. This gene is strongest in the non-refined sheep that have lived in the Falklands for a number of generations.

But it was a most surprising sequence of events that dashed all those dreams of 10kg fleeces and 17 micron wool. In fact, the first casualty wasn't a surprise. A shearer cut the pizzle off one of the rams. The second was more bizarre. Having survived his shearing experience, he lived on the green with a few pets, well away from any natural hazard and present for us to keep an eye on him and even feed him if necessary during the winter months.

Liam had a little pedal go-cart that he used to peddle up and down the green by the garden. On one particular day the only remaining ram took exception to Liam and charged him, knocking him flat beside his cart. Toni and I raced over, with Toni shouting for me to commit heinous damage to the ram's wellbeing. There was no chance that I could catch it on foot and so it ran away, but stupidly didn't vacate the scene entirely. Toni had rescued Liam but had returned from the house with the gun. The ram would probably have lived to procreate again and improve our wool but no, for some strange reason it had a death wish and came charging down the green towards Toni and with this charge disappeared all our extra kilos and super micron for this campaign. I often wonder about this event as we sit alone, just Toni and me, during the long winter evenings and I never dream of upsetting her.

Rescue missions

I used to go to the top of the mountain to cut peat. It was on the Head of the Bay land but we had rights to cut peat and take water from this property in our farm sale agreement. It was too far away to cut a few here and a few there, so if I went to the peat bank I would try and cut 30 yards unless the weather became absolutely atrocious. I sometimes, but rarely, cut more but occasionally I would to finish a bank or the job at the end. I would try and get up there before seven in the morning and cut until lunchtime and then I would find a lighter job for the afternoon.

I would cut for an hour and rest for five minutes or ten if I had a drink. I listened to the local radio, the Falkland Island Broadcasting Station, as I cut. On one particular day, I was scratching out my hour's worth, when an announcement came over the radio saying, 'if Richard is listening at the peat bog please come on the 2 meter.' I had the handheld and as I switched it on began to wonder what catastrophe might have befallen Toni. Everyone else must have wondered the same and so Toni had moved channels to speak to others.

I raced down the mountain on the bike, tore down the green, ran into the house only to find Andy Findlay, the son of the next-door farm owner. He was bogged in St Bruno's Arroyo and couldn't get out. He had got badly bogged and thought that the long walk to Sussex would be easier than jacking for ages.

The Land Rover was nearly always ready for a rescue mission and so we jumped in and proceeded east along the track. On my arrival, sitting patiently in the Land Rover, waiting for the Sussex answer to International Rescue, was Mally Spink. I heaved Andy's Land Rover out of the hole and he went on his way to Stanley. Mally was a lady who lived in Stanley. She had many years of experience in camp and she occasionally did the cooking on small farms during the shearing season to help out.

Andy was a young lad who was learning off-road skills, but at that time he would bog on a damp tea towel. I pulled Andy out more times than I pulled out any other individual. On one occasion he managed to drive over the beach bank below the house or below where our shearing shed was eventually built. I decided not to take the Land Rover this time because I thought if his vehicle rolled over it would take mine with it down to the beach. I took the lorry and pulled him up to the firm and flat ground.

On another occasion Andy called for help on the 2 meter. Again he was in St Bruno's Arroyo but he wasn't bogged, he had crossed the bridge turned right and then edged his way past some soft and rutted out places and then climbed the hill. When he was nearly at the top of the hill his gearbox had locked up. The funny thing was that the clutch wouldn't make it come free. I tried to drag him but it wouldn't budge so I jacked the front up as high as I could and because it was jammed it stayed there with the front right up in the air. I was hoping that this treatment would help unlock the bloody thing but it didn't budge. So with it still in the air I put the rope back on and gave it another pull. There was a big bang and it came free and we limped back to Sussex and Andy managed to get it home.

After this trip Andy got his Land Rover into the garage, took it to pieces and started working on making it better. Whenever I was passing, Andy would show me the progress. I am not sure what went wrong but I think I am right in saying that the Land Rover had to be dragged out of the shearing shed at the beginning of the next shearing season and it was dragged outside by the farm tractor. I didn't begrudge rescuing anyone because many people gave the same help all over the Islands but the demise of Andy's Land Rover didn't hit me that hard.

Andy's father Jock also used the track, although not as often as Andy. One night, Ron was over having his hair cut when there was a knock on the door. When you live where we do, miles from anywhere, it is an unusual event. Here was Bruce, Andy's elder brother. He was at least six foot three, towering over us all but clearly uncomfortable about asking for help. 'Dad's bogged on the mountain and needs a pull out.'

Off we went and picked up the San Carlos track, into our outer ram paddock and climbed towards the fence, which runs east west along the mountain. Jock was on the topside of the fence after driving through the gateway. We also noticed that someone had kicked the wooden planks from each side of the gateway and they were sitting under the wheels of Jock's vehicle.

We had had a bit of a dispute in the past with Jock because he had fenced across the riding track, which we used a lot in the early days. The only way with a horse now was a good dogleg to a gate built under a peat bank, which was soft and with no vegetation, and another to the west that was built on a peat bank and you couldn't drive a 4x4 tractor through it in the winter. I thought that here was an opportunity to make things happen. It was obvious what had happened and yet I didn't mention the wood from the gateway, but I did say 'One good turn deserves another, Gerald, how about putting that gateway in on the riding track?' He agreed that he could, but it never happened.

Mechanisation

The mechanisation from horse to machine was really started in the San Carlos area by Geoff and Marilyn Butler. A number of us had bikes, but in a supporting role such as chasing the horses in to the corral. Geoff took the concept a step further and had his Honda three-wheeler as the mainstay for his sheep work and quick-trip business.

I think this was a valuable bit of forethought by Geoff who knew he had to gather a large area of swamp and soft peat bank, and that on his own or even with Marilyn he would need more than horse power. Even armed with a three-wheeler that could go anywhere apart from the softest swamps, he also had dogs to help on these challenging gathers, Geoff had some very long days before he fenced his land up.

It wasn't only gathering because he made a small trailer and between the trailer and the three-wheeler they would travel as a family of six. I am not sure why they didn't get an old Land Rover in a military cast sale like the rest of us, but perhaps Geoff realised that even armed with the biggest of tyres to get to his farm would never be a doddle. Armed with thigh boots, a three-wheeler is relatively easy to un-bog.

Geoff would even do trips to town and that man could shift. Coming through Sussex ground, Geoff somehow managed to force a tyre off the rim of his three-wheeler. Being a tubeless tyre it was very difficult to get them back on the rims without a compressor. Geoff performed a feat close to a miracle of biblical proportion by getting his tyre back on, armed with a foot-pump. Geoff was incredibly hard on his stuff and on the premise of record trips and overloading and 24/7 hard work, we got one.

It was better than a bike in some respects because the wind couldn't blow it over and you could carry a dog or a small amount of fencing on it. We used it for many years, but like many things back then spares weren't that easy to get hold of quickly. The brakes wore out but it didn't really need them with engine braking. Or so I thought. We were gathering behind Bodie Peak because I used to round the sheep up into the southeast corner of the camp and then drive them around the back of Bodie, picking up other sheep on the way round. Unbeknown to me, driving between the grass bogs the gear leaver had been pulled underneath the bike and as I was going down a steep hill the bike jumped out of gear. It took me a fraction of a second to realise what had happened and threw myself off as the three-wheeler cart wheeled down the mountainside.

Our next acquisition was a blue Yamaha Big Bear ATV (All-Terrain Vehicle or quad bike), which gave us reliable service for many years.

The three-wheelers and the quads after them, had thumb throttles which was something I had never come across before. My first long gathers using the thumb throttle left me with a sore thumb for days but it is something you soon get used to.

The blue quad went for many, many years. It rode the rough ground better than the three-wheeler and it could carry a lot of stuff for those small jobs that were hard to get to with the Land Rover.

Riding a bike, two-, three- or four-wheel is always a challenge in the Falklands. Chasing sheep in rough and precipitous terrain always presents an opportunity for an adrenalin rush and I have had a few over the years. The most spectacular was after a long gather in Shepherds Brook and a long drive home. It had been a very hot day, flat calm and the dogs were exhausted and as we put the sheep into the ram paddock and took them towards the pens, the sheep spread up and away from the gate. I thought I would just drive along the side at speed and turn them down. As I was travelling along I hit a sharp hole that threw me off and sent the quad end for end. It could have been nasty if I had fallen in front of the quad but this is the kind of thing that happens on farms all over the Islands and one is usually thrown clear.

The only area where a quad is weak is on the side of a hill and because Sussex is mostly sharp valleys that does give us some challenges. We have mostly had reasonable dogs but that doesn't stop you from driving along the side of a hill to see what's going on. We have still had the odd roll, which means trying to get out of the way so you don't have the machine on top of you. Toni has had the luckiest escape when she was unable to jump clear and she went between the handlebars as it rolled over her.

On another really hot day, Toni and I were both on quads on the way to gather but needing to check on some horses. We split up to find them, with a meeting place arranged, before going on to gather the sheep. I got to the rendezvous first and Toni soon appeared and she was absolutely smothered in clay and soaked. She had been riding along the clay track at speed when she had turned off to avoid a big puddle. The wheel hit the bank at a funny angle flipping the quad over and Toni into the middle of a watery clay hole. I asked her about her wellbeing and on being told it was only her pride that was dented I couldn't help laughing.

Being a nice day it wasn't long before Toni had dried off.

Looking back over the years of gathering on horses and motorbikes, three-wheelers and quads there are merits and downsides to them all. Horses when they are fat don't always want to run straight into the corall and then they don't always want to be caught, they mill around and show their rear ends to you. Once caught, some horses are pricklier than others but equally the odd one was bomb proof. A horse beats all for covering rough ground or just plodding along behind a flock of sheep, but what I most enjoyed was this bond with nature, riding a horse with your dogs ready to round up sheep and bring them home. A horse is a commitment of time even if he is the cheapest form of transport. Even after taming all the dangerous parts, time and endless patience, some horses still don't make the grade.

Motorbikes aren't hard to catch and if maintained are pretty reliable even when there is plenty of water around. They are demons in big bogs and uncomfortable (with modern bike manufacturers reducing the size of the seat they are even more so). You can teach a dog to ride on a two-wheeler but you are limited probably to one dog. They are good on the side of hills but they are limited to the one job. They seem to always get blown off the stand, even if you weld an enormous foot onto the bottom of the stand. In my opinion a three-wheeler, once tamed, is better than a bike because you can carry materials or your dogs, although they are treacherous on hills.

Quads are great to do the small jobs and to convey a heap of dogs when gathering, but they are brutes to shift if you are unfortunate enough to bog one, but it has to be a mucky ditch or very soft swamp for that to happen. Quads at £5,000 a pop, spares that are pricey and a life span of about 10 years (plus all the consumables) does make it difficult to justify, especially on a small farm.

Probably the biggest plus for mechanisation is that after a long day, and the weather is wet and cold, even if it ends at the furthest point on the farm you can get home in double quick time.

Buying a tractor

We happened to buy a tractor at a cast sale and were very pleased with the deal. All of the tractors had done nothing in terms of hours and only light duties at that. The only downside, however, was the fact that they had been abused like being driven into the sea. Every single one had a damaged front differential where lack of maintenance had allowed the differentials to run out of oil, which in turn had ruined the bearings and some of the internals.

This cast sale was in Stanley and once we had found out that it was a runner we had to think about getting it home. In the Falklands, for some strange reason, you need a separate licence to drive a tractor regardless of all your other driving qualifications. I asked the Chief of Police whether Toni could drive the tractor out along the road with her full car driving licence, because the alternative was to be towed out which would be far more dangerous. Unfortunately, the law was the law and this wasn't an option.

So we went to the fall-back position, which was to be dragged out to the end of the road behind the lorry. We had a full complement of 2-meter sets and with the engine running on the tractor because it had powered steering, we headed out along the Mount Pleasant Airport Road. Caris was strapped into her car seat which was in the lorry.

Tractors aren't really designed to go much above 20mph and so it was a bit of a dawdle and when my mind began to wander the speed would creep up. Thank goodness for the comms, because Toni was able to explain in a very excitable voice that at any speed above 20mph the tractor would start to bounce and she would have her work cut out to hang on to the steering wheel.

Somehow, whilst going through a gateway at Swan Inlet, we got two punctures in the lorry. We managed to get hold of someone on the 2 meter and a guy called Smiler (Terence) Jaffray kindly offered to come from Goose Green with a spare for us. So that Toni and Caris did not have to hang around waiting as well, I took the car seat out of the lorry and, using some fencing wire, lashed it into the tractor. They then continued the journey to Burnside and waited for me there, where Gerald and Kay Morrison kindly put us up for the night.

The tractor was not needed for a while so I took it out of use and tried to strip it down to sort out the front axle. But when it came to pulling out the half shafts it was mission impossible. Not to be beaten, I thought I would thread a small chain between the universal joint and the half shaft and drive member and then with the axle fastened to something I could pull it out. I didn't want to damage anything by jerking but a steady approach wasn't enough to budge it.

I had a brain wave. I chained one end of the tractor axle to the towing hitch on the back of the lorry and then attached the chain on the half shaft to the Hiab near the biggest ram, which in my calculation should bring 3 tonnes of pulling power to play on the stubborn half shaft.

On came the power and the axle sat up and was rigid between the tow hitch and the Hiab. More power and things began to creak, but there was no sign that the half shaft was pulling out of the differential. More power and something began to move but it wasn't what I wanted or what I expected, because the power of the arm had just pulled the front of the lorry closer to the back, breaking the back of the lorry.

A while later I bought a two-wheel drive Bedford with power-assisted steering and a low mileage Turbo diesel engine and, more importantly, a decent cab. Mike McKay reckoned he could make a beast of a vehicle out of the two lorries.

I drove the broken donor lorry into town. It was like driving a mobile planetarium, sitting back and staring up at the sky.

Once in town we used the back of that lorry and the front of the new purchase, with a front axle from another four-tonner that we acquired from Mary Hill quarry. Mike was the brains behind the project and about two weeks later out of the garage came a hybrid. It had a tilting cab so you could work on the engine without taking the cab off, like you do with a four-tonner. And it had assisted steering, which to anyone that has ever driven an army four-tonner is a big bonus.

These lorries, which were surplus to army requirements, were used by many farmers and they had their failings in as much as they were powerless, the cabs rusted away quickly and bits would blow off them as the years advanced. However, they could shift an awesome amount and were pretty good off-road and their greatest asset was their fuel economy. I don't think they burnt twice the amount of fuel that our Land Rover burnt, but they could carry ten times the load.

There were a few things that had to be done to make them a little more robust. The steering rod that came from the arm on the steering box had to be strengthened, otherwise you were forever taking it off to straighten it. Equally the track rod took a lot more abuse if you welded angle iron along its length.

The one weak area that I never got to overcome was the king pins. To make our four-tonners even better over camp we bought wide wheels for the front (we already had double wheels on the back). This made the lorry really good on soft camp and stopped it sinking in. The downside was that the king pins just weren't designed to take the extra forces of a bigger wheel and would last perhaps 500 miles at the most and sometimes a lot less.

After my illness we half-heartedly ran the lorry for a while, but there were a number of issues that made running it less appealing. One was the end of army cast sales thus halting cheap spares and the other was having extra wool. To be honest there wasn't enough work throughout the year to justify me spending many hours keeping the cab from disintegrating and everything roadworthy, even to Falklands standards.

We chose to employ a haulier to shift our wool and haul anything that is too big for the Land Rover.

We had our tractor out on the farm while Mike ordered some spares. When they arrived, I decided to drive the tractor into Stanley to Mike's garage on Davies Street. Covering over seventy miles in a tractor is torture and it took forever. The steering began to get very strange during the trip, with it taking more and more turns to make it go in the direction that was needed. Just after the cattle grid at the bottom of Fitzroy Ridge the tractor gained a mind of its own and shot off the road and into the large ditch at the side of the road. One of the steel pipes, which held the fluid for the pump that operated the steering, had rusted through making it fail. I was surprised that with the gradient of the side of the ditch that the tractor hadn't rolled, but once again luck was with me.

Mike fixed the tractor axle as well taking it to pieces, but only after administering heat from an oxy-acetylene set and some strong pulling power.

7. CARIS AND LIAM

And then there were three

We planned our family with great care because as a family workforce we wanted to have our children in the winter months so that we would both still be able to do the main farming tasks in the summer. In the early years we didn't have the confidence or the expertise to be able to do it with one of our number absent for any reason. Like all couples without children we were very naive but having said that, we did read a number of books to prepare ourselves as well as we could. We even went to the doctor and asked him for advice. He laughed when Toni told him of our plans and told us that it didn't often happen like that and that some people try for years to have children. It did work for us in the terms of birth times, although the big plans of carrying on working had a huge dent kicked in it.

Our plans were realised and Caris was to be born in the winter. Once again, living miles away from anywhere, finding out that Toni was pregnant was a bit of a saga. She visited the doctor in Stanley and then the medical department wrote to her with the outcome. After this news arrived I happened to be in town without Toni and she asked me to tell her parents the good news. It wasn't the sort of thing one puts over the 2-meter radio. Tony and Heather seemed to be embarrassed and kept changing the subject, which was slightly disconcerting. It was their first grandchild after all.

All pregnant women living in camp had to go to Stanley a month before the intended birth. Derek came out and took Toni into town and they had to take the rougher track out beyond St Bruno's Arroyo, which we sometimes had to use when things got really chewed up on the main track. It was many miles of rough but hard off-road driving, with Derek on tenterhooks because of Toni's condition.

Nearer the time I went in to join Toni for the birth. Early one morning we were lying in bed in the Police Cottages when Toni's water broke. It was a really exciting time and we quickly got up and sped up to the Temporary Brewster Hospital. Nothing seemed to be happening so I went back to the Police Cottages and had some breakfast. I was told that if there were any developments they would let me know. I didn't get summoned but I didn't stay away that long either.

When I got back I sat on the bed opposite to Toni, chatting about stuff. Then a nurse came bustling in and gave me a right old ear bashing for sitting on the bed. However, it was going to take more than her to spoil this special day.

I went off again and returned with Christel. More excitement. The crabby old nurse returned full of misery and attitude. No, we couldn't both visit Toni in the ward. I jokingly remarked that wasn't that a little medieval, which didn't go down at all well. Instead Toni walked down to the waiting room to spend time with both of us. Toni wasn't in any hurry and so this nurse went off duty and the whole atmosphere changed in an instant.

After hours of being ready to spring into action I began to feel exhausted and it wasn't me that was doing anything. Toni was having the raw deal with contractions, examinations and gas and air.

The Falklands used to attract the oddballs that couldn't fit in in other places and so it was with 'Dr Death' as he was delightfully called. This doctor had come to the civilian hospital from Mount Pleasant Airport. His bedside manner was poor and his abilities were questionable. He came to put a drip into Toni's hand in the early evening to replace fluids. He was hopeless and couldn't find a vein, but was making a number of attempts causing Toni a lot of pain and distress. I am not one to make a fuss unless it is clear that something is definitely not right but even the nurse was grimacing. He then asked the nurse if she would do it but she refused saying that he knew that he shouldn't ask her. I asked him to stop and went to find another doctor. I know this put the second doctor in a difficult position, but it was clear that whatever Dr Death's skills may have been it wasn't putting in drips. This second doctor was summoned from a reception at Government House.

Toni had a monitor on her, monitoring the baby's heart, and late into the night the baby began to get stressed. In a matter of minutes, we were in an ambulance tearing down to the temporary military hospital down by the Canache. With Toni gulping gas and air from a portable bottle, we blue-lighted it down the road. I also took a few gulps of gas and air to help my flagging spirits.

In we dashed through the doors on the way to theatre and an emergency caesarean. It was as good as any hospital drama. I wasn't allowed over the red line and Toni, with her entourage of doctors and nurses, disappeared into the bowels of this linked Portakabin building.

We had always planned for me to be there for the birth and here I was pacing up and down behind the red line like a father in one of the old movies.

After what seemed like an eternity I was allowed to go through to the maternity ward and there was Caris being weighed. Then she was passed to me to hold. The nurse said that the surgeon was just stitching Toni up and she would be through presently. A while later Toni was wheeled through in a bed looking red in the face and inert, moving her mouth and lips as if she was thirsty.

Toni was determined to breastfeed Caris. We had both read *Breast is Best*, which like all those types of books was slightly fanatical. I can say that now, but at the time I would have been overwhelmed by the feminist movement that was very strong in our group. I certainly agreed with the concept.

Toni was completely zonked when the nurse said to me in a quiet voice, 'I'll just give baby a drink of sterilised water.' A small drowsy voice said 'No. I'll feed her.' It was tremendous willpower that made her speak when she didn't seem conscious.

I tucked this little bundle into Toni's arms and watched as they had their first bit of quality time. Toni remembers this vaguely because she was still very drowsy with the effects of the anaesthetic.

Caris was the surgeon's first caesarean and he hadn't messed around doing a bikini incision. He had gone in at the top of the pelvic bone and cut up to just below the tummy button, even though he cut the other way on the womb.

We were really lucky to have a strong healthy baby but, such is life that Toni felt inadequate because she had been unable to deliver Caris naturally. Toni had been conscious of her diet and she had not taken any prescription drugs, even though she had suffered severe headaches in the early stages of her pregnancy. She didn't smoke and didn't have any alcohol at all during the entire nine months. I tried to deflect this negative feeling towards the miracle that we had created and the family and friends that had visited and people like Angela and Christel who had projected such strong support.

The midwives were incredible at the King Edward VII Memorial Hospital and Christine had carried on after she had officially knocked off to support Toni, which negated the contribution of Dr Death.

We did have a brusque middle-aged nurse who came down to the military hospital bringing formula milk, and to be fair she was probably a wily old bird who had met many women talking about breastfeeding but who had failed for whatever reason. I have now heard and witnessed mothers that can't cope with breastfeeding. This is not the case with a student of the 'breast is best' philosophy and she tried to tell this nurse that she was determined to breastfeed. Instead of saying it was just in case or some other reasoning Mrs Self Bloody Righteous lambasted us with how many generations of her family had found bottle feeding satisfactory and how there was nothing wrong with any of them and how they were all going to live into their hundreds without so much as a loose eye lash. We both ignored her, but Toni was quite indignant with such an unnecessary disregarding stance. I began to think I was starting a nurse complex after my brush earlier in Stanley with the other forthright specimen.

The walls of this makeshift hospital were paper-thin. Dave Emsley, the Beaver and Islander pilot and one of the heroes of the local radio station during the war, was brought in to the ward next to Toni's. During the war he enraged the Argentines by playing patriotic British music and then finishing his broadcasting career by playing *Georgia On Your Mind* after the taking of South Georgia. He was abruptly heaved off the broadcasting staff after that but his thoughtful actions had boosted the moral of everyone listening to him.

Dave was fighting for his life in the room next to Toni and she had to listen to that fight after all that she had been through. It wasn't pleasant to hear the nursing staff doing their utmost to save Dave, talking to and encouraging him as they hooked him up to monitors and carried out the procedures needed to help him.

Sadly, after a couple of days they lost the fight to save this character who had frightened the life out of me in the Beaver float plane, but had been so inspirational during the conflict working at the Falkland Island Broadcasting Station.

Toni went back to the Stanley Hospital where she started on the road to recovery. She went for a bath after her op and as she lay there trying not to get her wound wet as instructed, a look of absolute terror crossed her face. It had suddenly crossed her mind that if the stitches got wet they might dissolve and her guts would topple out into the water. It probably sounds a bit silly but it was a genuine concern for Toni who was soon out and dried and back in bed.

Eventually it was time for me to head back to the farm and so off I went for the long plough home in the middle of winter.

Bringing home our newborn baby

During this time, there had been an accident within FIGAS and the Islander aircraft were not flying. Military helicopters were being used for civilian passengers as well as their military duties. We had hoped the military would continue their good work and bring Toni and Caris back to the farm. God knows, we have had every make of helicopters landing on the green here, but this time they were less obliging, citing safety reasons as we did not have a licenced airstrip. They did take them to JB, (San Carlos) which was something.

While Toni had been in town, Giles, Tony Courtney and I had been busy at Sussex putting central heating in. We had installed a big Bosky solid fuel stove with a gravity-fed central heating system. I still hadn't returned the house to a presentable state when I was called over to pick Toni, Caris and her mother up from San Carlos.

In the winter the mountain was a pain, but from frequent use we also knew it quite well so we rarely had any bother. Our neighbours had run a new fence from east to west along the top of the mountain and put the gates in where it was soft and from May to September they were impassable. The gate directly behind the Head of the Bay house didn't last long at all and the one towards Gin Rock gate was one of those 'we might just get through one more time.'

I got over and picked Heather, Toni and our newborn baby up and then headed back over the mountain. We went back up behind the Head of the Bay house, bumping and slipping up to the top where we laid the fence because the gateway was impassable. Then edging along a very soft peat bank, then heading inland and down towards the house. All written with the flourish of my pen, but it was cold and the Land Rover was bumping, sinking in and rolling around, with Toni holding tightly on to Caris and trying to go with the vehicles movement.

It was all going so well, but when Toni walked into the house she burst into tears. It was warm but it was also slightly untidy. Toni was happy to be home and also pleased that her mother was home to help sort out the chaos that I had manufactured. I would have liked to blame Giles and Tony but that would be unfair and although they had generated much of the mess I had had the opportunity to do a better job of tidying up.

'Breast is best'

Before the birth, three pregnant friends walked down to Surf Bay beach – Toni, Christel and Angela Moffatt. The other two had had other children and were reassuring Toni, telling her not to worry and that she would be fine. Within six weeks they had all had caesarean sections. When Caris was born Angela and Christel were some of the first on the scene. When Angela, a disciple of 'breast is best', heard that Toni might not be able to feed Caris she offered to breastfeed her until Toni could. Such generous spontaneity was something that I will always remember.

Caris had arrived in our lives by an emergency caesarean where they discovered that she had a true knot in her cord, which would have made a normal delivery very unlikely. We have always speculated about how this could have happened. Was it when Atesh threw Toni into the grass that day or any number of farm jobs that she continued to do?

Being pregnant in camp is totally different to having a child in the UK, or Stanley for that matter. There used to be regular doctor's visits where the doctor would stay overnight at each settlement and all those that needed to see him came in if they lived outside. So while Toni was pregnant she would ride over to have a check-up to see that all was well. Toni was planning on racing her mare Atesh at the Christmas race meeting in Stanley. She took Atesh, a very tame mare that she had tamed before the war, over to San Carlos to catch the boat to Stanley. Atesh was so tame that Toni didn't even put on a full set of gear and, although it now seems unbelievable, rode over on just a sheep skin. Plodding along coming up to the Hard Hill Gate, enjoying a lovely day with not a care in the world, a lamb that was asleep in the grass was disturbed by the passing horse and jumped up under Atesh's belly. Atesh shied and Toni fell off. On her next visit to the doctor for a check-up, Toni mentioned that she is planning on riding at the races, to which the doctor replied, 'No, you should not.' She thought perhaps she should not mention that she had recently had a tumble.

Toni continued to ride and work right up to putting the rams out in May and Caris was born in the second week of June. It was no big deal with us gently walking down on the horses behind the rams to put them out with the girls. Coming back, I went into an inconsiderate trot but Toni asked if we could walk the horses because her bump was really uncomfortable at this pace.

Life was to change after Caris came home but we were able to adapt fairly easily. As self-employed people we were able to take turns with Caris once she arrived home. Toni's turn was night and mine was early morning and so between us we were able to get enough sleep. Being breastfed, Toni would just pull Caris into bed gave her one side then the other and then put her back into her cot.

Our neighbours also had a baby at the same time as us and he was telling us how easy it was to bottle feed. 'I take a flask of hot water to bed and the milk mixed up in the bottle and when Rachael wakes up I just mix the two together and get it to the right temperature and feed her.' He had got it off to a fine art, but it wasn't as easy as breastfeeding. Toni just went and got Caris, plugged her on and when she was finished put her back into her cot.

One night the perfect system failed because I was woken. Toni had to go downstairs and Caris was in our bed. Searching for some poor humour as Toni came back I offered Caris my nipple. Caris latched on and gave an awesome suck, which really hurt. Funnily enough I got zero sympathy and I also didn't bother fooling around like that again.

We read all the books and even watched a video on how to bring up children. The best bit of advice I read was in *Toddler Taming* which said that, regardless of all the information and advice you have gleaned, remember that the children haven't read the books and so don't know what they were meant to do and that every child is an individual at the end of the day.

We were really neurotic with Caris. She moved out of our room and into a small room next to ours in the southeast corner of the house. If Caris didn't wake in the night one of us would go through and check that she was okay. More so in the mornings, if we hadn't heard a sound we would go through and make sure all was well.

Usually Caris would wake quite early and I would get up and take her downstairs. There she had a bouncy cradle thing, which was of a tubular frame in a tight bend with material on it. I would rock her in the chair talking and playing with her unless she was sleepy and then I would gently rock her and read a book.

I have always liked eight hours sleep to keep on an even keel. Too many six-hours-sleeps and my humour begins to fail, so this double act kept everyone in reasonable spirits.

I would mostly look after Caris when Toni was at the cows unless we were sorting a new cow and then she would be there on somebody's back or in the nearby Land Rover as we dragged the calves or chased the cow into the shed for the first time.

Caris was an early talker and you sometimes forget. Time and your memory can think one thing when reality is another, but with Toni having to go to the UK to have Liam, it ties in memory to a specific time. Caris was nearly word perfect with the nursery rhymes that she had learnt from a video she had. She was also a fan of AA Milne and liked reciting Alexander Beetle. In the book there was only half a beetle on one of the pages and this would fascinate Caris and she would want to know where the other half was. You could have quite a conversation with her before she went to England when she wasn't quite two.

I am sure the more sanctimonious would disagree, but working sheep with sheep dogs can bring the worst out in people, especially foul language, and I reluctantly share this failing of Toni's. Another downside is that our poor innocent and impressionable children would share a vehicle with this ill-gotten woman.

The concept of a pet and a working dog are completely different. If a pet runs off or is disobedient it's a pain and other people might be displeased, but with a working dog in the Falklands where areas are so big, a dog not doing as it is told can lead to many hours of extra work. For that reason, there are times when things get tense.

Toni had a bad day when her bitch decides a tactical withdrawal under the Land Rover was in order. Toni found some colourful words to describe this animal. Things calmed down and Lassie was coaxed out to do Toni's bidding.

The Lassie episode happened a few weeks before Toni and Caris were to depart to live with my mother in the UK until Liam was born. Because the medical facilities don't cater for every occurrence, mothers who have had a caesarean are sent to England just in case. It had been another very long day but the stock were in the pens and we were having a cuppa and a debrief after the day's work. A little voice piped up in mock anger using the dreaded 'f' word. We were thrown into instant guilt mode.

Pat Short was over a few days later and Caris' bricks went flying and so did the 'f' word. Again! What bloody awful parents and of course there was no one to blame. No salesmen, dustmen, milkmen, passers-by, other children.

Everyone has heard swear words and Pat thought it was amusing even if we didn't. Our fear was that Caris would arrive in Maldon, where Granny and Granddad Stevens lived, and try out this new word in her vocabulary. We are not people who swear a lot so it did seem a little unfair that this episode had made such an impression. Luck was with us, however, and she soon forgot the 'f' word and Toni, even when out gathering, didn't remind her. Once in England Caris had so many different things to see and experiences to worry about that she quickly forgot yesterday's excitement.

Running the sheep

The year after Caris was born our sheep were struck down with pink eye, a disease that makes them temporarily blind. To say it makes things a tad difficult is probably an understatement. Gathering, driving and drafting were made especially problematic. The gathering was awkward, trying to get sheep into one mob, but once in a flock they seemed to stay together because they could hear one another. However the sheep couldn't see the dogs, which is usually the controlling factor with sheep. Driving was difficult when sheep came out of the group and got disorientated and then the sheep would stumble into any hole or ditch. The sheep were able to hear running water, which made some ditches detectable.

Once Caris came on the scene we gathered with Toni in our old Land Rover and with Caris' car seat spragged with fencing wire into the middle between the driver and passenger seat, because by this time we had put a truck cab on the Land Rover with an open back.

Running the sheep through the drafting race is always an exercise in maintaining good humour. All the problems are magnified because you have to force the sheep up into smaller and smaller pens until eventually a small forcing pen and then up the narrow race, one by one, so that you can sort them. Halfway up the race are two small gates, which open into the race so that you can take sheep off. Let's say you are sorting your young sheep for shearing – you could let your male hogs go one way and the ewe hogs the other and let everything else carry on straight ahead. It is probably the one job that creates the greatest friction between man and wife on these small farms. Two really isn't enough to make the sheep run smoothly. Three is a much better number because the third person can keep the sheep flowing at the neck of the race.

Many people think that sheep are stupid, but perhaps they are really intelligent because they can wind a human up without too much trouble. There is always the sheep at the entrance to the race that turns to its mate and says 'you watch me wind these people up' and then turns round blocking the other sheep from entering the race. If you have a third person, he can just turn him around and encourage him up. If you haven't got that extra man power that sheep can be there for ages dithering about. Shall I, shan't I, stopping the flow on and off until he decides to go. There always seems to be a replacement, happy to carry that baton of contrariness. Sheep always follow one another so the skill of the person in the pens is to try and keep them moving through the pens following the ones moving out of the pens up the race. Stopping the flow stops the progress until you get them started again.

Try to imagine all the above when the majority of your sheep are blind and they can't see to follow.

One day to remember was when I was on the gates – because you need to be quite physical at times stopping sheep with your legs and pulling the stubborn ones towards you – and Toni chasing them up, with Caris in the backpack. Caris would have been around about 18 months old. The dogs were trying to move the sheep up with Toni and the latter were charging all shapes. Eventually Toni had them in front of the smaller pen behind the forcing pen. One sheep got a fright and went charging back behind. Unbeknown to Toni the sheep stopped and could hear the flock. It went flat out back towards them, skittling Toni and Caris over. Not many animals will deliberately knock you over unless they are cornered and sheep, apart from rams, certainly won't, but this one just could not see. Toni for her part was trying to get the sheep into the pen and so had ignored one sheep's antics.

Toni went down and Caris was fired out of the backpack and skidded along the ground, getting a mouthful of dust and sheep muck. Surprisingly, with a quick brush down she was ready for another session on Toni's back. In fact, Toni was more upset about the incident than Caris was. Even though a lot of these jobs were energetic, Caris used to fall asleep on Toni's back or at other times she would be cackling away as if it was a great game to be on mum's back.

Over the years, even in the Land Rover both Caris and Liam would fall asleep during gathers in their car seats where none of the ground is smooth. Of course, if Toni hit a big bump or jolt they would wake up, but soon be back to sleep. They would also sleep in the Land Rover at the pens, but once they were mobile they would get out and go exploring looking for goose nests or getting soaked in the nearest ditch. We didn't encourage them to come into the pens because you have to be quite big before you can push sheep around and make them do what you want.

Toni was driving back home from town and in the 1980s and early 1990s you used to drive through Mount Pleasant Airport to get home (although there was a rough track that went round that hardly anyone used). This day there was a military exercise on and Toni wasn't allowed to drive through the military complex. The guard that stopped her must have had kids of his own because he was profusely apologetic about turning Toni back to use the rough track which would throw the kids around. Toni ended up reassuring him that our brats were made of stern stuff and that they would be fine. She didn't elaborate and tell him how they spent hours driving and sleeping through the roughest of terrain gathering sheep on our farm.

Toni wasn't too worried about the rough ride, although she tried to minimise the discomfort by being careful. Her biggest nightmare during gathering was that they would get out of the vehicle and go 'exploring' and fall in a ditch or hole and she would be unable to find them. Our fields were thousands of acres big and with the regular winds making hearing limited, finding a lost child would have been like looking for a needle in a haystack. Gathering in the Land Rover was not as free and easy as on a horse or a bike/quad and there were places you could not go. She would therefore get out of the Land Rover and walk here and there with her dogs, turning the sheep into the way of the gather. Usually Caris and Liam were good and stayed put and only once or twice did they go walkabout.

As I have already mentioned, when Caris was little we spragged her chair into our old leaf sprung Land Rover. We had just spent a little money getting the vehicle revitalised. The wiring had needed a little something and we got some spot lights wired in on the front, basically because it was easier than paying someone to rewire it to get the regular lights to come alive again. So once more our day on the farm had found us out and about, miles away from the house and it was dark. The tide was in and we were coming up the second valley out of Hells Kitchen. I decided to use the fancy new lights that we had paid to have installed. I put them on and nearly instantaneously the wiring burst into flames behind the dash and smoke billowed out.

I switched the lights off as Toni grabbed Caris and we both exited the Land Rover at speed. Turning the lights off saved the day because the smoke eventually stopped and flames didn't consume the whole vehicle. We cautiously returned to the Land Rover and drove back to the farm in the dark, aided very slightly by the light of the stars.

The children's adventures

It is strange to remember that when Caris was small she called Toni and I by our Christian names, as she did for a number of years. It is a precious memory, which was probably driven by the fact that that is what Caris heard us call one another. There weren't enough of the normal visits that one would have in even a village where the mum and dad word/concept could be reinforced by other mothers and family and friends. By the time Liam was talking it was 'Mum' and 'Dad'. I thought it was quite novel, but Toni preferred to be called Mum, although she didn't dislike being called Toni if that makes any sense.

As they got older, Caris and Liam were often out making their own entertainment, which would have them having their mini adventures. They always liked messing about in the sea and they would spend hours in the small arm of the creek below the house. On one particular day they had been gone long enough for us to become concerned and Toni went off looking for them. As she drove down towards the sea, staggering up and over the hill, coming from the creek, was Caris with her sleeves rolled down over her hands carrying a large mullet. Apparently they had built up the fish wall and managed to trap this fish and then they had chased it up and down in this pool until it was exhausted. Then Caris had started to carry it home. As any fisherman will tell you, fish will flap for ages after they are caught. This fish didn't move a muscle or a scale, it had been totally played out.

The next day Caris was having her radio lesson and told the tale to her radio teacher about how she chased this fish up and down behind the fish wall until it was 'knackered.'

Another great game was disappearing over the hill on their bikes looking for a juicy swamp to play getting bogged and returning soaked to the skin smothered in mud but having had a whale of a time. These sorties sometimes got completely out of control with Caris or Liam having lost articles of clothing. It was usually a sock but it could be a boot or a glove. Toni would heave them into the bath and wash them off ready for the next day's episode.

We had very few hard and fast rules apart from if they went out and about as youngsters we liked them to go together. We also told them to keep away from the small cliffs, which run along the creek because they are dangerous. We were assured that the cliffs couldn't be further from their thoughts.

We had been told of the secret beach and had assumed that it was one of the small coves that are everywhere in our creek.

A group of military friends from the Motor Transport Section at Mount Pleasant Airport were visiting one weekend when the children asked Elizabeth and Martin Davies if they would like to see the secret beach. Everyone else, including us, thought this was a jolly good idea and we all dutifully trotted off to see said beach. Where was the secret beach? Only down one of the out-of-bounds cliffs! Caris and Liam went bounding down a track that is hardly discernible, like a couple of mountain goats, with the adults squawking and sliding and reaching the beach with a lot of fuss.

During an event at Sussex the children came running up to the house from the beach. They had all been fishing and they were telling us about the biggest fish they had ever seen and what was more it was red. We all knew what a good fish yarn was and so asked them why they hadn't carried it up with them. Apparently the fish was too big and so an adult was dispatched. This fish was enormous and someone phoned the Fisheries Department for identification. It was a Moonfish and apparently good to eat. It turned out to be very good on the barbeque.

I suppose you would have to be extremely unlucky to kill yourself on what are high beach banks but you could easily break a bone or stun yourself and reach the water during the high tide. Children do have a strong sense of what they can and can't do but parents don't trust this instinct, although unwittingly they do help their children's judgement by bringing dangers to their attention.

I am not sure where Caris got this saying from but she would always want to help and say 'I'm helping, Mummy, aren't I?' or 'I'm helping, Daddy.' What she actually said was 'helpin' and this became a family saying. If somebody was 'helpin' it wasn't as beneficial as helping. In fact, there was a little bit of getting in the way, but in the nicest of ways. If Caris was really sure her helping had significantly resulted in something, she would highlight her help by saying 'It's a good job you borned me Mummy.' Of course, a few years down the line Liam was equally vocal in how indispensable he was and how lucky Mummy was to have 'borned' him as well.

Don't cry over a broken egg

Despite being born into a world of technology, even in the Falklands, it was the simplest things that Caris and Liam enjoyed. Strange as it may seem, Caris loved to find eggs and, by the time Liam was able to participate, she was an expert at finding hen eggs and extricating them from within the gorse or calafate bushes with a serving ladle. Calafate is a sprawling prickly bush, which is rumoured to have been brought to the Falklands by a member of the Coutts family from South America. When Liam was old enough they would toddle up to the hen yard with Toni to feed the hens and collect the eggs and they would triumphantly walk back to the house carrying an egg in each hand. Liam went through his egg collecting training in front of one of the hardest critics: his sister.

Liam would go up to the hen house at an early age with Toni and his older sister and much against the better judgement of Caris would be trusted with an egg. Although they were both very good there was the occasional accident. Caris had made her mistakes in front of a partisan. Liam wasn't as fortunate. To be fair, when it did happen to Caris there were usually tears and Toni would say that it didn't matter. If Liam fell down and broke an egg however all hell was let loose. Liam's name would be shouted at the top of Caris' voice and then in an accusatory, exasperated I told you so tone, Caris would dob Liam in to his mother.

Try as Toni might to defuse the situation, Caris obviously never felt that she was taking it seriously enough even when her mother gently reminded her that she had also broken eggs at Liam's age.

The question remains. Why are eggs so fascinating to children?

The other simple pleasure that they both had was digging potatoes although sadly this phase vanished before they were big enough to do more than get in the way.

Toni and I used to dig the potatoes together. I would dig and Toni, with the help of Caris and Liam, would pick up the potatoes. I don't know what the fascination was other than it was like a hidden birthday present, wrapped and unknown at what was under the next fork full. If there were a lot of potatoes, they would shriek their approval and put the potatoes in the bucket. If there were some big ones we would all shout out 'chippers' and if one or two were really big we would have to stop and admire them. Of course, there would be times when one or the other would want to dig but this could be rather wasteful because potatoes would get speared, which again was a crime for which innocent parties wanted capital punishment to be introduced. This has also been the case with visiting children up to the present day, where electronic games are put aside and willing volunteers are eager to dig potatoes.

Although there was always heightened activity when we were digging the potatoes their focus didn't last for too long and after three or four rows they would be throwing a few worms to the garden thrush and then off to do something else.

With the interest in eggs came the knowledge of hens and ducks sitting and bringing out chicks and ducklings and the collective effort of catching mother and all her offspring. These are surprisingly fleet of foot and difficult to find let alone catch if they reach thick calafate or gorse, and then there were always the waifs and strays that needed to come into the house for intensive care. Many of these critters would just need some water, warmth or food and rest and they would be back with their mothers within hours. Other long-term patients never made it back and although there were many that didn't make it, there were others that joined the menagerie of pets that were part of our yard. It was always a bit of an emotional roller coaster even if some never made it past a ball of fluff.

On one occasion Jemima Puddle-Duck was nursed to full fitness from a cracked egg, peeling this wet life from the shell over a couple of days. Slowly and surely she grew into a drab-coloured brown duck. It was at a time that we seemed to be overwhelmed with ducks and geese and hens and pet sheep that all seemed to have one ambition – to bankrupt our frail business by eating tons of expensive food.

Mel Lloyd was passing one day and asked if we could part with a few ducks because he wanted to have some at Swan Inlet. No problem, so Toni rounded up a few put them in a box and gave them to Mel.

Unfortunately, the 'middle management' didn't see Jemima as a drab, brown duck much the same as many others, but a vibrant duck with colossal individuality and personality who would eat corn from your hand. She just happened to be the most favourite duck of all time and they wanted her back, and to reinforce the need for its return a large tantrum was thrown.

Through protracted negotiation with Caris and Liam we found a duck that didn't have a hermetic-type bond with the farm and we were able to swap it for Jemima.

The story doesn't end there. Jemima returned home as the prodigal duck.

I think it was the following year Jemima had laid a nest full of eggs up by the stable and the egging team had found her and great excitement had members of the household buzzing.

It was at the same time that Mike was in the vicinity building roads and we had asked him if he could drive in a post for tying horses or bullock to outside the horse corral. Mike trundled over with his tracked excavator and we got the post in place. Then Mike reached up to the top of the post with the bucket and using the teeth he shut the bucket to drive the post into the ground. Once it was down a few feet he rolled the bucket over and used the bottom to carry on pushing until it lifted the front of this large machine off the ground, whereupon he used the bucket to give it a few bangs to finish the job.

Everyone apart from me knew where Jemima's nest was and so Caris decided to take time out to show me. Up we went, but we couldn't find Jemima. Things looked a little different after Mike had driven through some of the bushes making his way to the post job.

I happened to be the first to spot Jemima and all was not well. Unbeknown to Mike, he had driven over Jemima and her nest of hatching ducklings. Poor old Jemima wouldn't leave her brood and so there they all were looking like a set of feathered Frisbees.

In an emotional congregation at pets' corner we buried Jemima, about six ducklings and the same number of eggs.

Toni somehow got her hands on some Muscovy ducks, which seemed to prosper quite well. The ducklings were a lot stronger than the Mallard variety, and duck and ducklings would cover miles in pursuit of flies and other goodies that they could find. Although the majority were robust there was one that was introduced into the top rung of intensive care and never returned to the flock. I named this creature Sir Francis and Toni would carry it around wherever we went tending to its every quack, squawk and very irritating whistle.

I know all pet lovers would see this attitude as slightly severe but then I, unlike them, had to go on a camping trip up where Rabbit Mountain meets the Flats at what is called the Forkings. Sir Francis did nothing but whistle and make noises the whole 48 hours, especially during the hours of darkness.

He was a favourite and the ladies took turns at having him sit inside their quilted boiler suits. During Trudi's turn, as she was stirring a big pot of *casuela* on the camping stove, this duck got miss-mothered and escaped out of the boiler suit and was running around in the dark squeaking. Poor old Sir Francis had just missed falling into the pot and certain death by a whisker.

A year later Sir Francis laid a nest full of eggs and so we imaginatively renamed her Duck-Duck.

Travelling abroad

As a family we did occasionally get back to the northern hemisphere to say hello to our family and friends. We are not unique in the Falklands apart from the fact that our link with the outside world was with the military and their air bridge. Although perfectly adequate, not many people would describe it as commercial and for many years there weren't any films for entertainment.

With an 18-hour flight coming up we would always put a lot of thought into how to entertain the children. It wasn't just the flight, it was also the early morning check in and the hours journey out of Stanley.

Sometimes we would get a lift out with someone, but occasionally we would catch the bus at silly-o'clock in the morning and, with the other passengers, head for Mount Pleasant Airport.

On one such occasion Caris and Liam were woken up really early and as Toni and I split resources – I was put in charge of cooking toast. As is my wont I get sidetracked waiting for the toast to cook and it burnt. No problem, as we open a few windows and get another batch underway.

The smell of burnt toast followed us into the bus, however, and with all the excitement of getting up early and going to England, Caris tells all on the coach why we smell of burnt toast.

Somewhere in those early years we found ourselves in Crete enjoying the hospitality of my sister, her husband and daughter, plus the blistering heat by the side of a pool less than 20 feet from our apartment. Caris had moved to Crete a few months before I came to the Falklands, married Yianni and had a daughter Zoe, who was a little older than our Caris. They have a villa with a number of apartments surrounding a pool and situated close to the sea. Their generosity had us with a free apartment and most of the evening meals cooked by Yianni who was a very good cook. It was an arrangement that we still enjoy today.

Caris and Liam could swim, but living by a pool in 30 degrees was like having intensive tuition and their swimming developed enormously. Liam was just six and Caris was eight, but they were diving down to the bottom of the pool at the deep end picking up coins. Caris, being a little older, could touch the bottom every time but Liam had to work hard to swim down the ten feet.

On the last Sunday of our visit we went to a beach on the north side of the island. Caris and Yiannis often went to this beach where Yiannis would read a paper and Caris and Zoe and whoever else would swim. I was teaching Toni how to snorkel and with Caris and

Yiannis on the beach and the children Zoe, Caris and Liam all playing together we put our snorkels, masks and fins on and swam out to sea. At this beach one has to swim quite a way for a reasonable amount of water.

We had been out for a little while and I was trying to pass on the principle of getting Toni to get her legs high in the air to get her under the water with the least amount of effort. I became aware of a child shouting but at first I couldn't see anyone. Then there was a small head bobbing about making for us. It was Liam complaining bitterly that Caris and Zoe had run off and left him.

We were at least 100 yards from the shore and it is the one thing I think about as the closest thing we ever came to a major catastrophe. He was a reasonable swimmer but this episode put the fear of god into both Toni and me.

We brought Liam back to the shore and explained that what he had done was very dangerous and why, but at that age you are never 100 per cent sure it had sunk in. We bought an ice cream for everyone and then went and sat in the scorching hot sand, on our towels. As we were finishing our ice creams and thanking our lucky stars, a bit of a commotion started up at the far end of the beach, which in Greece could mean something but equally it could be just a family reunion or something equally mundane.

People were running from all corners of the beach converging on something and so we joined the masses. Lying on the beach, having been caught from a smallish fishing boat, was a large hammerhead shark.

With the combination of Liam's exploits and discovering that this size shark swims in the Mediterranean Sea we concluded snorkel training for the rest of the day.

A medical situation (part one)

At the time we never seemed to realise how vulnerable we were living five miles from the nearest airstrip for assistance or medical evacuation to the town 70 miles away. The military were always there for extreme emergencies, but even then depending on many variables you would still be talking the best part of an hour at best. The local hospital has dedicated and motivated staff but they don't have the capacity to deal with the more serious issues.

The children spent a lot of their spare time down on the beach or in the small water courses that ran into the sea 'minnowing'. This could mean anything from catching a large mullet to a small minnow. One day, unbeknown to us, Liam (who was about three) took a glass jar with him to catch minnows. He got some dirt on the jar that he then tried to shake or knock off, breaking the jar which in turn sliced his thumb down to the bone.

I was fencing far away from the house when Caris arrived home with her arm round Liam – a definite sign that all was not well. Caris always kept up a high ethical standpoint when it came to physical contact with her fitness and mentoring client. It took a few minutes for Toni, busy doing some farm chore or other, to realise how serious it was and how a Winnie the Pooh plaster wasn't going to bring a miraculous recovery on this occasion.

Toni got on the phone to the hospital and explained the problem. They asked how Toni knew that it needed stitches. 'Because I can see the bone,' said Toni. FIGAS found a duty pilot and a doctor and nurse were duly dispatched to San Carlos. Toni left a letter for me, including a diagram of said cut, and drove over to meet the plane. Without roads again this was a challenge with Caris, who was only five, opening gates and standing on the fence to get over it on top of the mountain. On the way over Caris asked Toni if Liam was going to die.

It was clear that Liam did need stitches and so the first job was to inject local anaesthetic around the cut. This was such a cruel operation that some feel that stitching without might be kinder. Liam was screaming the room down and had to be held down with Toni lying across him. The sweat was dripping from the doctor, under the pressure of a screaming child.

Much to the relief of all those involved the stitching was finally done. Toni drove back over the mountain and home with our walking wounded. Until this moment, Liam had sucked his thumb, and did not mind which one. After having seven stitches in his left thumb, the sucking was restricted to his right.

If that saga wasn't enough within a few months Caris had broken her leg.

It was the end of the shearing season and we were tidying up the shed and pressing up the last bales of wool. (This is putting wool into a machine that squashes 200kgs of wool into a bale four-foot long, by two-foot six-inches wide and deep.) Derek and Trudi and family were out visiting and Derek was helping me at the shed. We had lifted the circular wool table up onto the raised floor to get it out of the way. This is where the shearers shear the sheep raised up above the level of the wool handling area. This means that the rousie isn't bending down all the time and it is meant to be easier.

The circular table spun around and it was wider than the raised floor, so Caris and Liam were taking it in turns to jump on the table spinning themselves out over the floor and landing back on their feet on the other side. It was such good fun that they decided to jump on together. Disaster. The combined weight tipped the table over onto the floor below, with Liam thrown clear and Caris underneath.

Caris couldn't get up. Although the break wasn't severe enough to have the leg at a different angle, there was a swelling like a goose egg behind her shin. I carried Caris up to the house and Toni got on to the hospital. It was too late to fly that day because it wasn't a life and death situation. The advice was to put some frozen food, from the deep freeze, onto the swelling, which got the patient into a strop because it made her leg ache.

Next day FIGAS was meant to fly out with a stretcher, but unfortunately for us (and in particular Caris), FIGAS was very busy flying people home from sports so a decision was made by the senior pilot not to carry a stretcher. We bounced the five miles over the mountain to the San Carlos airstrip. The plane arrived and Toni, the world's worst passenger and Caris had to sit on the seats to fly to town.

On arrival the luggage handler carried Caris to the ambulance.

It is silly but because of the effort you question your judgement and we wondered if the leg was broken. X-rays confirmed our suspicions because Caris' tibia had a greenstick fracture and she was put in plaster from the tip of her toes to the top of her thigh. In fact, they had three attempts before they were happy with everything.

At this time Caris had a week in the Infant and Junior School and although she was noisy and liked to be in the limelight, her broken leg gave her a novelty status that had everyone milling round her and she was totally overawed and did not like this smothering popularity. Caris would turn up at the school gates and everyone would be calling her name as she disappeared, crutches, plaster and personage into the crowd.

Back at home the plaster cast couldn't stand the attrition because Caris was a very active individual. By this time the crutches had been abandoned as she did not like them. They had been running in and out of the house, playing in the yard or off to their hut and even down to the beach. We just happened to be building a fence cutting off a small point that we had bought from Pat and Isobel Short when they owned Maryfield. It was a small piece of land but it helped us cope with the problem of being jammed into the corner of our property. Originally our cowshed opened up into the neighbouring land.

Caris and Liam had been out on the fence line 'helpin'' when they decided to go home because they were cold or bored or both. Caris would go like the clappers swinging out the leg in plaster as she negotiated the large grass bogs. It would take over a mile to get home.

The bottom of the cast was constantly wearing away and needing to be repaired and strengthened. Caris was in plaster for a good six weeks. Another trick we used to try and extend the life of the cast was to wrap it in plastic shopping bags to keep the plaster dry.

Caris was always active and she was quite muscular and for many years she walked on tiptoes, which made her calf muscles very prominent. She was still walking this way when she started school, which worried our conscientious first travelling teacher Ro.

Come the day that the plaster came off and out of the cast came this wizened hairy leg that looked strange alongside her good one. Needless to say her active lifestyle soon had her leg back to full fitness but there was one thing that remained and that was Caris' limp. After a few months, Toni and I began to get quite concerned and worried that she might have it for life and when we consulted the medical professionals, no one would say categorically that it would go in time. But disappear it did and the funny thing is that we didn't see the change it was something that we eventually realised 'Oh, Caris isn't limping'.

The travelling teacher

Ro Kells was Caris' first travelling teacher and she came to live with us for every two weeks in six, as part of Caris' education. It was a funny feeling wondering how this had all crept up on us. We always talked about the children's education and what would happen to them as they grew up but everything seemed to be years away when we started our family.

Ro was a small lady in her twenties who was full of enthusiasm and easy to get along with. Ro brought with her a guitar and a flute, which she used to help with nursery rhymes and things. It would be nothing for us all to sing songs in the evenings with Ro on her guitar. She was also great for extending the repertoire of songs sung in the vehicle as we travelled here and there.

Liam loved Ro and was so jealous that Caris had a teacher and he didn't. Liam would ask when could he go to school and we would say when you're this tall and hold a hand above his head. He would stretch and then jump to be as tall as that hand but he never quite made it. We would tell him that if he ate up all his dinner he would soon be able to go, which was a little unkind but Liam would nosh back vast amounts of food in the hope that he would grow overnight.

We used to have a policy of 'hands-off the teacher after school' unless explicitly asked to join in so that they could have time off. On a busy farm it wasn't always possible to supervise this rule to the last second but the children usually respected it.

One day we came back from working to find Ro fast asleep on the sofa and Liam fast asleep on top of her. I can't remember where Caris was, but obviously somewhere else because she saw Ro as exclusively hers.

Ro did a number of things that involved all of us and the most memorable was the 3D dragon that was built in our stairwell. Our stairs go around on three sides of a square. The head was at the top and the body in the middle and the tail at the bottom. The dragon's scales were made from handprints colourfully painted and cut out. We all made handprints to stick to this dragon. The belly part was another piece of paper with crumpled up paper inside and covered with scales on the outside to give it bulk. She also helped them build the Hungry Caterpillar out of woollen pompoms, which could then be passed through all the fruit they had built with holes in, which hung all along the passage way.

We had some really good teachers that all contributed to Caris and Liam's skills. John Fowler deserves a mention because he was teaching at Sussex and sharing with us stories of his family's adventures in the southern seas. I think John was covering for full-time staff, but anyway he happened to be here when Liam was just about big enough to start school. Caris would have the morning and Liam would join the party in the afternoon sometimes for a story but often to do something like painting. It is the painting option that makes the story interesting because Caris and Liam were painting and a little bit got splashed onto Caris' painting from Liam and so Caris flicked a little bit back. The occasion of his first taste of school went to Liam's head and he mega-splashed Caris' painting and John sent him out of the room. As far as I know this is the only time in Liam's school career that he was asked to leave the classroom.

Eventually time passed and Caris moved on to board at Stanley House Hostel in Stanley and Liam had a teacher to himself. Heather Norman and Liam hit it off big time and Liam used to get hyper as Heather's visits got closer. There used to be laughter and sounds of people enjoying themselves and everything seemed to be a game but they also got through a large amount of work during the two years before Liam also went to Stanley.

When Liam went off to join Caris at the school hostel he found life in school a little boring because he was well ahead of the work they were doing in his class.

Camp education is a family affair and in between the two-week visits was a month where Toni used to supervise Caris and Liam's homework and 2 meter and, later, phone lessons. In the case of 2 meters it was open to anyone who wanted to tune in. The younger the children, the more input there was from mum but as they got older the responsibility for writing down homework and completing work on time moved to Caris and Liam. It was a job that needed full concentration from the parent at times especially when children were experimenting with phonics like searching their minds for 'sh' words. Threats from mum of 'Don't you dare,' as the pupil, with a mischievous twinkle in their eyes, listens to the teacher speak waiting for their turn to say something.

With things always happening on the farm it wasn't easy to meet the schedules but we did everything we could to be there on time and ready to work. On one journey home in the lorry the wheel bearing collapsed and the wheel and half shaft wandered out away from the lorry. No roads and no help available we had to get home and then the next day, rob a piece from one of the other lorries on the farm and go back and fix it. What were we going to do about Caris' lesson? The Land Rover had a 2-meter set so we packed Caris' school stuff and while we were fixing the lorry Caris was chatting to Mr Fogerty, reading her book and telling him her news which on this and many other occasions wasn't in the least mundane. Lesson over, the lorry was fixed and it was just another day living in the Falklands.

On another occasion we were putting a new cover on a polytunnel. One has to pick the right day in the Falklands and then get cracking. The children were doing phone lessons as we got the plastic sheet into position. The wind waits for no one in the Falklands and it doesn't take much to make this job difficult. Up the wind got and so we had to call the kids away from their education to stop the cover blowing away. Camp Education were good like that and understood how things worked. They were soon able to catch up if time was missed.

Time soon whistled by and both the kids were off to the hostel. I loved the West Falklands and the outlying islands, when I worked and lived there, but living on the East was easier to cope with the children living in Stanley at the hostel because they could get home every weekend. We would head up the track and the hostel staff would meet us halfway. Many times we would pick others up and take them back to meet the hostel staff on the Sunday. It was a great arrangement that wasn't available to the parents on the West and outlying Islands. Sometimes it was difficult for the hostel staff to move everyone if a lot of children went to the North Camp and on those occasions we would ask family or friends if they would help us.

Caris and Liam adored Granny Heather and she reciprocated this love. Caris started staying with Granny from an early age. It was not a case of us pushing Caris because she saw it as an adventure and jumped at the chance when Granny asked her to come and stay. We saw it as an opportunity to do big jobs on the farm if our little helper was helping someone else. Another consideration was that we knew that Caris and Liam would be going to the hostel, which is where camp children are encouraged to attend so that they can be educated in Stanley. We might not like the concept but it would be our self-indulgence if we allowed them to stay at home and not in their best educational interests.

The very first time Caris stayed with Heather and Tony we left her but didn't go home. We stayed in Stanley with friends. We wondered how she was getting on but we didn't want to show our true colours and phone to find out, realising that if it went totally pear-shaped we would know. Next morning, we again discussed the possible outcome of Caris' solo run as we ate breakfast. We stretched our morning out until nine and then tore down to Davies Street to find Caris unconcerned and totally at home hardly acknowledging our arrival.

It was an easy road for Liam because he would follow Caris anywhere and so he tagged along with his sister. Caris and Granny Heather had that special relationship and maybe it was because Caris was her first grandchild but they always seemed to be on the same wavelength.

Farmers' Week

Farmers' Week is an event in the middle of winter where farmers gather in the capital to drink too much, argue about dogs, sheep and horses and then go home to recover over the following week. It always seems to snow on this week or be at least one of the coldest weeks of the year.

We would head into Stanley for Farmers' Week and stay with Tony and Heather, and the children would go to school in Stanley. Some years we would take in some of the pets. The episode that I am thinking of in the early to mid-1990s we had taken Caris and Liam's two rabbits into town.

Returning from this particular Farmers' Week we got into the Sussex area and the tide, which always makes it difficult, was really high and there was at least six inches of snow. This doesn't stop you, but does hide the soft patches that you need to avoid. So we had a high tide track, which would get us home even if it was a full moon high.

About 400 yards from the Low pass and Hells Kitchen we would take a right, go across a spongy valley, then climb up onto the top of Hells Kitchen valley and head inland. Here you go down a very steep hill into Hells Kitchen where you drive down the valley and through a 'once more' ditch before the beach. This day we didn't make it and so Toni and I were out in the hole, me jacking the Land Rover up and both of us throwing rocks under the wheels. This job was cold. The metal bumper jack is cold and you felt it sticking to your fingers. The rocks were equally freezing, with the water and ice perishing and so were we.

After nearly an hour Caris asked if they could come out and play in the water too! Shortly after, they were getting fed up and demanding 'we want to go home now.' We managed to get the vehicle out and get onto the beach, drive around and up the next valley, across a small bridge and through yet another 'we'll make it once more' pass. Then there was 150 metres of soft valley, then a steep climb out of the valley onto the flat. In the winter with the tide in, you still couldn't drive straight home because you couldn't drive around the beach below the house and so you had to turn inland again and go right round and come in from the opposite direction.

Inland we drove blindly because of the snow into the outer ram paddock, doing another horseshoe-shaped diversion before going into the inner ram paddock. We then headed away from the house for 70 metres or so and followed a fence going east and west which splits the pen paddocks; through two soft runners fairly close to one another and then along a peaty flat heading west, so eventually we would have driven around our farm house and the valleys and approached the homestead from the other side. We didn't make the next gate because we sank down all four wheels and were mega bogged. It looked like a few hours of jacking plus the possibility of a major bogging if the vehicle slipping off the jack and the jack damaging the bodywork so, as the farm was only ten minutes walk away, I went for the quad.

I ran back to the farm as Toni got the children and their rabbits out of the vehicle and started walking along the track. No question of leaving Strawberry and Flopsy behind.

I managed to get back to the weary travellers as humours were beginning to deteriorate. There was another ditch with a good pass that's access was boggy on the west side. Toni was getting the kids and the rabbits over the ditch at a narrow point when Liam fell over in the snow and started to grizzle. He would have been about three or four years old, maximum. My arrival saved the day and we all clambered on the quad, the rabbits in front of me, Caris on the back and Liam sandwiched in the middle.

That was the trip over and done with, but although we had a very efficient central heating system, it was peat fired and the fire needs to be fed even when it is banked down so we didn't come back to a warm house. We had a Bosky solid fuel stove that threw out a huge number of BTUs and warmed our house better than today's oil-fired boiler by miles when it was going. We got the paper and wood and opened up all the dampers for a quick response. The fire was soon roaring and the warmth started to spread through the house, although it would be a good eight hours before we were back to optimum warmth in every room.

Next day we go back and heaved the Land Rover out with the 4x4 tractor and got it back to the house. So endeth another run.

The children get around

Caris and Liam were driving the quads from as soon as they could reach the throttle. The Yamaha Big Bear was ideal for would-be speed kings, because it had a low range. We would select first low range and even with revs that threatened to have the piston escaping from captivity the bike would still be doing only two and an onion in speed terms.

Admittedly, this didn't last too long because Caris soon learnt to lean over and change gear with her hand, but it was still long enough for her, and subsequently Liam, to learn the fundamentals. By the time they were shifting the low to high they were fairly proficient.

Fast forward a few years and Toni's brother was replacing his vehicle. This Land Rover was a bit of a banger and had had a tough life with numerous owners, and the chassis was in such a state you could see through the side of it. There were not that many miles left in the vehicle before the chassis would break. This Land Rover was on tyres that had got Derek the nickname of Damien Hill because the tread was non-existent and therefore slicks. In fact, to give one the idea of the status of this vehicle I had nicknamed it 'The Skip'. Derek proposed that if we bought him a set of tyres for his next vehicle he would give us his old one. We were getting the bum side of the deal but went for it anyway.

Derek had certainly got value for money out of the tyres because they were past slicks, in fact you could see the canvas in a couple of them. As if to demonstrate the point, Derek had calculated the optimum use of these tyres to their last few revolutions and I got two punctures before I had driven the thing home.

Now in new ownership and having recognised Derek's skill at getting the last ounce of value from his possessions before he sold them on, I invested in a good, if slightly lozenge, chassis and Turpin (David Ford), with my assistance, changed the body work and running gear onto the new chassis. We invested some money into the brakes and steering to maximise the safety angle and she was ready for a new dawn.

To celebrate the work and new ownership we renamed the vehicle Skippy, and Caris and Liam had their own truck.

The Land Rover was fairly gutless and so wasn't very quick, but it was a cheap vehicle for the brat pack to learn to drive and in which they had many adventures.

A medical situation (part two)

The last major medical incident concerning our brats was not long after I had survived necrotising fasciitis (more on that later). I had been killing sheep for mutton and dogs' meat and the kids came down and picked me up at the end and gave me a lift up to the house in their Land Rover. The next night was Bonfire Night and the children had used their vehicle to pick up wood and were going to drive over to the Head of the Bay with it, which is where it was being held that year.

The kids tore off and then moments later, 'Dad, Dad, Dad, Liam's sat on your knife and there's blood everywhere.' I rushed over to Liam and lifted him off the knife and got him out of the Land Rover and then exposed the wound by pulling his trousers down a bit. There was blood pouring out of the wound in his right buttock. Having seen my own blood pumping high and freely in the intensive care in Monte I knew exactly what to do and without fear paralysing me I applied direct pressure and the flow of blood stopped.

We jumped in our Land Rover and headed for town with Liam more concerned about missing out on Bonfire Night than his current predicament. What had happened was that my knife had fallen out of its sheath and fallen between the seats. Add to that that the children's Land Rover was a bit of an old banger and the passenger's door was wired up so everyone got in the driver's door and shuffled across. On this occasion Caris was going to drive and as Liam shuffled across to the passenger's seat he sat on the knife.

We got to the hospital and the surgeon suggested that he put a small probe into the cut to see how deep the wound was, but Liam forcefully suggested that he wasn't that keen. They put a drain in and a stitch. Liam asked if he was allowed to swear during this procedure. Toni and I forbade it but the doctor unwisely said 'why not.' We did still make it home in time to attend the Bonfire Night party.

So once again we were at the end of a medical drama and all was well. Bringing kids up in the Falklands, and camp in particular, takes some beating because of the space, but with the children having access to bikes and quads at an early age there could have been more stories. We always felt that as long as they were together there would be a natural control and also one could either help or come for help.

Teslyn has an accident/s

Caris and Liam used to bring friends home for weekends and many if not all of them had their lives enriched and ours also at times. Teslyn was Caris' friend and she was terribly accident-prone. Thankfully she always arrived covered with bruises and she generally left with many more.

One day Teslyn, Caris and Liam were cycling up and down the green. Conditions were good and everything seemed to be going well. I was mending tyre punctures and just happened to look up when Teslyn, coming down a small slope back towards the house, lost control and does an endo (where the back wheel comes over the front and slam dunks the rider hard into the ground). I didn't even bother to run in Teslyn's direction, but ran away from the impact zone towards the house calling on the expertise of a veteran, with enough medical soaps to her credit to qualify as a state registered nurse –Toni.

It looked bad, but after a brush down and a hug the victim was fully recovered and ready to add to her collection of bruises.

There is a small bank running along the seashore. Sometimes the grass just goes to the beach and in other areas there are small cliffs, which can be as high as 20 feet and occasionally straight down but mostly just steep enough to test for osteoporosis or some general weakness in one's constitution. Step forward someone to test this assumption. One Teslyn Barkman.

Teslyn managed to fall down the last few feet of the beach bank and onto the beach. Caris arrived out of breath having run round from the impact zone to summon the farm medic. Toni drove around but this time it needed more than a brush down and a few patriotic songs to rally the victim. We had to take Teslyn into town to get some sinew pushed back in and her leg stitched up.

One of the greatest games for the kids, apart from the odd attempt at the junior land speed record for a 350cc quad, was to build a very small shed on a sleigh. The idea was for one person to drive the quad, and then the other, or the rest if there were more, to sit in the shed as it was being towed.

It was shed evolution at work. It was also debilitating to the availability of farm nails. Mk1 didn't go 100 yards because the rope was not tied to much more than an ice cream stick-sized piece of wood. The next version went a bit further and the next further still until the elite model was created and was virtually indestructible. The deluxe model had a pallet base with a wooden frame and a bit of old canvas lashed and nailed together to make it wind and waterproof and to keep it all together.

Once the ultimate sleigh was built they seemed to lose interest and went back to dragging a tarpaulin behind the quad on a long piece of rope.

Caris and Liam did have their own motor bikes and three-wheelers where they used all the space at their disposal. On the bikes and three-wheelers helmets were mandatory. The bikes were designed for kids so were low-geared, easy starters and good for the experience of powered two wheels.

The 250cc three-wheeler was not so child friendly and went like hot snot. It was much lighter than a quad and so could easily outperform the quads even giving 100cc away. A three-wheeler is a completely different concept to two and four wheels. Once you have ridden up the back of your legs a few times and careered off the intended path on numerous occasions you start to get the gist of where to put your weight and then they are brilliant to ride.

I was working on Caris' three-wheeler, trying to get the choke to work properly, and decided to take it for a spin to the top of the green. I had ridden a three-wheeler for many years, even riding this one home from Walker Creek, a farm in Lafonia, so I believed I was proficient. Not proficient enough, however, and after hitting a series of bumps the three-wheeler came to rest on top of me and, more importantly, out of sight of the house. I thought someone would make some tentative enquiries about my whereabouts and wellbeing after a while, but no such luck. Eventually, when the pain of the accident wore off, I was able to extricate myself from underneath and drive back to the garage to replace the front mudguard and carrier.

Caris and Liam's Land Rover

Caris and Liam's Land Rover wasn't very flash but it was reliable. It had its funny little ways like jumping out of first, third and fifth gears. The first gear was a bit of an issue because the safest way of coming down a steep slippery hill was to put the diff lock in, select first low and let the engine breaking slow the vehicle.

Caris was a little bit older and so was able to reach the controls comfortably but for Liam, being a little bit smaller, it was a steeper learning curve.

We had a visit from other children and Liam took them off behind the farm into the Head of the Bay ground where it is flat and has less hazards. A while later the children came walking back in. Liam was bogged. Off we went to recover them and back we came with Liam's pride slightly scuffed.

But not to be put off he carried on driving against all the ribbing he got from one and all.

The following weekend Liam took his cousin April for a spin and coming around the tight bend where the fence comes up from the shearing shed and ends close to the generator shed he crashed. The passenger wing was stoved-in and the exhaust of the generator was bent right round. April was not at all impressed and Liam was mortified. On top of that his personal development officer and co-owner of Skippy was outraged.

Liam was never going to drive again and April was able to point out that she didn't intend to ride with him for an equal length of time.

I did spend a while explaining to Liam that if it had been our vehicle of course it would be very serious but that is why we bought them a cheap rough and ready vehicle, which could afford to take some rough treatment and not really matter.

They were both very good but we did always keep an eye open for them. If they went fishing at the point I would give them ten minutes to arrive before I started to get twitchy. They did get stuck occasionally but to us it was all part of learning their driving skills.

One weekend things did get rather hectic when Lucas, one of Liam's muckers from the school hostel, came out to stay. Every time I turned around Liam and Lucas would be walking into the farm needing to be rescued and pulled out of this hole or that.

After bogging close to the farm on a number of occasions they went for a longer drive down towards the Bodie reseed, which was through the old Hells Kitchen road with the gate in the valley. They had been off for quite a while so I thought I would go and have a look and see if I could locate their whereabouts. Miles away up by the Bodie reseed I could see the white of the top of the Land Rover at an unnatural angle. Toni was despatched this time to pull them out.

Although we were fairly relaxed we did like to know where they were. I didn't feel as comfortable when there were two bikes, quads or anything because although one likes to extend trust, temptation is a powerful force. I thought two vehicles could lead to yet another force which can sometimes lead to one's downfall and that is competition and who can beat who, or go the fastest.

The Land Rover was very underpowered and you needed a tail wind and a very steep downward slope to get anything near fast out of her.

Having said all the derogatory stuff, she was maintained to a very high standard and all the lights worked and we put her on the road (insured and road taxed) and to work on the farm.

On the farm we used to put the big track grips on her and load her up with fencing or even transport small numbers of sheep and use her for those types of farm jobs. There were miles of road now and the big track grips were just not the tyres for roads and so fitted to Skippy with minimum road use we got a reasonable life from these tyres. The tyres would wear very quickly on the roads because only a small amount of rubber was touching the ground at any one time and also the vibration they generated was uncomfortable and noisy.

I was always changing the tyres backward and forwards when Skippy was supporting the farm effort, rather than the children's leisure time. On one run we are returning from Goose Green in the dark after some social function and a wheel overtook us and went whistling out into the camp, disappeared outside the loom of the lights and vanished. Fortunately for us at Skippy speed we just juddered to a standstill.

Toni and Caris and Liam dashed off into the night to try and find the wheel, but it was really one of those nights that was pitch black with not a star showing. I robbed a nut from all the other wheels, jacked the vehicle up and put the spare wheel on. I could hear the search going on in the dark somewhere. The search did come to an end without the wheel being found but walking back to Skippy Caris fell over the absent wheel. The children were complaining about how dangerous Skippy was and how they were not getting back in and would walk home, only to decide – when they got out of the range of the lights and it was so dark – discretion was the better part of valour and perhaps they would ride home after all.

The Sussex fishing club

We made some good friends with some civilians from Mount Pleasant Airport who worked for Turner Diesel and one of their number managed the power station. I met them by chance as one day we looked out to see people fishing in our creek. I said to Toni that I would go and sort them out, jumped on my bike and headed off. They were all jolly sorts that liked to come and fish at the head of Sussex Creek and have a barbecue and have a few beers and bottles of wine. On this occasion I helped them out which resulted in me weaving my way home much later in the day. As Toni likes to point out, I didn't much sort them out, but we did make some good friends. After that, we used to go down and join them if time allowed.

At first we would lay on the east-facing bank on the western side of the Sussex Creek basin. It gave perfect shelter from the prevailing winds and only winds from the east or straight from the north or south ruined this appealing aspect.

The Sussex Creek comes in between Ponds Rincon and Terra Motas and then runs up past the house for quite a way, tapering into a bottleneck by the bank in question before opening out into a basin. At the neck there are two spits which are at the east and west end. Both these areas are good for fishing. If the tides were bad for fishing the opportunity arose for alcohol to be consumed by lying on the bank, sheltered from the wind, sampling wine of many countries.

It was like the Sussex fishing club and many happy hours were spent at this kind of recreation. We were still building up the farm at that stage and so life was mostly work so this occasional distraction made a welcome change.

It was a time when you could get many favours for the right currency. I don't know what the trade was, but from somewhere they got a Portacabin and then the cabin got a lift on a military ship and finally it was lifted by a Chinook to the place under the bank where we consumed our leisure time. These must have been some favours to get all that. I can only think that it must have been some decent trout for a mess dinner or two. What else would the Turners have that the others didn't?

So the start of the Sussex Leisure Industries Complex was started. From being a location that depended on reasonable days and summer time, it was transformed into a summer and winter retreat, undisturbed by the climatic surprises that could spoil the day. Everyone mucked in to make the cabin comfortable and I took up a small container, which was made into the engine shed, on the lorry and managed to lift it off with the Hiab hydraulic arm.

For a few years we used to do a mid-winter supper where all the Turner guys would come up to the house and we would have a banquet. It was a do of all dos, where everyone would eat and drink far too much and feel awful the next day.

One memorable mid-winter feast became more colourful than the others. We had got delayed in town so the guys came up to the house. By the time we got home, Derek Miller and the others had cooked enough food to feed a full Wembley stadium. We had just got it served up and were tucking in when there was a knock at the door and there was a local guy called Chutney. 'I'm stuck in Hells Kitchen.' A few of us dropped everything and went off to rescue him.

It was bitterly cold outside with a strong wind going right through all the layers and chilling us to the marrow. It became apparent that Chutney, who was working in the San Carlos area, had driven out without a starter motor. He had tried to get out of Hells Kitchen valley, up the steep track. He had charged it a couple of times until he stalled and because his brakes weren't much either, he ran back down the hill and out into the creek. When we arrived back at the scene the Land Rover was out in the sea with the water lapping around the bottom of the doors. Since Chutney's incident and during his walk back to the house the tide had come in. Chutney took the rope and waded out to his vehicle and attached it. A quick pull and he had bump-started and driven up onto the bank.

Over the years we had put in our own bridges in different places to help us get home and we were reluctant to tell others. Not because we were mean spirited towards our fellow travellers, but it was just a fact that if a lot of people used our tracks they would soon, with the extra traffic, become unusable. On this night in question I reluctantly took everyone back on one of these routes so that we could return to our meal before it was totally ruined.

Chutney's tyres were bald with very little tread and so once we got through the valleys he had problems getting up and out of them and he couldn't get high enough so that we could get a rope onto him. Chutney was another one of these people with a 'can do' attitude and he began racing up and down the sides of these valleys trying to zig-zag up. I really couldn't believe my eyes that he didn't roll over and down to the bottom. Eventually we got back to the house and Chutney was soaked to the skin, covered in oil and chilled to the core. He was sent to have a bath to thaw out and to clean and brush up.

After Chutney had finished washing off the evening's grime he must have left a tidemark around the bath as though the Exxon Valdez had run aground there. Chutney believed that Toni's face flannel was the cloth for cleaning the bath and scrubbed the oily slick from the bath's sides. By this time the rest of us had eaten well and were into the magic.

Next day, Toni discovered her violated flannel and picked it up between thumb and forefinger, gingerly walking with it through to the kitchen. She lifted the lid of the peat stove and without a word flicked it into the flames.

During these dos, over a number of years the Turner guys got fewer and fewer as they decided to move on and work in other parts of the world, including Britain. Norman was the last and he stayed until he was retirement age and by that time he had met Kathy and had decided to settle down with her in Nottingham. The cabin was really neglected during this period because Norman would come and stay with us. We inherited it as the last user left but although we had big plans, in all honesty we had enough to do without establishing a second home a few miles from the house. Derek and Trudi were interested in buying and developing the spot and so we decided to sell to them.

8. COUNCIL 1993–97

The seed is sown

I can't remember how I got involved directly in Falklands' politics. I remember after the camp returned their number unopposed and approaching the next election, the Governor of the time suggested to me, on a camp visit in this area, that perhaps I might consider standing. I don't think I did on that occasion. Perhaps this is where the seed was planted. I did dabble in the committee setup, which is an important part of the political function when I sat on the Camp Education Managers' Committee.

Even at this lower level, we as the Camp Managers' Committee were quite revolutionary for that time and promoted openness and sent out minutes to all camp parents. This was many years before the public drive virtually demanded openness. At that time, it was very controversial and the Director of Education received a few fiery phone calls before everyone became reasonably comfortable with the concept. It seems funny in today's political climate to remember how pressure was bought to bear to stop this practice of sending out minutes. We did compromise and continued to send them out with a disclaimer at the beginning encouraging parents to contact the head of Camp Education, or a member of the committee if there were any concerns.

A lot of the workings of this committee were fairly mundane, and we had a number of sessions at the outset of these three management committees telling us what our parameters were. I always hated these get-togethers which the establishment tried to control.

One of the issues that we got our teeth into was when Government wanted to build some public toilets in the grounds of the school hostel next to the West Store. Parents got involved and the committee were outraged, but strangely everyone else seemed to think it was quite acceptable.

It was unwisely tasked to me to write a letter to the Councillors expressing our views through the Chair of the time, Ann Robertson. I did my best in vividly describing, in graphic terms, what we felt these toilets would promote.

My letter did the trick because the Council of the day obviously suddenly saw what everyone with a vested interest saw and how unsuitable public toilets would be on hostel grounds. Our Chair was not that impressed with my style but told me in such a gentle way that I wasn't quite sure until I got home and thought about it. I was also not trusted with the good name of the Camp Education Managers' Committee again.

So really this was the only experience I had before clutching the nettle and putting myself forward to become a Member of the Legislative Council.

How Council works

It is not my intention to delve too deeply into the workings of the Council but a brief explanation of the working might be of some interest.

The first Council I was on was made up of a fifty/fifty split between town (Stanley) and the camp (the countryside) The four members for Stanley were John Cheek, Sharon Halford, Charles Keenleyside and Wendy Teggart. The members for camp were Norma Edwards, Eric Goss, Bill Luxton and I.

There aren't any political parties although there have been attempts to form them. So every politician is an independent, having various views on all the topics so there is not necessarily a left-wing stance or right on any subject by each individual, however each person's own politics, or situation might have a general influence on how they think.

Gilbert House was a historic house converted to offices with one half belonging to the archives with the manageress, Jane Cameron. In the other half our research assistant Jenny Luxton, and Maria Strange coped with the demands of the elected members. The two departments shared office equipment like the photocopier.

Members wanting to meet people could use Gilbert House and on occasions have meetings of committees but as a council it was where we would all sit down and work through the Executive Council papers. It was also used to work on any issue collectively and to meet the VIPs visiting the Islands.

One of the first things a council does, after getting in, is to vote three of its members on to the Executive Council (Exco) and these members have the executive power of the Falkland Islands. One has to be voted in from the camp constituency, one from town and the third from either camp or Stanley. This happens once a year.

Executive papers are prepared to go before Exco, and all Councillors get their chance to comment at the General Purposes Committee (GPC) the day before at Gilbert House. The Executive do not have to take the views of the other members into account and even if they do, the expertise delivered by officers at the executive meeting sometimes alters the logic of things that have been discussed at GPC. If the decision goes against the views of a majority of Councillors, made by the three at Exco, there is an opportunity for the other members to halt its passage if there is money involved by voting against it at the Standing Finance Committee (SFC), which is held on the morning after Executive Council.

Executive Council was conducted at Government House and the frequency has increased as years have gone by. For a number of years now it has been monthly with additional meetings being held if need be.

Executive Council sat around a large wooden table with the Governor as the chair but without a vote. There are a number of government staff supporting this meeting like the Chief Executive, the Attorney General, Financial Secretary, Government Secretary, Clerk of Councils (secretary for the meeting) and the three councillors. The three Councillors are the only people that can vote on a paper. Other members of the Government could be called in to support any item at this meeting. Other Council members can stand in as executive members in the absence of an executive member or if a member has an interest in any papers

Depending on the number of papers, and the chair, the meetings could be wound up before lunch but occasionally a bumper session could have you leaving in the early evening.

Although the day's business would be carried out with much thought and dedication it wasn't devoid of humour at times. If the meeting looked as if it was going to go past lunch the Governor's staff would provide lunch for everyone. This usually entailed an opportunity to have an alcoholic drink which could liven up the debate or even extinguish it for certain individuals over the years.

The Legislative Council was where the legislation was enacted and where all eight members were involved. The meetings were held in the court and council chambers and we sat in a three-quarter circle with the speaker of the house, which was the Governor during my stint in the 1990s, and an elected speaker of the house in later years, sitting in the middle of the circle with the Clerk of Councils. Leading out on one of the wings of the part circle was the Attorney General, Chief Executive, Financial Secretary then the three Executive Councillors (who are also Legislative Councillors.) Leaving the Speaker of the House and leading out the other side there is the Commander British forces and then the five Legislative Councillors.

All members can ask questions of the House, and it used to be asked of the administration, but since members have taken on the responsibility of leading departments members ask one another, and each councillor answers on behalf of their responsibilities. Every member has the chance to ask supplementaries (other questions).

Bills are read out and Councillors are able to speak on them and suggest amendments if they so wish, which are then put to a vote and eventually pass or fail. At the end of the business all councillors, the Chief Executive and the Commander British Forces have the right to speak to the Motion for Adjournment with the Speaker of the House commenting on occasions.

Many members use this motion to highlight issues, which are concerning their constituents, and also to praise government departments' achievements, or even individuals or highlight any subject that they feel they wish to air in public. When members of the community that have contributed to the society die, it is also an opportunity to note their passing.

What surprised me most in local politics, on my first foray in the 1990s, was that a lot of the business was conducted on a personal basis with individuals grouping not only with like-minded people, which is natural, but also against people they didn't like. To me then and now it seemed a funny way of doing government business. On this Council there were many issues that we voted on and were split down the middle, four each way. Recent suggestions that all members should be on the Executive would have been a nightmare then because there would have been so many stalemates.

Because there were only eight elected representatives some of the officers would work the system to their advantage knowing that the right member being away could allow their pet project to succeed.

Working as a Councillor

Work on the external links of the Islands was a very important development at this time. There were ideas about airlines working out of Uruguay and Punta Arenas, Chile, which was happening to a degree in the 1990s from the latter.

A proposal came to us about paying for seats on LAN Chile, so that they would get the revenue for a specified number of seats even if they were not filled. It was a scheme to kick start a reliable and regular connection with the outside world. I voted for it, primarily because I thought if tourism was to succeed we needed a proper link with South America. I felt that many tourists visiting the southern cone would probably tag the Falklands on to their holiday. I always felt that a stand-alone holiday to the Falklands was going to be very exclusive and would need some very clever selling strategy.

I think it failed at least once to get funding from MLAs, (Members of Legislative Assembly)partly because there was still a lot of suspicion about South America in general, and even a fear that it might undermine the air bridge and move us back towards relying on South America for our external link. Everyone knew that relying exclusively on any part of South America gave the Argentines an opportunity to manipulate it in their favour. This turned out to be fact years later when Pinochet was arrested in London, and Chile and Britain had a difference of opinion and the Argentines persuaded the Chileans to close the link.

If my memory serves me correctly the proposal to subsidise LAN came back to be considered while a certain member or members were overseas and through it went. This has developed into one of the greatest success stories in terms of improving links for private and economic development. I don't think the seat numbers went low enough for FIG to buy seats or if they did it was very rarely.

Another surprise in the way the Council worked was the stuff that came to Executive Council, like blocked drains or something equally mundane. I always thought these issues were bizarre, and that our managers were paid to sort this stuff, and Executive Councillors shouldn't be doing their jobs. Others must have thought the same and this wasn't the case in the next Council that I worked on. Although even now some members still get involved in management.

Another area that was carried out straight after being elected was who would sit on which committees. Again as a new member I didn't push in any direction but I was pleased to be on the Education Board, but I think my inexperience led to me chairing the stamp committee.

As a novice Councillor I went at it like a bull at a gate and with no subtleties. I knew, or I thought I knew, what the problems were and I had plenty of ideas about the remedies. I felt that we did a lot of complaining but didn't try and contribute a will to find solutions. We did have plenty of money so we were able to subsidise the rural sector which had major problems with wool prices, viability in size and the balance of quality to marginal ground on a number of the newly created farms. We were able to fund direct subsidies, mortgage relief and a huge replacement fencing programme and probably most important of all for the rural population, to carry on driving the roads to all inhabited properties on mainland East and West Falklands.

The Education Board

My time on the Education Board was very interesting with Phyl Rendell as the Director and John Cheek as the other Councillor and Chairman. They were big on academics but I felt that vocational skills should not be ignored, and we should work towards increasing this provision. One of our greatest achievements was to raise the age of children leaving school to 16, but once again I thought we were neglecting the needs of the children with practical skills. I felt that without some focus for this group of children they could switch off and their frustration could develop into bad behaviour.

I took a bit of a battering from the united front of the director and chair who didn't give any priority to the issues I was raising. The laymen of that time, seeing a strong response, followed their lead. Things were to change however when Dr Barry Elsby joined the Board, and began raising the issues that I had had over the previous 18 months to two years. The tide had turned, and because of the change in the makeup of the Board the issue of vocational training began to be taken more seriously. To be honest, my views had taken such a hiding that there were times that I questioned my beliefs, but the more I read the more I knew that there was some merit in my stance, but it was Barry's participation that helped broaden the educational thrust.

International conferences

I was soon learning the ropes on the international stage under the expert guidance of Norma Edwards when I had the opportunity to work with her at the party conferences in the UK. Norma was a great communicator, not just at home in the Islands but wherever she went.

We were sitting in Paddington Station in London waiting for a train when she got talking to a complete stranger, and in the time it took for the train to come this chap knew the major fundamentals of the Falkland Islands and went away a convert to our cause, i.e. we are British and we want to have the right of self-determination like all other countries and peoples.

Of course, I wasn't neglected, and Norma would tell me endless stories from previous councils and about her work as a nurse in the UK that were hilarious. My two favourites were the prostitute who had 'pay as you enter' tattooed on the skin of her pelvic bone. It was weak on story but high on punchline, and the other story was about false teeth. A chap had died on her ward and as they were rounding up his personal belongings they found his false teeth and popped them into his mouth for safekeeping. Unfortunately, these teeth turned out to belong to the gentleman in the next bed who soon alerted the staff to his missing teeth. Quick as a flash Norma realised what had happened and sent a nurse to recover the dentures, explaining to the owner that denture cleaning was all part of the hospital service and that they would be bought back to him in pristine condition. One would hope that they would have given them a good clean, but one can't help thinking that the nurse asked to do the running probably gave them a cursory rub and handed them back to the owner who would then plonk them back in his mouth.

Coming back from Blackpool on a train from a Labour Party Conference, Norma again sprung into action in winning another member of the British public over on to our side. The train was packed and there was Norma, Sukey – the government representative in London –

a total stranger, and me. Train journeys can get a bit tedious after many hours passing fields of cows, sheep and the odd rabbit, pheasant and houses. So what more welcoming sound than Norma proposing that she buys us all a gin and tonic. This included the total stranger who couldn't refuse this kind motherly approach. I then bought a round just to keep it going and before there was time for the guard to say we were going to be hours late getting into London, Norma, with some small help from Sukey and I, were giving said stranger the heads up about the Falklands. Of course, he asked us what we were doing at the party conferences and what we were trying to achieve. After a few G&Ts everyone was in the best of fettle and this chap hated the Argies and loved the Falklands and the people. He got off at about the halfway stage and staggered off down the platform and out of our lives. Probably wasn't even his stop.

The party conferences were hard work because you are on your feet all day meeting people, some, even with it being not that many years after the war, that didn't have a clue about where we were and let alone that the Argentines still claimed our home. One lady that I was trying to explain as tactfully as possible to that the Falklands weren't off the Scottish coast just walked off in total embarrassment when the penny finally dropped. The hardest task was to convince people that there was more to the Falklands than the war in 1982 and that the images of the war in mid-winter, with horizontal sleet and snow, didn't portray the climate accurately.

People just loved Norma and her relaxed, warm style and would talk away to her as if she was a long lost relative. Most people wanted to know if you lived in the Falklands and the next question was usually whether you were born there.

We would have a stand that had a portable display with some stunning pictures of wildlife and some of the newest infrastructure, like the new community school. With this and some basic facts written alongside we would try and answer and fill in all the gaps about life in the Islands and where we were going in development terms.

The first time, and the first conference, the hotel we stayed at was rough and rundown. The receptionist was a vulgar individual that made suggestive remarks while he booked us in, asking Norma and I if we needed 'extracurricular' services. Norma was a respectable middle-aged lady who you would have thought projected a dignified personal signature. This ignoramus didn't pick it up.

I might have been mistaken however, because I ended up at the other end of the Hotel Grotsville from Sukey and Norma.

My part of the hotel was pretty shabby with every floorboard creaking and groaning under the lightest footstep, and the walls were so thin you shared the lives of everyone else in neighbouring rooms in all directions.

The couple in the room next to mine did not recognise the limitations of the room's flimsy walls. If they did these people didn't suffer from shyness or the fear of violating the sensibilities of other hotel users. Every night they came back to their room after midnight and there would be all this moaning and groaning with the bed shrieking for some quality oil. It was hard to try and sleep even after a long day on the stand and I would wake up completely shattered after a night in bed. My only consolation was that unless the people next door were trained athletes they would be feeling even worse than me.

Norma and I did have a little time to ourselves, and we would go downtown to see the sights. There were arcades and novelty shops and other seaside entertainment. In one of the novelty shops, a salesman was delivering his silky patter about the quality of his products. He had a number of clockwork and electrical toys that he was demonstrating, and was encouraging people to pick out a toy that he would demo. In our minds the products were pretty awful but this young man was giving his sales pitch his best shot. A wicked gleam came into Norma's eyes as she had spotted a clockwork willy way up on one of the top shelves. She was quick to ask our man for a demo. To be fair he only hesitated for a fraction of a second before he reached up and brought this quality item down for a quick show. Needless to say, neither of us bought one but it did make us laugh. In hindsight, I think for the effort the salesman put in we should have bought something. It would have given us hours of fun at Gilbert House on our return. There would have been 50 per cent laughing and 50 per cent outrage.

The party conferences are all about meeting and greeting during the day and eating and drinking at night, delivering the Falklands' message to all party members and hopefully making a memory for up and coming politicians that might one day wield power and influence.

We got the heads up that Guido di Tella, the Argentine foreign minister in Carlos Menem's government, was going to visit the stand on this particular day. Guido was an anglophile eccentric and had been sending presents to everyone in the Falklands for a couple of years in an attempt to break the ice between the Falklands and Argentina. One such present was a *Pingu* video tape, which was a cartoon penguin that doesn't speak properly and which was very popular with youngsters at the time. Another present was a video about life in Patagonia.

Norma had suggested that we did not shake hands and when he arrived that is what happened. Norma told him in no uncertain terms that she wasn't going to shake the hand of a politician of a country that claimed the Falklands. He looked genuinely taken aback, and as he was reeling I handed him a tourism video about the Falklands saying that this was a video about real penguins and the real country the Falklands. He recovered from the initial shock of being rebuffed by us and said some complimentary things about the Falklands and then left. I must say looking back on it, it was hardly power politics but at the time Norma and I were pleased with our performance.

The next year I went to the party conferences with Sharon Halford, who had her own distinctive style – very matter of fact – and an 'up and at them' politician. I had worked with Sharon first of all at an ABC (Argentine, British Council) conference in London. This group was made up of businessmen with interests in Argentina trying to lobby British politicians. The conference had many individuals from Argentina, including the Argentine president Carlos Menem's brother, Eduardo. We were meant to debate some meaningful topics but the core subject of the Falklands' sovereignty kept raising its head.

That evening we all had a dinner get together. It was fairly daunting in some ways, because the majority were really people that thought the Falklands and their people were an insignificant and inconvenient blemish in the relationship between Britain and Argentina and the problem should be sorted by handing the Islands over to Argentina.

Sharon was invited to join the top table, I felt because they thought Sharon as a female could be won over. As I was pussyfooting my way diplomatically through their 'let's be friends', and 'let's be realistic about where the Islands lie', etc., Sharon was delivering broadside after broadside at her table. I am not sure of women's roles in Argentina, but the Argentines (99 per cent were male) this evening didn't know how to handle this forthright lady as she had them reeling. Sharon didn't beat about the bush. I am sure if I had spoken so clearly they would have hung me from the nearest light fitting.

So back to the party conferences, and this time Sharon was the novice and I had a year's experience.

In a way Norma still had an influence in the proceedings because during this year's campaign both at the Labour Party and Conservative Conferences, Norma's fan base would come along to demoralise Sharon and I with 'Where's Norma? 'Where is that nice friendly lady from the Falklands?'

'We are from the Falklands, can we help?' Usually at the point that Norma was found to be absent they would lose interest, and we would be calling after them 'Would you like a pamphlet or a badge?' No, what they really wanted was a chat with Norma. I think Sharon and I felt inadequate and certainly undervalued at these exchanges.

Regardless of us being second best to Norma, we soldiered on and did our best to communicate with the many people who came to visit us. We had had an upgrade on the stand with bigger and better pictures and text and a carpet with the shape of the Falkland Islands on it in a different colour. We made a vow on the first day not to let any visiting Argentine stand on the Falklands.

Sukey was very house proud and would cast her eyes over the stand constantly checking that all was in order. She seemed to spot the smallest speck of dust or notice that the pamphlets were not in neat piles nearly as it happened. There were times of near frenetic activity at the stand, but sometimes when there was some key speech going on in the conference hall things would be very slow indeed. In fact, things could get quite boring, but you still had to stay on duty.

To raise spirits, I would test Sukey's response times to some encroachment on her patch and would roll up a sweet paper really tightly and flick it onto the carpet. It would be seconds before the hawk-eyed Sukey would see the offending article and quickly swoop down and pick it up. I do not exaggerate when I say that Sukey could detect detritus on her stand down to the size of a tealeaf. She was, and I guess still is, very particular.

Downtime

During these conferences with Sharon, the Stevens family had taken the opportunity to come to the UK and do the family thing with my side of the family, but with having the farm

Toni had to return home before I was able to. The children decided to stay with Granny and Granddad and come back to the Falklands with me.

During our family time I had done my best to steer clear of all shopping malls and campaigned strongly against some of the things Toni was thinking of buying. Toni had other ideas and managed a serious shop while I was busy with council duties.

During the Labour Party Conference, the contact phone went off and it was the bank wanting to speak to Toni. I told them that unfortunately she had flown back to the Islands and could I help. They weren't that keen until I explained that, as it was a joint bank account I couldn't understand their reticence. They decided that as I was one of the signatories they could share their concerns with me. They felt pretty sure that Toni's debit card had been stolen, because it had hundreds of pounds withdrawn and many transactions carried out over a couple of days. I was able to reassure them that this serious abuse of plastic was not the work of some notorious credit card extortionist, but Toni on her pre-departure shop before returning to the Falklands.

This contact point was used once more. By the children this time, but equally serious. Most of my chats were done in the evening after the conference and before the night-time events. Liam, who was usually unflappable, was in a terrible state. They had been out painting in the garden and they had left their works of art on the table to dry when a seagull had flown over and crapped on his picture. Not on Caris' but his, and it did it on purpose and it was the best painting he had ever done and now this gull had ruined it.

Well I tried to say that I was sure that a gull wouldn't have singled him out and that it was just one of those things, but he wasn't having any of it. I spoke to Caris, who could usually work the magic with Liam, but she was unable to placate him.

It was one such incident that after I had calmed him from ten on the Richter scale down to about six, a call was made to his mother, in the Falklands, to finish the consultation.

Sharon and I also had downtime and I had, half-jokingly, suggested that we go on the Big One, the highest big dipper in the UK at the time. Sharon seemed to be up for it, so one evening we joined the queue. Sharon did have second thoughts about the ride but I was able to convince her that it must be safe or it wouldn't be allowed to operate and that they let people of her age on, although I am sure she was at the upper limit so this would probably be her last chance.

Into the cars you get and they crank you up to the top. The drop is so severe that you cannot see the descent until you are descending, and then when you are accelerating from 0 to 1 million in less than a second on the way down your mind is on controlling one's bodily functions. It was hairy, it was safe and it was brown-alert material.

It was in Brighton that I left my favourite tie. If it hadn't been for that I would have left the other assortment of clothing. Foolishly, I asked Sharon who was living in Brighton, before she flew home, to pick them up for me. Unhelpfully the hotel didn't tape the bag up in any way. Sharon, even to this day is still happy to gleefully tell everyone and anyone about the time she had to go and pick up my shreddies.

I enjoyed working with Norma and Sharon and can't remember a cross word or a dull moment.

The UN

During my political life I represented the Falkland Islands four times at the UN. The first time was during my first stint as Councillor with Eric Goss.

Eric was another larger-than-life individual whose day job was managing one of the biggest farms in the Falklands. He had a wicked sense of humour and amusing catchphrases. We sort of had the same bigger objectives, but our ideas on how to achieve them were poles apart, although on foreign affairs we were both on the same wave length even if Eric was more hard-line.

We flew up to the UK on the air bridge that was operated by the RAF in those days with an aging fleet of TriStars. They were comfortable, direct and the quickest route to England.

During any one term, a Councillor's spouse can accompany them on an overseas trip. I have always seen this as recognition of the spouses' part in a supporting role. Times do get tough for numerous reasons and during periods when members are making difficult decisions which affect people, this does lead to the inevitable angry phone calls and personal attacks. The spouse is pretty hard-skinned if they don't feel the pressure at all over the four years.

On this trip to New York our wives Shirley and Toni came with us to take up this perk of the job.

We flew Virgin Atlantic from Heathrow to JFK and I was impressed with the staff. They seemed so willing and helpful and pleased to see you. They convinced me of their sincerity, unlike some of the other airlines I have flown with whose people just seem to go through the motions with their mouths in the smile position (apart from LADE of course).

Coming into JFK, Toni asked me what something was that she had seen in the distance. It looked like the sun going down, but it was too quick. Perhaps it was a flare. It was something out of the ordinary.

We struggled through arrivals with queues that seemed to go on forever. Eventually we got to the surly American immigration staff that grunted ill-humouredly through the documentation bit and the 'welcome to America' process. No cheery 'welcome to America and thanks for making this your work or holiday destination and creating jobs and contributing to our economy.'

We went off to the taxi rank where we had to wait in another queue, while a person gave us a chit with the expected rates on it which also encouraged us to challenge the driver if he over charged. The person then picked the taxi for us when it was our turn. Hiring a freelance taxi is, I believe, illegal. As we got into the taxi the breaking news was of a Pan Am jumbo crashing into the sea and we realised that this was what Toni saw as we were coming in to land. As we were all flying back in a few days it was a double shock realising even in this day and age that things can go wrong. Shirley at first said she wasn't getting back on a plane again, so we imagined her getting a couple of horses and following Tschiffely's Ride in reverse, back down to the tip of South America and getting a boat across. It was a shock but we did get back on the return flight.

We were soon at the Beekman Tower Hotel which was old and slightly run down. It is a historic building without the frills that you would expect from a new building. It was however perfectly comfortable. It did have a few virtues. One being a bar on the bottom floor, and one right at the very top that had some good views over New York as you supped your drink.

One of the downsides was the air conditioning that was really noisy. It was like living with a small jet turbine going off in the room at regular intervals.

Eric, the born and bred Falkland Islander of countless generations, was not someone to just sit idly by and do nothing, He thought there must be a reason for this mechanical cacophony and so proceeded not to call the hotel maintenance staff, but to take the thing to bits. Eric deduced that it was obviously a simple case of the fan rubbing on something inside as it was spinning round. Eric had it partly dismantled when he felt that he might need a few pointers from the resident engineer. Funnily enough, the maintenance staff were less than impressed with Eric's can do, DIY attitude and refused to put it back together. Eric was equally unimpressed because he felt that he had done half the job for them.

Eric and I did have our other responsibilities to attend to so, leaving the air conditioning unit strewn across his hotel room, we left to pick up our Foreign Office minders and pick up our UN identification tags and then off to the UN building and numerous embassies to meet different countries' ambassadors and mission leaders to fight the Falkland Island corner.

On the one-to-one bilaterals everyone was particularly supportive, understanding and friendly although this was rarely replicated at the Committee of 24 where people just aligned to their political interests.

We met the Chilean ambassador, who was a charming man and spoke highly of the honesty of farmers, which Eric and I were, and how we were the salt of the earth, etc. We had our say and spoke of our community, but there was nothing to hang it on like Argentina who is a serious trading partner with Chile. Eric did mention our strong Chilean community and our trade with Chile through Punta Arenas, but of course compared to Argentina this was a drop in the ocean. Chile and Argentina have had their differences over the years and it is almost certain that if Argentina had prevailed in the war of 1982 the three Islands that they claimed from Chile in the Beagle Channel would have been next.

While we were doing our bit, the ladies were enjoying the sights and sounds of New York, walking the length and breadth of Manhattan shopping and touring. They did the UN guided tour that they found all very interesting. They came on to the minefields of the world and how many had been indiscriminately laid in many cases. The guide in Toni and Shirley's group skipped over the Falklands' mines, but Toni had heard the group in front when the Falklands were mentioned in fairly strong terms. As anyone that knows her will tell you, Toni is not an extrovert. We leave that to our children but, even though it cost

Building the insides of the new shearing shed.

Liam & Caris learning to use the quad (ATV).

Liam with a big mullet he caught at
The Estancia.

Lamb Marking BBQ with l-r back row Liam, Martin Carey, Steve Malik, Trudi Pettersson, Patrick McGeough, Martin Davies & Tony Pettersson. Front Row Ron Dickson,
Iris Dickson, Keith Dickson, Toni, Hilary Hutchinson with Daniel Hutchinson in
front, Paul Hutchinson with Faith Hutchinson in front, Barbara Cheek (now Bates),
Steven Dickson with dog, Me. Caris is behind the BBQ.

Mike McKay getting into his bogged excavator.

The D6 after being rescued from the creek. The cab of our tractor is still visible in the water as it goes under for the third time.

After all the hiccups we get the D6 on site and use it, block and tackles, a tractor and the lorry to pull the excavator out.

With all equipment now in use we continue with the road building.

Tipping a load from the Moxy , with the D6 ready to spread on Sussex Mountain.

End of phase 2, packing up to go home.

Derek and the Moonfish

MLA's with Douglas Hurd. Back Row L-R Eris Goss, Wendy Teggart, Me.

Middle Row L-R John Cheek, Charles Keenleyside, Sharon Halford, Bill Luxton, Norma Edwards and ? Front Row L-R Ronnie Sampson, Douglas Hurd and the Governor David Tatham.

Photo courtesy Norman Clark.

Family and friends on one of our many camping trips. Back Row L-R Tonisha Goodwin, Cody Betts and Ted (Michael) Jones. Next Row Trudi Pettersson, April Pettersson holding Michael Goodwin, Turpin (David) Ford, Shelia Jones, Marie Ross, Derek Goodwin standing. Front row Robbie Todd, Me, Liam, Caris, Toni and Bonita Goodwin. Photo courtesy Derek Pettersson.

Sign on gate at North Arm when we went camping.
Photo courtesy Derek Pettersson

Pupils, including Liam looking directly at HRH and his friend Ashley Jaffray in the orange jacket, meet Prince Charles outside the Falkland Islands Community School. Photo Courtesy Norman Clark.

Meeting Tony Blair at the party conferences. I am shaking hands with Tony whilst Norma Edwards greets Cherie. Photo David Carrol.

Horses and jockeys lined up at the cemetery during Heathers funeral.

Head shave for charity. Derek Goodwin, me and Derek Pettersson
with Toni the shaver.

Accident in Hells Kitchen. The casualty is still laying by the ditch.

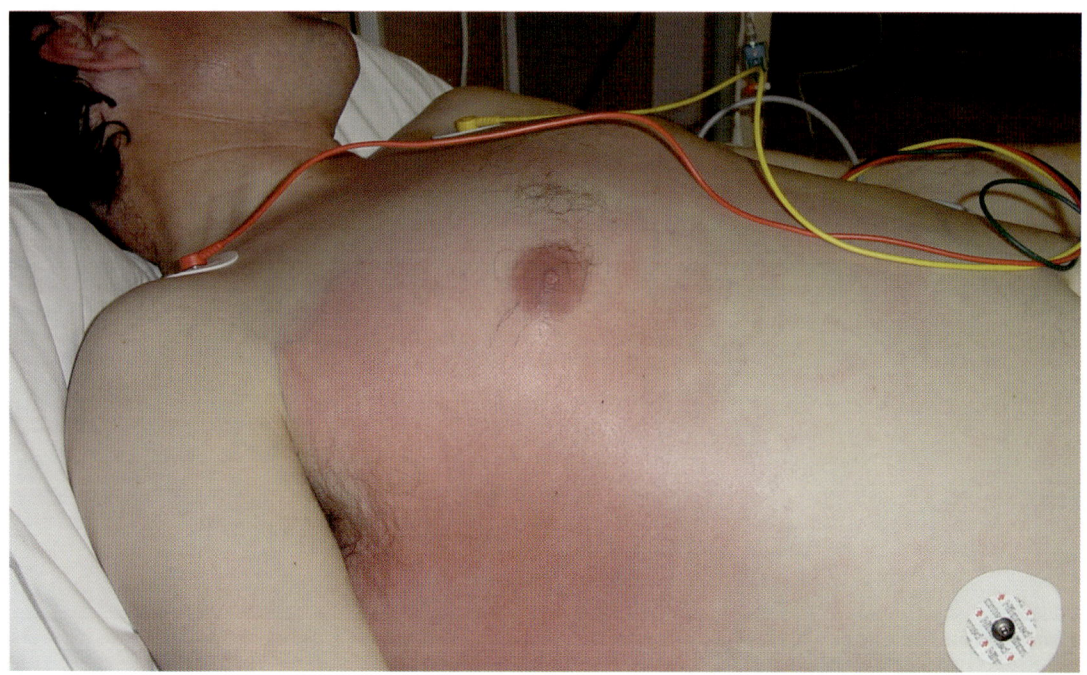

Me ill before my evacuation to Uruguay. Photo courtesy Derek Pettersson.

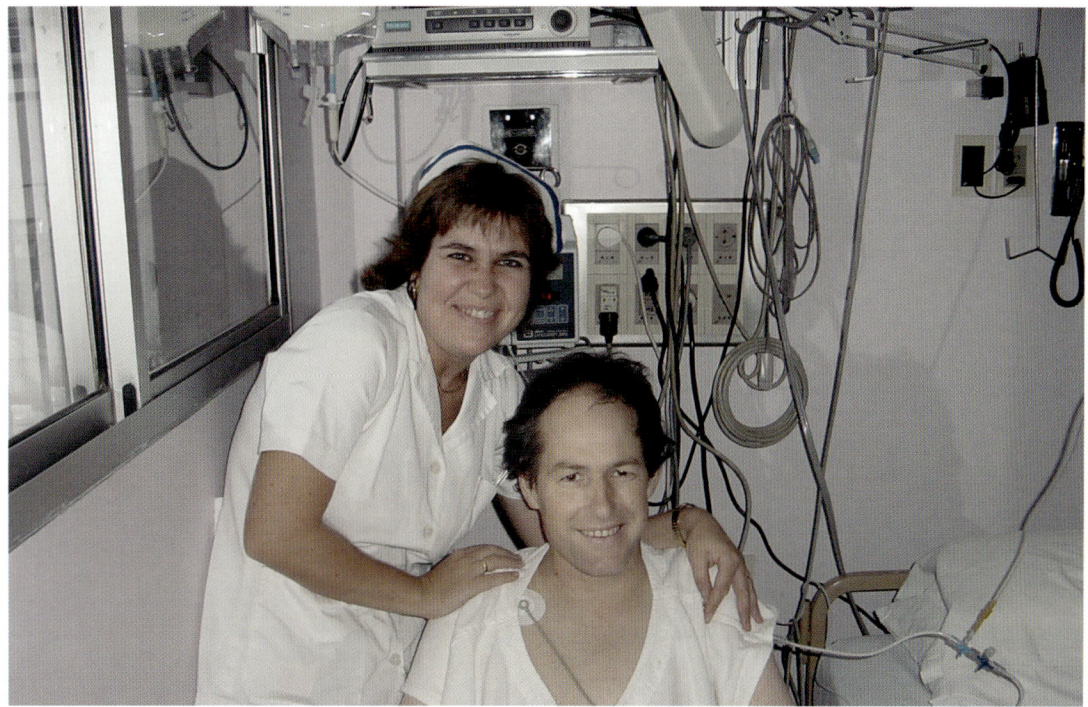

Me with Claudia, one of my nurses in Montevideo. Starting to get better.
Photo courtesy Derek Pettersson.

Feeding me up because I am a bit skinny, at Derek & Trudi's.

Dr Stanham with me and his wife when they visited the Islands in February 2002. I am back to full health.

One of the fishing competitions. Back Row L-R April Pettersson, Ron Dickson, Gina Tyrrell, Gary Tyrrell, Marie Ross, Derek Goodwin, Diana Aldridge, Hew Grierson, Tony Pettersson, Sue Smith, Trudi Pettersson, Me, Lucas Berntsen. Middle Row L-R Iris Dickson, Toni, Caris, Turpin (David) Ford, Ted (Michael) Jones, Robbie Todd. Squatting down L-R Bonita Goodwin, Brian Aldridge, Liam, Roy Shepherd, Shelia Jones and Derek Pettersson. Kids to the left James Tyrrell, Tonisha and Michael Goodwin. Family photo.

During my second term on Council. Standing L-R Clerk of Council Claudette Prior, Attorney General David Lang, Councillor Mike Rendell, Councillor Mike Summers OBE, Councillor Dr Richard Davies, Councillor Ian Hansen, Financial Secretary Derek Howatt, Councillor Richard Cockwell, Commander British Forces Rear Admiral Ian Moncrieff CBE, Chief Executive Chris Simpkins, me. Seated Councillor Janet Robertson, Speaker of the House D Lewis Clifton and Councillor Dr Andrea Clausen. Photo courtesy of Penguin News.

Gibraltar with Richard Cockwell during the CPA conference.

Outside the UN Building with Janet Robertson when we went to address the C24.

Opening the ferry terminal at New Haven. L-R Mike Rendell, John Birmingham, Janet Robertson, The Governor Alan Huckle, Me and Mike Summers.

The Governor rolls GH1 with his wife and two Dachshunds on board, after leaving the opening of the ferry terminal.

Building the cattle yards with Mike McKay and his team. L-R Basil Farria, Kenneth Jaffray, me.

Moving stock through Hells Kitchen now we holistically graze our farm.

Family at Wineglass on the North Coast of East Falkland.

Toni dearly to pluck up courage to do her bit for the Falklands, she educated the group on how the Argentines had laid mines rendering large areas of our home out of bounds.

We did have the opportunity to recharge our batteries and do some of the touristy stuff. We all decided to do the Liberty Island trip with Toni and I queuing to go up to the crown in the Statue of Liberty. I have never queued for so long. At one point there is a sign saying 'three hours from this point', but it is satisfying to say that you have done it, especially today while it is shut. Eric and Shirley were unable to join us because of Eric's sore knees, which was a shame. There were also signs saying 'no chewing gum on Liberty Island. No chewing gum in the Statue'. Talk about closing the stable door after the horse has bolted. This horse would have died of old age before the door was shut. There was gum everywhere. On every path stuck into any accessible nook or cranny. I reckon if the gum was cleaned off the Statue of Liberty it would amount to many tons. We made it to the crown but were not allowed up into the torch because of some safety issue. The latter part of the climb was a bit disconcerting because the whole statue vibrates in the wind as the thousands of us made a continuous chain from the bottom to the top and back again, each moving a few steps in unison every few minutes.

One of the spectacles of the whole trip were the showmen who entertain you as you wait for your turn to board a boat to take you out to the Island. There was one contortionist who I have never seen better on a TV speciality act. He was truly amazing at turning himself into all kinds of positions. Standing on his hands, putting his head back onto his bottom, standing up without using his hands from the splits position. He had such flexibility and poise.

Then you got the comedians working the crowds, getting great swathes of people laughing and joining in. There was a common theme to these guys – if you didn't laugh or join in they would suggest you came from Newark. Then there was a guy with a HUGE snake as thick as your leg that you could have draped around your neck and have your picture taken. All this and more was taking place as you moved closer and closer to the boats.

We did the Empire State building, although it is hardly the tallest structure in New York these days. In those days the twin towers dwarfed it. It was on the to-do list and I suppose the views were still pretty special overlooking the city. Eric and Shirley joined us on this excursion and Shirley looked at some souvenir spoons, although I think she put them back because she felt that they might be overweight for the flight back. Toni's mum was a keen collector of teaspoons so Toni bought one instead.

Toni was determined that we should go to a musical on Broadway. She had read somewhere that you can queue for cheap tickets in Times Square, and so that is what we did and got tickets to go and see *Smokey Joe's Café*. Eric and Shirley were unable to join us on this one because Eric suffers from tinnitus. It was a great experience and Toni and I clapped and participated until our hands hurt and our throats were dry. It was very special as a one-off.

Derek Millar and the Queen's stud manager

To finish this part of our story, one has to go back to Sussex Farm. We were home one weekend and Derek Millar, a friend from Mount Pleasant Airport, who had a cabin on our land, came walking into the farm. Derek walking was pretty unusual, he was out of breath and a bit red in the face. We gave him a beer and then after his rare exertions this meant that he needed to consume another. There was apparently no rush, but eventually he shared with us the fact that Sir Michael Oswald, the Queen's stud manager, was bogged at the head of our creek. He was out in the Falklands as the guest of Commander British forces and the driver had got the CBF's vehicle stuck.

Unbogging people was charity work and we did quite a lot, especially in the summer months when people would follow the clay track until they got to Sussex and then the valleys, ditches and soft mountain would claim most of the military drivers. The boards, jacks and rope were permanently in the Land Rover in those days before the roads, so we went off down to the head of the creek to see if we could be of service.

Sir Michael had got a little bit impatient, not understanding the social etiquette of drinking beer, having a chat and then moving on to business. He had walked down to Hells Kitchen and looked mightily relieved to see Derek and a rescue party.

So down we went. It wasn't that serious and we hooked on and yanked the Range (could have been a Discovery) Rover out of the mud. What amused me was Toni was able to pass the driver his wellies from the back so that he could get out of the vehicle. It was all good fun for us and an unusual experience for the CBF's driver and Sir Michael. The Queen's man said, 'Thank you very much, whenever you are in the UK pop in to Sandringham and have a look at the Queen's horses.'

Before we went to the UN, we had been invited to a garden party at Buckingham Palace but after much consideration we cancelled because it seemed impossible to meet the deadlines. Once in the UK however, tight as the deadlines seemed, it looked possible to fly back from New York on the morning and attend the garden party in the afternoon.

Once in the UK we phoned Sir Michael and they invited us to have lunch with them, which we pencilled in during our flying visit to see family and friends that seem scattered to the four winds throughout the UK. Coming down from Cumbria we were in casual mode, in fact we were a bit travel weary and looked it. So that we didn't disgrace ourselves we called in to Kings Lynn and purchased a shirt for Liam and me and then carried on for lunch with the gentry.

We found the place no problem and started driving up the long drive to the manor, stopping to change a few hundred metres in. We didn't think about security cameras or the like and I often wonder if in fact we gave the luncheon party a warm-up act courtesy of the people from the far-flung Islands in the South Atlantic. After we had changed, we threatened Caris and Liam to be on their best behaviour or else, and then carried on up to the house.

We were met like dignitaries, as the heroes that had come to Sir Michael's rescue when all hope was lost. Well not quite, but we did feel as if our efforts on that day had been appreciated which was very satisfying.

We had a lovely meal and somehow the conversation got round to hamsters. My take on hamsters is as long as they don't breed, the little bastards don't live for more than about 1,000 days. So you are just getting fed up with their perpetual scratching and wheel squeaking when they snuff it. One of the guests told us when she had a hamster and was cleaning it in the bathroom, she balanced the cage on the cistern behind the loo. However, the hamster managed to get out of the cage, fall into the loo and shoot around the S-bend, never to be seen again. What a grotty end, even for a rodent.

The children were allowed to leave the table earlier than the adults and for our two they had done miraculously well. They were ushered off in the direction of the nursery, that was rather grand. We were drinking coffee and talking about how great the Falklands is when Caris and Liam ran through from the nursery unable to contain their delight. 'Look what we have found!' They had found a burping and farting gun. Just as we thought we were going to lose our hero status and the Falklands' people were always going to be looked down on by the Oswald's, Lady Angela exclaimed, 'Oh yes, that's my grandchildren's favourite too.'

During the meal we just happened to mention the garden party and our dilemma and how we could have attended if we had only known. 'Oh, have a word with the vice-chancellor,' said Lady Angela to Sir Michael.

A few days later I get a call from Sir Michael saying that it is all back on for all four and could I ask Eric and then confirm. We spoke to Eric, but he didn't seem to be that keen so I phoned back saying we would definitely go but Eric and Shirley wouldn't. I had just put the phone down when Eric rang. He had had a change of heart and they wanted to go. I was in an obliging mood so I got back on to Sir Michael and he must have been, as well, so the garden party was back on and the debogging moved from being charity work to 'paid in full' category.

We had a lovely afternoon looking at fantastic horses that were as good as you are going to get. They made our old farm nags seem less-than-ordinary, which of course they are in comparison. However, I did imagine shepherding on these tall creatures and the work just getting on and off one and whether they would be good in the soft and peaty ground of the Falklands. The ultimate test would be trying to carry a sheep up front or all your dogs milling around as you're leaving home with perhaps one ruffian hanging from the horse's tail, something that wasn't unknown.

Everything seemed to flash by and it was soon time to say our goodbyes and we tore off to our next meeting of friends.

Back in New York, we went looking for an outfit for Toni at Sears for the garden party. The store was absolutely enormous, taking up a whole block in New York. It had so much choice it was confusing and something we were not used to in the Falklands. Eventually, with me on the verge of climbing onto the roof and throwing myself off, Toni chose her dress.

The Committee of 24

It does sound as if the New York UN experience was one big jolly, but most of our time was spend conducting bilaterals and attending functions trying to rally support for our cause. So the day came, after days of lobbying, to address the Committee of 24 at the UN.

Just Eric and I sat in seats to one side of the hall, looking over the area where the countries' representatives sat. Over to the far right sat the Argentine petitioners. When the Argentine delegation entered the room I thought they had bought the population of the South American mainland with them. Their group was huge and they all gave us a penetrating stare when they crossed the room to their area. In reality, there must have been 40 in their contingent and most of them glared at us as we delivered our speeches.

Eric's speech spoke of the Goss family and their part in the Falklands' early days. One Jacob Napoleon Goss built one of the most prominent stone buildings in Stanley in the 1800s. My effort was a little more abrasive, pointing out that both populations in Argentina and the Falklands were from immigrants including their present president whose family came from Syria, and then the similarities change with the Europeans wiping out the southern indigenous people – an act that was still going on long after the British settlement in the Falklands. Then the Argentine petitioners spoke and after them Guido di Tella, the Foreign Minister of Argentina. Guido hadn't been staring at us and when he stood to stand he soon left his prepared text and addressed us directly, changing from speaking Spanish to English. He spoke of the meeting with Norma and I, and how Norma had refused to shake his hand and then I had given him a film of Falkland propaganda. But his address was calm and again he appealed to us to find common ground. Then all the Latin American countries supported Argentina's claim, which I found the hardest part of the whole process, and I couldn't have felt worse at that moment than if I had been hammered with a length of alkathene piping. But during our long trip back to the Falklands I realised it isn't about ideals, it is all about politics and influence. South American countries' economies intertwine. Why would you upset a significant trading partner? 40 million people is a huge trading partner, which is slightly different to our 3,000 souls. It costs nothing to put the boot into the Falklands. It was a hit that first time, but we did have our own friends that spoke out for our rights.

The garden party

We had to fly out of Newark where it has been suggested that they don't have a sense of humour by the comics of Manhattan. I can't comment on their humour, but if our seats on the aircraft were anything to do with the folk of Newark, they are great people.

Somehow we managed to get promoted to the upstairs in the Virgin jumbo. When we had first got the tickets we thought we were the usual cattle class right at the back of the plane, but in fact I have never flown in greater comfort before or since that date. We had huge armchair-like seats, legroom of unheard of length, our own TV screen (pretty novel back then) and four stewardesses at the beck and call of perhaps thirty people. Toni and I took a lot of pictures to record the day that we flew first class on Virgin Atlantic.

Once back in UK we quickly made our way to the London office where we changed for the garden party. I couldn't help teasing Sukey, who I have already mentioned had such a keen eye for detail but also an awareness of social etiquette, which she delivered to you in a friendly, authoritative way you would expect from your older sister. We went downstairs all dressed up with me wearing my tie showing a chicken laying an egg into a basket. Sukey's eyes nearly popped out of her head as she spotted this affront to any sensibilities. 'You are not wearing that' in a sort of voice my sister Caris, used to use. So we left looking as smart as we could to attend a garden party, something many people would love to do.

We were just terribly impressed. Here we were among people who saw attending a garden party as the highlight of their year. Or one of their ultimate goals in life, and we were joining them.

Incredibly we hadn't been there very long when the heavens opened and it just chucked it down. Hard, steady, English rain. It wasn't long before we, and most of the other guests were drenched. Only a few wise souls had an umbrella. If that wasn't enough, thunder and lightning began in earnest. Most people just carried on making the most of things.

We had been told that we might be able to meet the Queen, but there were no promises. We went to her tent and were offered some unpronounceable tea (certainly unspellable). Eventually the Falklands' contingent stood before Her Majesty.

Unfortunately, as we were getting closer and closer to meeting the Queen, two old ladies sheltering under a tree got struck by lightning. An ambulance was driven onto the royal lawn and the ladies were picked up and taken away. Watching it all I had to pinch myself to make sure it wasn't a dream.

Apart from that, how was the
Royal Garden Party?

The Queen, unsurprisingly, seemed a little predisposed but then having two people struck by lightning in your garden must have been a new experience even for Her Royal Highness.

It wasn't long before everyone was leaving and we were all filing out. No one wanted to walk because it was still bucketing down so people were just piling into taxis and sharing the costs to train stations and other destinations.

Toni and I just legged it, through the streets, splashing through puddles and laughing all the way back to London office.

Sukey met us at the door and said 'Oh, and you looked so smart when you left.' She didn't have to say any more.

Toni's light coloured dress was ruined. The filth in the rain left rings aground the fabric that resembled the damp you see in old houses on the walls. We attempted all the tried and tested remedies to shift these marks but to no avail. The hat was saved because, as a true gentleman, I had wrapped the hat up in my suit jacket.

I should imagine that the royal household has long forgotten Eric, Shirley, Toni and myself, but I am sure the memory of two old biddies being struck by lightning lives on.

More tales from Council

There are a lot of amusing tales about Council but it would be difficult to write about all of them. One of the Councillor's spouses was a hard drinker and a bit of a comic.

We had a cabinet minister visiting the Falklands and so we organised a legislative dinner. The tables were spread through the room with six or eight people to a table. This individual thought it was highly amusing to pretend to blow their nose on the serviette, which was perhaps amusing the first time but lost its edge on the next twenty or so occasions. They then drank a considerable amount of port and kept bellowing for 'more port'. Eventually fed up with the responses from the present audience, they went down on their knees and asked their other half for money to go to their local.

This wasn't the only time that they showed that they weren't the most perfect ambassador for the Falkland Islands. In fact, they were closer to the Australian Cultural Attaché Sir Les Patterson, played by Barry Humphries.

It all came to a head and all spouses were banned from formal functions like legislative dinners because no one would front up to this individual and say that this kind of behaviour was unacceptable.

Everyone else from the officers and councillors and their spouses made a huge effort to make our guests at home and give them something positive to remember.

As Councillors it was an unwritten rule that you would take turns at sitting next to the VIPs, with the Executive Councillors taking pride of place. Spouses could have a mixed time unless they were extremely forceful. One kind and considerate soul, but who was a nightmare to sit next to because of his inability to talk about anything other than shop, was one to avoid.

It wasn't long into the term before the quiet and thoughtful Charles Keenleyside ran up the white flag and left the Islands. This was a most surprising event for me. I liked Charles. He always seemed so caring and considerate and dedicated to the Islands, but here he was off to pastures green.

So we had a by-election where John Birmingham was voted in. John was very different to Charles, and I would describe him as a good nuts and bolts man and he was to become, in my opinion, the hardest working Councillor at that local level. He would always be found ferreting around, finding out the ins and outs of things, responding quickly to the concerns of his constituents.

In the second half of our term it became apparent that John Cheek wasn't a well man, but he bore his illness with such fortitude it was hard to tell. John was pretty matter-of-fact about dying and came to meetings without a groan or complaint. Even at the very end he was 'just breathless' coming up the stairs in the secretariat.

John was not an easy man to get along with. He said what he meant and he didn't give a jot about what you thought, and any debate contrary to his view put John into instant attack. He was certainly one of our better politicians for having a wide political view of all the aspects of the Falklands. He had that rare gift of looking beyond knee-jerk politics and was a definite strategy man, i.e. if we build a new school and invest in education the end result will be a well-educated populous. This vision was present in most things.

John resigned nearly at the end of the oil legislation, but I knew he was all in because he would have wanted to be there at the end of this process. I phoned him up to say I was sorry that he had resigned and that I would pop up and see him when I was next in. 'When will that be Richard?'

'Three days,' I said. He just matter-of-factly said that he wouldn't be there then. No puffing, no moaning, no dragging a leg, he just got on with it until the end of his life. I could never imagine me dying with such dignity.

There were some that thought he was irreplaceable but of course no one ever is.

So our next by-election was held and on to the team came another big hitter and independent thinker – Michael Victor Summers. Mike was easier to get on with than John, but he had that same difficulty with handling a contrary view.

The four years at Gilbert House were marked by its porous nature and very little remained confidential. It seemed as if some people had a hidden microphone in the meeting room. There were several accusations, but nothing was ever proved and no one ever admitted to the crime. Everyone had his or her suspicions, and I had mine, but how could you ever prove it. I would drive home to Sussex, which would be at least a couple of hours plus, and someone would phone saying that they had heard this or that.

Guido di Tella

There was one secret we did keep in house however, and that was our dealings with Guido di Tella. We all knew that if it got out people would jump to the wrong conclusions and we would be hated with a passion.

Di Tella was trying to build up contact and trust between the Falklands and Argentina by sending gifts. Most of us used to laugh at some of these gestures and possibly many of his countrymen did too. One of his most serious proposals, which wasn't his idea but he delivered it, was buying every Islander out for £2 million each. It was a very divisive suggestion. Many Islanders were outraged that he was offering money for their birthrights but the wily Islanders had their own suggestion, which was to come up with the money to see if you're serious.

Eventually he made contact with Bill Luxton and they agreed to meet at a London restaurant. It was surprising in some respects because Bill was meant to be the most extreme hardliner when dealing with the Argentines, and had unflatteringly called di Tella 'a greasy dago' or words to that effect during his election speech in 1993. Di Tella suggested to Bill that it may be possible to get what we were after. That was self-determination.

That got the ball rolling and so the British Foreign Secretary, Malcolm Rifkin, and a group of Councillors including me met with di Tella. Di Tella believed he could deliver some kind of acceptance in Argentina of our own status but we had to work together. There were a few things that didn't make sense to me, but basically the core theme was that Argentina would drop its claim.

I know people said we were being naïve, but then we were being offered what most Islanders wanted and it was in our interest to pursue it until it was delivered or we called their bluff. If we had told the Falklands' public there would have been a rumpus, which would have certainly scuppered any work if di Tella was serious. The Menem government could have used that internationally to say 'look we gave them this opportunity to have self-determination and they deliberately worked against it.'

Di Tella, for all his eccentricities, gave us an approved status in Argentina, recognising us as part of the equation, something that the Argentines hadn't done in the recent past or since di Tella either. Before and now the Argentines think we are unimportant. Di Tella's initiatives were very hard to counter because they always seemed so reasonable even if, as some people have suggested, he was trying to hoodwink us.

Di Tella came to the Islands after Menem's government was succeeded. Menem had done two terms and under Argentine law he had to stand aside. Many Islanders tolerated di Tella but others saw him as another Argentine manipulating the situation for his country's needs.

Unless he was delivering a pack of lies, not just to us but also to the British government, I think he would have liked to deliver more but was unable to. If Menem had had more time who knows, but consistently Argentine politics conspires to ruin any initiative because it is never stable enough, for long enough, to sustain a hearts-and-minds campaign. A few more years of di Tella and who knows, perhaps there would have been a better understanding between them and us.

Before leaving this episode, I will always remember di Tella's daughter coming to the Islands and staying at the Malvina House Hotel while Guido di Tella was still Argentina's foreign secretary. She was sitting on a table next to our collective one as we were having a legislative dinner. Where else in the world would that happen??

Hay Management

One of the most controversial events of this Council was Hay Management, which was the name of the consultants that came down to look at pay and conditions in the civil service. The idea was to try and tie in the pay and conditions into a world structure so that the pay we offered would attract quality people to come and work in the Falkland Islands, and just as important if not more so was so that our own people would remain on the Islands and would only be tempted away by exceptional offers. This would apply particularly to the increasing number of students that were studying in the UK.

Of course the whole concept is difficult to deliver because everyone thinks they or their profession is worth more than the next. Also in the Falklands, we tend to personalise positions and instead of saying the fair wage for this post is this, we say that person isn't worth this or that.

I believe a lot of management jobs of those times got significantly increased.

One of the downsides of all that work is that the economy has not been able to keep pace with the wages in the rest of the world, so all the principles that made it a sensible programme have been by-passed and we no longer pay equivalent wages for management positions and so we struggle to fill some posts. The same could be said of all wages which affects the local community and the corporate standard of living.

Changes to representation

At the next election I was unceremoniously booted out of Council along with Eric Goss. There had been a constitutional reform that reduced the camp representation down to three and increased town up to five. Norma and Bill were returned and Richard Cockwell was voted in as the third representative from outside Stanley. I fought against the constitutional change, but I can't argue that there wasn't some numerical justification for doing it. The debate on the fairness of representation is bubbling away once again because of the disparity between numbers in camp and Stanley and there have been more moves afoot to reduce the rural representation again. Is a change fair numerically? Will it lead to an assembly that thinks of the Falklands as one entity? Hearing recently that at least one current member thinks that camp should be satisfied with a lesser telecommunications system, which is a huge change from past governments, I think not.

It will always be hard to deliver a one-country outlook when the camp experience on Council dwindles. Up to now, many of the town Councillors have some experience of camp but with the number of people outside Stanley shrinking rapidly, mostly in the late 1980s and 1990s, it is difficult to see how this first-hand knowledge will be maintained.

I had made some errors of judgement. I was too direct in challenging the future of the government farms that own one-third of the Islands' land mass and was being badly run with a top-heavy management team that the business couldn't afford. I am annoyed with myself even now that I couldn't convince my colleagues that I was right, even though Eric and Sharon worked for the corporation. Of course, I had an interest as well and lived on a non-viable farm, like a number of other properties, and my thrust then was to let farms in non-viable areas sell up to their neighbours which could make more farms have a future and the family in transit would move to a viable piece of the government property. To me this seemed a way of breaking the perpetual subsidies.

Of course, people on the government farms have felt vulnerable but it was clear in the 1980s that in local human resources FIC/FLH were going bankrupt. History has shown that there weren't enough local people prepared to work on these state farms and so people have come onto the Islands from Chile to take up work opportunities. There were local people interested in buying parts of FLH but they in turn have sadly been part of a process that has replicated buying small farms and most of the time for more money than the price that caused years of government subsidies in the first place. Many of these new farmers and the old guard have found other ways of diversifying to make ends meet, but with some of these new enterprises come new challenges like the slowing of farm development and the pressures on families as they work too hard or work apart.

Success and a medical emergency

Among my successes, which would be hard to challenge, was a first that I achieved in modern technology. The head of the computer section encouraged me to try and send an email back to the Falklands when I was overseas on government business. As a total technophobe I am one of the last people that you would expect to be involved in this way. So I dutifully sent an email back to Mike Peake. It was such a new and untried method of communication I didn't hear anything more until I returned home.

Mike was very excited but I was totally perplexed as he showed me the actual email that I sent. It was just a load of symbols and marks on a page. Apparently this was not a problem and Mike knew what had happened and how to put it right.

One really serious thing did happen in my first term which to Toni was life threatening. It was past the halfway mark in the Council and I had to go in for a few days. Caris and Liam had been asking for a flight in the Islander, so for a change I flew to town with them, with Toni joining us later coming overland. Toni hadn't felt right with a pain in her abdomen. She had a good idea what it was but after a call to a doctor they didn't make the same diagnosis, even though Toni put forward her fears.

While I was in town the farm work continued for Toni and one of the jobs was to saw down and cut up a cow to feed the dogs. It had already been slaughtered and sorted. She took the big bones around in a barrow. She then carried buckets of water around to fill up all the water containers as one does when leaving the farm for any length of time and probably carried out other heavy work besides. On top of that the drive to town was still quite arduous.

On arriving in town, the powers that be couldn't possibly see her until the next day at the pre-arranged appointment time. Toni went up to the hospital at the stated time and was taken in immediately, even being wheeled in a wheelchair up to the ward. Toni had suffered an ectopic pregnancy which if it ruptured could have been very serious indeed and the last thing you should do is to do anything strenuous.

We had told the children why mum was in hospital, which resulted in me being put on the spot. Heather, myself and the children were getting into the vehicle to go down to the hospital to visit Toni, when Caris piped up with 'anyway Dad, it's your fault mum is in hospital.' 'No it's not Caris, why do you think that?' 'Well, if you didn't put that baby there, who did?' Caris was only about eight at the time, but I guess growing up on a farm she knew how things worked.

It doesn't bare dwelling on, but this was another very important time when the gods were smiling down on us.

Toni went on to make a full recovery, but unfortunately my flippancy has never been forgotten when I suggested jokingly at her hospital bed that she would soon be home carrying peat buckets into the house.

9. ROADS

Bogged down

In my first term on council the road wasn't anywhere near Sussex. During that time the Property Services Agency were contracted to build a road from the L'Antioja to Goose Green. We, at about the same time, managed to get funding, before I got on Council, for a link track out to a non-existent San Carlos road.

Mike McKay bought his plant out to Sussex and we began putting in a road through our Horse Paddock. The original track came in from the east down a very steep hill, around the beach and up to the house. It was possible to get as far as the beach, but you were unable to get round to the house if the tide was in to any degree. If the tide was high you drove inland, through soft ground, from before Hells Kitchen, going up and down hills that most people outside the Islands would believe were too steep to drive on. All trips to and from the farm were planned on the tide. This new track was designed to overcome all these shortcomings and give one the ability to come and go regardless of the state of the tide.

These machines were a little tired and consisted of an old JCB-tracked excavator and an old Mercedes ex-Argentine lorry. We began winning material from the side of the hills and dumping it in the valleys after putting a culvert in. We hadn't really got warmed up before the excavator got stuck in a swamp and the more Mike tried to get her out the worse it got and she began settling down further into the ground. The problem really was that she was old and tired and didn't have the power to get herself out. Every time Mike asked her to track, and also pushed with the arm, the engine revs would disappear. We had to admit defeat once Mike found it hard to get in and out of the cab because the machine had sunk so low.

A solution was not easy because we were miles away from a road and it had already been a major undertaking to track the excavator there. It was time to think of all the options, which looked fairly bleak at first.

Government happened to have a very clapped-out caterpillar D6 bulldozer that North Arm Farm had managed to get to do some advanced road works out in their direction. North Arm had returned it, judging it to be next door to junk and useless.

I approached the government and asked if we could try using it. We knew it had been returned, but Mike felt that there was plenty of life and work left in it. Mike was a mechanical guru and machine resurrector and so we got our hands on the aforementioned machine.

I had to go to town, so Toni and I met Mike at Burnside, or to be accurate the hill in the Mares Park with the corral at the top. Our lorry was there with drums of fuel and excavator buckets and Toni was going to drive it home. Mike was there in the D6. Toni jumped into our four-tonne Bedford lorry with its large load and headed up the hill and I headed in the opposite direction to town.

I had only been in town a wee while when the phone rang. It was my father, who just happened to be out on the farm, to say that the D6 was bogged in the creek and what should they do. I suggested Toni should get the tractor and find some chain and tow some heavy posts down to the D6. The idea was that Mike would chain the posts to the tracks and he would be able to move back and out.

I didn't realise that it had been an eventful trip and that Toni had had enough. On the journey up, one of the gates hadn't been wide enough for the D6, so they had laid the fence. This entails lifting some standards out or cutting the wire that holds the battens onto the standards so that you can flatten the fence and drive over it. Mike had warned Toni about the tracks and how they might catch in the wire and to be careful, but when he went back for the lorry he wasn't as careful and went roaring over. To be fair, unbeknown to Mike, one of the Hiab legs was down and hooked up on the fence and sent Toni flying, painfully bringing the wire across her legs. The Hiab was a hydraulic crane that sat behind the cab of the lorry and had legs to put down on either side of the lorry when you were working the crane.

After this drama they carried on and then once again at the boundary they couldn't fit through the gateway. The fence was laid once more and the D6 driven across. They then backed up to the fence to hook on to a large, metal, luggage moving rack that we had got in a military sale and that we hoped to use as a cattle grid. Things didn't go well, resulting in Toni having to leap out of the way so as not to end up under the tracks and the fence getting torn down.

No one is sure what happened next but Mike drove down to the Creek and possibly followed the old horse track that cut across it (and was a much shorter route than following the coastline) and got bogged.

Toni had carried on in front only to look back and see Mike bogged in the sea. She continued towards home explaining the problems over the 2-meter set to my father. She left the lorry on the town side of the creek and walked back to the farm.

My father then spoke to me and I thought that the best bet was to pick up some chains and to drag some wooden telegraph poles down to the creek behind my tractor. I thought that if Mike chained them to the tracks of the D6 he should be able to back out.

Luckily for us, Mel Lloyd happened to be in the vicinity and he was happy to pick up the tractor, the bits and pieces and come to our aid.

Back in town I had made my apologies and gave the 110 everything to get back home as quickly as possible. I don't think I ever did the trip quicker under the same conditions.

It wasn't quick enough, however, because as I came over the hill I noticed not one machine out in the sea but two. As I got closer I could see that one of these vehicles was our farm tractor. Mel had driven our tractor down to the site of the bogging, driven to the front and tried to turn round. I just couldn't believe my eyes or Mel's stupidity.

Needless to say the D6 that we borrowed from the government, and which had not as yet contributed to our road effort, went under at high tide. The next day, bright and early, I took two long and thick nylon ropes down to the scene and Ron Dickson came over with his 4x4

County tractor. We drove the lorry back from Hells Kitchen, still with the drums of fuel and excavator buckets on board.

The Falklands can never be described as a place where water-based activities like swimming can be seriously considered, even on the nicest days due to the low water temperatures. So imagine the rescue party wading out in very cold water to the D6, as the tide was receding, to start the recovery attempt.

Mike took out the injectors as I drained the fuel tank and replaced the contaminated fuel. We then lashed Bedford wheels to the tracks because we couldn't get the posts close enough. The idea being that the machine would climb back onto them and, pulling them through the mud, would move us backwards and out.

All this work took hours but eventually we were ready to give it a go and miraculously the starter motor worked. Mike managed to get the engine fired up but a certain amount of salt water had remained in the fuel. So every time Mike tilted the machine by lifting with the blade or began dragging the wheels under the tracks huge columns of whitish grey smoke poured out of the exhaust and the engine would lose its power. Most of us were soaked and cold from chaining the wheels on to the tracks and one can visualise the sorry-looking team, as we still had to attach ropes. Chris Lloyd, Mel's son, was a young lad and deserves special mention because he was soaked up to his shoulders where he had been reaching into the water doing numerous tasks and although frozen to the marrow carried on helping.

The D6 just couldn't generate enough power to drag itself out and the tide was coming in. The final throw of the dice was to put the two large white ropes onto the D6 and to our lorry and Ron's tractor. I backed the lorry out as far as I dared without doing a Mel and then I charged up the beach as fast as the lorry would go, hoping with all the weight on board we would shift the bulldozer. Ron did a more sedate pull with his County. The lorry got to the end of the rope and then, with the weight of 12 drums of fuel and a couple of excavator buckets, we stretched the rope for a number of extra feet before the weight of the rope pulled the lorry back. Try again.

We were running out of time. With the second pull everything seemed to come together. The D6 engine, without white exhaust, the coordinated pull of Ron and me and there she was, tracking back up the beach to terra firma. So now the main event was over it was just a case of rescuing the tractor.

Mel had optimistically thought the tractor was sitting on the surface but we were unable to pull it up the beach with the white ropes. We had run out of time and the tractor suffered another saltwater bath as the tide came in and over it for the second time. It was time to adjourn for the day, cold, wet and partially satisfied.

The next day we did the same to sort the tractor by taking the injectors out and getting it going before we were able to drag it out. We learned from the D6 and brought a separate fuel source. It would have been difficult to sort the fuel tanks because they are very low on a Massey Ferguson.

Although we did use the tractor again for a few years it was never the same. The starter motor failed and the light metal like the cab, bonnet and the steel hydraulic pipes disappeared in front of our eyes.

Unbelievably, a couple of months later Mike and Adrian Minnell came flying over the hill heading east. We were returning from town. Mike said that that he had got the D6 bogged in the creek again. I was sure he was winding me up, but Adrian Minnell agreed. I was still reluctant to believe them, I knew if I went and looked and it was true I would be livid. Mike once again wanted to save time, and our fence, and because he was on his own he thought he could sneak around the crates of the boundary fence where it went into the sea. So he drove down the fence from the crates and gave it a go.

Once I got home I went up to the east-facing bedroom and looked down the creek and true enough there was the bulldozer bogged in the creek.

By this time, we also had a wheeled JCB courtesy of the government in support of the advanced road works. Mike dug a hole with this into hard ground behind the D6, and then pulled it back into the hole using the arm. Once the tracks were on hard ground she just drove back and onto the grass. As this happened the JCB ran out of fuel. Wing and a prayer come to mind. To this day I can't help admiring Mike's ingenuity and 'can do' attitude but wonder why he hadn't learnt from the first episode.

Back to the D6 on the beach, after the first rescue, Mike gave it an oil change and then headed off to the job at hand, which was to rescue the excavator.

We tried the easy options first like a straight pull but, even with the pulling power we now had, nothing happened. We then conjured up some blocks and tackle from places like the Estancia. Then Mike intentionally got the D6 bogged in the swampy valley above the excavator and attached the block and tackle. He put the loose end to Ron's 4x4 tractor and our lorry, which were joined together. These huge blocks just peeled apart and broke before anything meaningful happened. Mike then found some heavier ship blocks in town, we tried again and out she popped. Writing about it seems so easy but it was another cold and miserable few days wallowing in mud to put the chains on, trying this, trying that. It was around this time that I saw an advert on someone's satellite TV promoting a keep-fit stepper to mould you into the physical shape of your life, although how this could happen beats me. All it was, was a piece of plastic to step on and off. After all the jumping on and off the different pieces of plant, none of us should ever need to buy one. EVER. The operation was successful which made it all worthwhile and so now we moved on to building a road.

Building a road
Every cloud has a silver lining and the D6, which the FIG didn't want back, once on site was a huge asset for the money invested, which helped us carry out far more work than if we had carried on with just the excavator loading and spreading.

Although the front of the D6 flopped all over the place in an alarming manner the machine went on for years, doing a great job at spreading and compacting the road surface.

Now it was only the Mercedes lorry that was really the weak link. The body was incredibly tough but the clutch was more than suspect and with a big load you would let the clutch out and the lorry would take a while to move.

We did persevere with the kit at our disposal and built the road through the three valleys in our Horse Paddock, out and along 400 metres of flat stuff, then through another steep valley and then a few more hundred metres to where the San Carlos road would eventually come. The government employed Mike to improve the existing track from the Goose Green road towards San Carlos with a causeway in the Mares Park and joining up the old clay tracks at each valley.

We worked out of Sussex, which was a very interesting time. We would leave early in the morning with a packed lunch and a flask and travel up to the road head. Mike had an ex-military one-tonner, which he had put a tall hard top on the back of. He had then loaded it up with the tools of his trade. Spanners, socket sets, big cutting and welding gas bottles, oil and every other conceivable thing. We would work all day and return home for an evening meal.

Occasionally Mike would go to town and then I would meet him at the road, but this could be quite eventful.

One day I arrived and there wasn't any sign of Mike. As a workaholic he was always up in the middle of the night ready to start work so I thought that he had been held up by something, which could be anything. Puncture, breakdown, someone needing assistance. Still no sign so, because there wasn't much I could do on my own, I drove towards town thinking that if he had had problems I could help. I went right back to the gate at Burnside which was the first gate from the road in those days. I could see that he had been through because of the fresh track-grip marks made by his tyres.

I thought, 'that's funny, why haven't I seen him?' The track spreads all over the place but not that greatly. Anyway, Mike was behind me somewhere and I must have driven passed him. So back I went looking for his tracks. I began to notice every now and then in the grass very strange tyre patterns. It was as if someone had turned violently, stopped and reversed up. These marks vanished. After a bit of searching I found where Mike had turned off and, eventually, behind a ridge was the one-tonner.

I drove up and looked into the vehicle. There was no sign of anyone. I looked around and couldn't see anyone walking. I was wondering if Mike had just carried on to the road head on foot when another thought struck me. It's unlikely, but it's worth checking in the back before I go back to the work site. I opened the back and, in amongst all the tools, oil drums, rope, chains, jacks and other stuff was Mike, sound asleep.

It didn't take much to rouse him and he was soon ready for action. What had apparently happened was that the track rod end had come off and because he didn't have a spare nut he had tried to hammer it on tightly and sprag it. This would then last a hundred yards or so before it would come off again.

This unreliable feature did become a pattern over the period he worked in the San Carlos area. Arriving on site or coming home it was all a bit hit and miss. I wasn't always working with Mike and so I often found myself tracking him down to see where he was. Inevitably I stopped looking, thinking he would arrive when he was ready and this nearly cost him his life. If he hadn't been travelling in company it most surely would have. Coming down the track before the Creek at Sussex, in view of the bogging in the creek, was a gate. Mike was driving our four-tonner loaded with fuel on the way to the road. Mike got out of the truck to open the gate. The hand brakes on four-tonners are for decorative purposes only, so Mike turned the engine off and put it into gear. As he walked in front, to open the gate, the weight of the lorry pushed the engine over its compression stroke and it moved forward, trapping Mike against the gate. A fellow traveller realised what had happened and went and drove the truck back. The gate did have a tongue that fitted into a slot in the wooden post. Maybe it would have bent before Mike was crushed but I wouldn't like to bet his, or my, life on it. Mike's lucky star had remained with him, thank god, and I felt that I shared his good fortune.

Mike had proved that he could build roads and overcome working in isolation miles away from any assistance. He was rewarded by being given more work and eventually built the road through to San Carlos, from the PSA road that had been finished to Goose Green. He spurred off from north of Burnside. He did improve his kit by getting a bigger and better excavator, a D5 (the government 6 did eventually expire) and three Moxy dumpers for carting spoil. The Moxys beat the old lorry hands down and when three were working the road just shot ahead in leaps and bounds.

Mike got his hands on some mobile homes and built adequate accommodation for a small gang. I continued to work for Mike with what time I could spare.

Mike was married to Jeannie who would try and help Mike to keep focused. She would come out to see that all was well. Not wanting to get between man and wife the gang would scatter like goslings being attacked by a hawk, returning after a discrete period of time.

Mike was a driven man and if it wasn't for his determination the road would have been many years away.

The Moxy
During the campaign of building the road to San Carlos, one of the Moxys needed to have an engine change. So we lifted one out and another one back in with the wheeled JCB, in the middle of nowhere with the minimum of what you would expect in a workshop. On another occasion, the D5's engine gave up the ghost less than 100 metres from the Cantera Boundary Gate, slap bang in the middle of the road. Mike just left it there and concentrated on finding the bits to rebuild it. This he did with it still sitting in the road. Once fixed it carried on the job of spreading and consolidating. I don't think it was the big jobs but the nonstop fire fighting to keep stuff going, or upgrading a feature like the brakes in those early days that was impressive. I can't think of anyone else that nearly single-handed could have made this road happen with this kit.

We all got something out of this road programme. Toni drove Moxys and was promoted to operating an excavator in the quarry. It can be a monotonous job where you dig stone from the face and then swing round to put the load into a Moxy. After the first full day, Toni was still moving backward and forwards in her dreams. In this operation the excavator sat on top of the quarry, digging from the face as it loaded the lorries, moving back as the material was loaded. Toni found it disconcerting to sometimes find the power of the machine pulling her closer to the edge of the face.

The Moxys were okay, and they carried large quantities of material, but at first their brakes were not at all at their best. Slowly and surely Mike brought spares and improved many aspects of these machines. The downside of driving these vehicles before the brakes were adequate was that if you reversed them back down a hill the only way to slow them was to select a forward gear and, unless your timing was immaculate, the machine did a huge lurch ahead much to the annoyance of Mike, or stalled and went flying down backwards under no control what so ever.

The latter happened to me when reversing downhill from the Corral in the Mares Park near Goose Green when we were upgrading the old track. I didn't stay to find out what would happen. I knew that no engine meant no steering either, so I leapt out of the cab and watched as the Moxy charged backwards with a full load on board and the back end tip over. I waited for Mike to come over and call me a useless so and so, which he wasn't shy in dishing out, but he just said I should have stayed with the machine which is meant to be safer.

On the more level areas Caris and Liam used to ride shotgun and even steer when conditions were reasonable.

Building the culverts could also be fun if you work on it. The culverts are large diameter corrugated pipes made out of sections that you lay into the bottom of ditches and streams and the really big ones are put in to rivers to take the water through under the road. It is an art form to get the first few sections of a culvert together but once you get the tube shape started it is fairly straightforward, although more of a challenge because all sections have a thick coating of black tar. We went to pick up one culvert that was complete outside Goose Green which someone had burnt, getting rid of the tar along with any reasonable life expectancy. Once you had built more than about five feet one person would have to get inside the culvert to push the joining bolts through, as someone from the outside lines them up with a podger. A podger to those that are interested is a solid round three-quarter inch bar that has a point at one end. You put the point into the holes in each sheet of the culverts and then you lever the holes together to line them up. You can't bolt the hole that has the podger in, but the other bolts pull the sections together to get the remaining holes each time.

Lucy Ellis, straight from the Wild West Falklands, joined the team and she and I built many culverts with good humour. We made the time go quickly, telling the yarns of shepherds and settlement life when there were still a lot of people on the farms. It was a breath of fresh air when sometimes driving day after day could become a little boring. Lucy had been a shepherd at Port Stephens when it was a large farm and she had tried to work freelance after the farm was divided up, but like many family farms at that time everyone tried to do everything to keep costs down and work was patchy particularly outside the shearing season.

Some of Lucy's tales of working with a gang of shepherds were hilarious and some were disgusting in the extreme.

Most dogs like nothing better than to find a fresh cowpat or anything else with a ripe smell and get down and roll in it. Don't ask me why because that is a question for an animal psychologist. I just know that they do.

One of the shepherds in the Port Stephens' gang was notorious for leaving home a little unprepared and getting caught short and having to find somewhere discreet for their morning's constitutional. Imagine the scene as the gang were waiting for their absent friend to return to the group with them, all having a good idea for the reason for their absence. On one occasion one of the shepherd's dogs came running over the hill with a shirtsleeve stuck to his back confirming everyone's suspicions.

The roads improve

Mike had an aversion to sport, but I liked to listen to football on Saturdays and Sundays. He believed that it was impossible to think about your work if you were listening to a game of football. He had a novel way of telling you when your Moxy was full, if he was loading, by rapping the bucket onto the side the tipper. To stop this happening, you had to make a judgement on which bucket was the last and start off before he struck. If you were switched off through boredom or at an exciting part of a game or miles away thinking about something else, Wham! Your wakeup call.

Mike was a likeable rogue who would do anything for anyone but he did have a few rough edges.

So those days, of one day's travelling to get to town or home again at best, three days at worst, are over. A legal trip today is probably one hour forty minutes, less if you have a vehicle that can maintain that average speed of forty at all times. Yes, all the roads deteriorate during the winter due to water lying on the roads and frosts but it's a case of slowing down a bit to avoid the potholes. It isn't a case of bogging, waiting for or missing tides, beating the hell out of your vehicles on beaches and stony rough ridges or mile after mile of soft ground that works all of your engine, gearbox and axle components hard. These days there are numerous travellers throughout the year. In the days before the all-weather tracks, travellers were few and far between, particularly in the winter. If you broke down or got bogged, you were on your own unless you were lucky enough to be on the track at the same time as someone else. Today you are unlucky if you have problems and don't have another vehicle turn up.

So in most respects the roads during the Council 2005 to 2009 were a treat compared to the time before but with this Council the workload was many times greater so I was travelling a lot more.

Commemorating the war

There are many memorials dotted around the Falklands relating to the war and commemorated throughout the months that the war was conducted in 1982. We don't celebrate the invasion of the Islands by the Argentines, although for those that were involved we will never forget that day. The thing that we do celebrate is not the deaths on both sides, which to many demonstrate the foolishness of war, but the day the Argentines were beaten and their soldiers were returned to their own country.

Some people go to a number of these services but many go to the commemorations at the locations that they were involved in. The first of these services is probably the one for Nick

Taylor, who was shot down and killed attacking Goose Green. At Blue Beach it is Landings Day that many people Island-wide go to. Then there is the Liberation of Goose Green where people celebrate being freed by British forces. People in the settlement were rounded up and locked in the community hall for most of the duration of the war. Then there is the service at Fitzroy to remember the attack by the Argentine Sky Hawks on the *Sir Galahad* and *Sir Tristram*, which was so devastating. There are a number of other smaller remembrance services culminating on June 14, which is Liberation Day.

Because we live just over the mountain from Blue Beach, the place where the British troops started their campaign to remove the Argentine forces, we have made the trip to pay our respects at the British cemetery on May 21 each year. There has been the odd year that we haven't made it, but most years we are there.

In the early days, and for the best part of fifteen years, we would drive over in varying weather and track conditions to show our respects. The people of San Carlos would usually have a few drinks as they relived some of the events of 1982. Today, not all the section holders were even on the Islands in 1982, but most pay their respects.

Since the road goes all the way to San Carlos more people have driven out from town and Mount Pleasant Airport and, while this is always good to see strong support for this special day, it has led to a serious accident on the San Carlos side of the mountain.

Accidents on the roads

Toni and I do not profess to be experts on driving off-road or on the dirt roads but I think we are proficient and with years of experience do have a thorough understanding of what is involved.

We were driving over to Landings Day at San Carlos a few years ago and the conditions were very icy with a covering of snow. The thing to do is to keep the vehicle in a low enough gear so that you can keep off the brakes unless you really have to use them.

As we got near to the foot of the hill a vehicle was off to the left-hand side and it was obvious that it had rolled because it was a little battered and the windscreen was out. There were two people in the front seats and they were looking a bit dazed. Toni and I went over to them and they told us that somehow they had come off the road and rolled twice, maybe three times but they weren't sure. It was obvious that they were in shock.

Toni stayed with them and I went to get help. I drove up to the back of the cemetery and ran into where everyone was gathering and told the Commander British Forces what had happened and he dispatched a helicopter, with me along as guide.

While I had been away Gary Clements and Dr Davies had appeared on the scene and the latter went to see if he could give some assistance to Ivan Short and his wife. While they were assessing the situation and thinking about getting them out and into Gary's vehicle they heard another vehicle arriving fairly quickly. A military Land Rover came over the hill and, seeing Gary's vehicle on the road in front of them, jammed on their brakes and lost control. Gary was alongside his vehicle and the Land Rover headed for him. He jumped headlong into his vehicle but not quickly enough and ended up being caught by the front of the military vehicle. This vehicle hit Gary's vehicle as well and the impact threw them off the road and over a ten-foot drop.

Toni went to Gary because he was now a higher priority than the Shorts and Dr Davies jumped down the bank to see what he could do for the Land Rover full of service personnel. The people in the Rover were shaken but not badly hurt. Gary was.

Everyone seemed to be in panic mode and one of the people in the military appeared with a thermos flask and they were offering the victims hot drinks. Toni suggested that a hot drink wasn't advisable, which was confirmed by Dr Davies when he came up to see how Gary was. Toni then prompted someone from the crashed Land Rover to send a person to the brow of the hill to prevent any of the vehicles that were still heading to San Carlos causing more mayhem.

I had left with just the Shorts a bit roughed up and in shock, but returned to see a Land Rover off the road on the other side and the road full of people from the affected and passing vehicles..

Poor old Gary was in a bad way but Toni was able to bring all her nursing experience to bear and stood holding Gary's hand and reassuring him straight after the accident and during the painful operation of getting him onto a stretcher and out of the vehicle. They then strapped him onto a stretcher and then carried him onto the helicopter, which whisked him off to hospital

The story does run a bit further, when Toni was asked to give a statement to the police. We all were. My story was quite simple as I had missed most of it. Toni, however, had witnessed the whole event. She recalled what she had seen and the police officers took it down, but they suggested that it was far too detailed. Toni just told them that this was what she saw from an unobstructed view and that she couldn't help what she had seen. She felt that the police were saying that she had collaborated with Gary and this hurt her sense of honesty. I felt some sympathy for Toni who doesn't like even telling white lies.

We have always had a fear of coming upon a serious accident when people are badly hurt and then trying to cope. It isn't as if you can get on your mobile phone, although having said that there is patchy reception on the Mount Pleasant Airport and Darwin roads. Every accident is different but we have always felt that one would stay while the other went for help.

I always used to worry about Hells Kitchen before the roads, because even locals had their moments there. We have gone to rescue a few that have been on the point of balance on the side of these valleys. Then we got a road, which wasn't perfect because there was a cutting down to the floor of the valley where there was a gate until the government paid Mike McKay to come back with his equipment plus the government's D8 bulldozer and sort it out once and for all. Even then there weren't enough culverts to be able to sort out the second valley on the west side which creates a bottleneck in wet weather.

It was the first road into Hells Kitchen that caught a military family out in a big way.

We were lamb marking in Shepherds Brook and one of Caris' friends had run away after a disagreement concerning murdering goslings for the barbecue. We carried on and delegated the task of rounding up Teslyn to Mother and Father so that we could carry on. So off they went to find Teslyn and going through Hells Kitchen came across a short-wheel base 90 Land Rover off the road. We later learnt that its driver had tried to drive through this place in top gear and had lurched off the road. The children were strapped in their car seats and so were okay and so was the driver, but the woman had been thrown out through the back window and was lying by the stream. She was a physiotherapist and she said she had hurt her back and shouldn't be moved. The force of the crash had also ripped the back axle from the vehicle to give one some idea of the forces involved.

Mother and Father went to Sussex and rang the emergency services and then Bonita, who had also gone back to the house for something, came back to tell us what had happened. We weren't being unsympathetic but we thought it was pointless us all dropping everything and going down because a helicopter coming from Mount Pleasant Airport would be there probably quicker than we could get back, and so we carried on.

About an hour and a half later we had finished and packed all our stuff and headed home. Unbeknown to us the emergency services sent out a military police vehicle to confirm our diagnosis that we had a serious incident. I just couldn't believe it. What's more, they were breathalysing this squadron leader, as his wife lay badly injured in the grass. If it had been outside the summer, I think this lady would have suffered full blown hyperthermia rather than the mild case she had.

As the police were going through their questioning, our quads roared past with three children on each plus the clapped-out children's Land Rover with the driver looking through the steering wheel. The police just couldn't believe their eyes.

Once again we tried to give the lady some support as she lay by the stream and her young children ran up and down seemingly oblivious to the seriousness of the situation.

When the helicopter came in, it was flown with incredible skill into this valley onto a small piece of flat ground. After the medics got her onto the stretcher and had made her ridged and secure, a number of us picked up the stretcher, carried it to the helicopter and manhandled her in.

They had a very lucky escape and although she suffered from crushed vertebrae in her back she made a full recovery.

Today Hells kitchen is sorted and as long as you don't drive over the side it is perfectly safe.

Accidents continue to happen on our roads but they are so different from driving on tarmac. Since the introduction of road restrictions during adverse weather conditions like high wind speed, plus speed limiters on military and Service Institute Fund Rovers, the accidents have been greatly reduced. Our dirt roads are pretty good during the summer when they are graded and rolled but even then you do have to be aware of the loose stone that can build up into ridges.

For many years in the Falklands the road safety was very good, although there were some fatalities in Stanley. Outside Stanley, with the limited opportunities to go fast and vehicles not designed for speed, I can't remember any fatalities even when drink driving was involved. People would drive to and from two-nighters and drink a lot but usually the drunk driver would get stuck.

One of the practices in the runs before the roads was to have a beer or a tot at every gate. As you can imagine this wasn't designed to get you to your destination sober or slightly merry and did lead to some drunken escapades.

10. GROWING MUSHROOMS

And a medical situation (part three)

1999 was an eventful year for us because while looking for a diversification idea we were encouraged to pursue growing mushrooms. Most farms struggled in the 1990s to make ends meet and the smaller units were only kept going through different schemes produced by the government.

The mushroom idea was sitting on sound economics, with many tinned, dried and fresh mushrooms being imported into the Falklands at very high prices. So we did a bit of homework and decided that we should give it a go. Steve and Elizabeth Oliver had just done their tour in the Falklands and their niece and her husband were growing mushrooms in Yorkshire. Next thing we know we are off to Yorkshire to learn how to grow mushrooms.

It was a great thing to do, but sadly the more we got into it the harder it seemed to be for us to copy in the Falklands. Growing mushrooms in climate-controlled, triple-insulated tunnels was simple as long as you followed the recipe of when to heat and when to cool. Bags of compost would arrive in lorries with the spores already in them. These bags would be distributed in three lines. Two bags wide up each side and a row of four up the middle, and the tops would be turned down as they were placed. The temperature was then turned down and within days the first flush would begin and the mushrooms would appear.

When we first arrived we were put in a shed at the end of a growing cycle when things were slowing down. As beginners, being slow and ponderous, we could easily pick the mushrooms back so that there were no more to pick. As a picker, you sit on a trolley with a table at the front that has a hole to put a bucket and then different punnets for different-sized and quality mushrooms. You are armed with a little knife and the idea is to push yourselves along the rows picking and sorting as you go. So you picked, cut off the bottom of the stork into the bucket and then sorted them into button, medium and any that were misshapen into the 'bargain basket.'

We had a few days of speeding up and getting the hang of harvesting and began to think that we were the real deal. Then one day we arrived and encountered our first, first flush. This is the first cycle where you can see them growing in front of your eyes and even experienced pickers struggle to keep up with the growth. There was a team of pickers and we picked from morning to 10 or 11 o'clock at night.

The children were over in UK and had been staying down south with my mum and dad but they had bought them up to this lovely part of Britain to meet up with us. They had been with us for a few days all living in our accommodation. We came out of this long day and night picking and there were all these messages on our mobile phone getting crosser and angrier. Father was getting quite incensed. 'Where the bloody hell are you.' We hurried home to explain our inadequacies with the mobile phone and to explain the phenomenon of first flushes.

In the evenings, we would pop down to the pub, about 100 yards from the cottage that we were staying in. Dad and I would have a pint together and we would sometimes all have our evening meal there. On the wall of the pub there was a blackboard with a huge list of things that you could choose from to eat.

On one of these occasions, we were no more than 20 feet away from the door when father went a purler. When we went to help him up, even though he hadn't hit his head, he was unable to stand up.

We got him into the pub and sat him down so that he could collect himself, but he couldn't speak properly and he didn't improve. We didn't know what was happening but suspected that it was something serious. In the setting of a pub everyone thought Dad was pissed but we hadn't made it as far as the bar. We made our way back to the cottage, but were worried so Toni returned to the pub and phoned a duty doctor who advised that we take father to Catterick Garrison for a check-up. We felt that he had jumped to the conclusion that dad was drunk.

I rang Phil and Jane, who were part of the family that was teaching us about mushrooms. Phil advised that we call an ambulance. The kids were worried in their own ways, wondering what was going to happen, and Caris was anxious but also caught up with the excitement of the ambulance's siren and flashing lights as it entered the house courtyard. Father made a big show of smiling and waving as they carted him off. The ambulance took father to North Allerton Hospital. The service was very slow and Father waited a long time to see anyone.

We had just moved from the mushroom side of things to the compost operation, which was in Lancashire. We would leave Yorkshire early in the morning and bomb over the moors to Lancashire to work and study the compost business and then tear back to base to wash and brush up and then quickly up to see Father in North Allerton General.

The hospital was grim and short of a sense of urgency. There were bottles of pee propped up behind the doors and we were witness to some poor sod asking incessantly for a thing to pee in and eventually wetting the bed.

Poor Dad was in bed but remaining cheerful, which was difficult to cope with as he didn't know Mother's name or mine or Caris', my elder sister. It was awful and doubly so surrounded by institutional squalor and neglect. Dad was unable to coordinate the actions of his left side and while eating a meal swept the food onto the floor.

Father, who was in such a pitiful state, wanted to leave the hospital and was vocally demanding his clothes. One had to admire his spirit. Then we had a classic catch-22 concerning the ambulance to take him down south back to Essex. The system made it virtually impossible for an ambulance to be able to take Father home. They needed the ambulance in North Allerton, and a bed to be available in the hospital in Chelmsford at the same time, but the two never seemed to coincide. Along came the dependable Tom King, my brother-in-law from Essex, and he and Mother between them got Father home. The hospital that had been unable to arrange the transfer helpfully waived all responsibility. I am sure if we had had to wait for an ambulance Father would be buried in North Allerton.

Back to the 'nothing is ever easy', on one of our many flying trips between Yorkshire and Lancashire the exhaust fell off our hire car. Low Cost car hire, surprisingly had never been heard of before in Yorkshire so I had to phone the Low Cost only office, where the owner and only employee of Low Cost said that he was prepared to pay for the repair.

We went back to mushroom growing.

A medical situation (part four) with a sad end

Meanwhile other issues were unfolding on the other side of the family and Heather was diagnosed with liver cancer. She and Tony were down in Bristol while Heather went down the path of radiotherapy and chemotherapy. On Friday nights we would get in the car and head down to Bristol.

We did have a little bit of time to ourselves so we were able to shop in the local town, Leyburn, and have a look around. We happened to have a look at some of the properties in the area, in a couple of estate agents. We were totally gobsmacked by the prices of property in this lovely part of Yorkshire. Even a pile of old rocks was worth £30–40,000 or more as barn conversions. It seemed that a lot of wealthy folk from the Midlands had second homes in the area. Great for these folk getting away from Birmingham and places, but not so good for the young local, first-time buyers trying to get on to the property ladder.

As we would be heading for Bristol we would meet the hordes leaving the Midlands for their weekend retreats. We would spend quite some time gridlocked as this migration eventually dispersed in a northerly direction. If an accident occurred, and it often did, everything ground to a halt for hours. So we would fight most of the length of England to get down to see Heather and Tony only for our return run to coincide with everyone else's. We found it a living nightmare and also such a waste of life. In our case, we only had to suffer it over a number of weeks, but most of our fellow road users must have had this experience anytime they wanted to get away.

It was great going to see Heather and Tony, but it was pretty boring sitting around looking at each other. We did try to get out and about but the treatment didn't leave Heather with spare energy.

Eventually we toddled back to the Falklands, care of the air bridge, and slotted straight back into life.

Heather and Tony followed us a while later. Heather had seen her specialist and she told us that he said she was cured, and that she didn't need to go back for any more treatment or check-ups. It didn't sound quite right but none of us challenged this prognosis. I think it is what we all wanted to hear, but when cancer is involved one always seems to need check-ups.

Sadly, over a short period of time it became apparent that Heather was getting weaker and frailer. In my own way I try not to dwell on illness and the pessimistic viewpoint and I still had Heather returning to full fitness when it was obvious to the rest of mankind that this was never going to happen.

The prognosis was not good heading towards Christmas and we were advised to get the Christmas period behind us and then take it from there. We carried on living our busy lives but popping in as often as we could.

Heather was in and out of hospital but Derek and Tony kept us up to date. I was still thinking that we had a couple of months. A few days before Christmas the phone went and it was Tony, 'Get in as quickly as you can. Things aren't that good with your Mum.' We rounded up the kids and headed for town as fast, but as safely, as we could.

Heather died while we were coming in. We weren't even close to arriving before she died. We were taken to a small room and told as a family by Dr Barry Elsby. It was very, very sad. We all hugged one another and cried. Then we were asked if we would like to see her. Caris initially wanted to go and see her Granny but thankfully she decided against it at the last moment. I thought this was good judgement and would enable Caris to think about all those good times rather than the body lying on the bed all empty and vacated.

We were all quite stunned because Christmas and the races had always been a special time for Heather. She always took great interest in the horses and gave a prize for the best-dressed horse. She wanted us to carry on and we did our best to carry out these wishes, but it was far easier said than done.

Toni felt guilty that she hadn't given her Mum more time, especially on our last visit to town before Christmas. Heather had stayed at home waiting for her, because by this time she was mainly living at the hospital. However, like all busy mums at Christmas, Toni had been trying to pull it all together for her family, buying gifts etc, and only got a fleeting visit to the hospital before we headed home again with promises to see Heather for Christmas. Of course, as a mum in her own right Heather, I believe, would have understood perfectly, but Toni still felt that she could have made that extra effort. Hindsight is a wonderful thing and is often referred to but if the hospital's outcome had materialised we could have invested a lot more time. It wouldn't have been beyond our means to take December off if only we had known.

So Heather's funeral came and we all trooped down to the church and sang hymns and thought about Heather's life and the contribution she made to ours. I remembered the time that I was walking back from San Carlos and Heather came to meet me riding Silver and leading Bluey. Heather knew that I didn't like riding Bluey and so when I ungratefully said that I would rather walk she thought it was the biggest joke ever and swapped the gear over as she had intended to do all along. She often told this tale with great glee.

Heather was a dedicated horse and dog person and was forever looking after farmers' dogs that had been sent into town to the vets. She would also help people move horses from yard to yard in Stanley if people went away.

A couple of jockeys approached Toni at the first day of the races and asked if they could ride behind the hearse on the way down to the cemetery to which she agreed. The funeral was to be held on what was the second day of the races, so the Committee suspended the afternoon's races as a mark of respect to Heather, and so people could attend.

The funeral was well attended but as we came out of the church there were not two but eighteen horses there ready to follow the funeral procession down to the cemetery. Even Diana Turner, who hadn't ridden a horse for years and wasn't particularly well herself, climbed on a horse and rode down. Heather would have loved to be taken down to her final resting place in a horse-drawn carriage, but to me this spontaneous acknowledgement and demonstration of appreciation by these horse folk for another member of their fraternity couldn't be beaten and was what made Heather's funeral special. This act made Heather's funeral one of the most moving that I have witnessed.

We did carry on through Christmas and, although not a total success, no one succumbed to the emotional upheaval that we all felt. Heather was only 58 and far too young to die.

Heather had been a big part in our lives and like many things we took it for granted. But when she wasn't there we all missed her sorely. Toni had spoken to Heather on nearly a daily basis from when we moved to Sussex and she was one of the first people to share our successes and failures. Before the phones, Toni used to relay on the 2 meters through the Estancia. Then Toni spoke through the Education Department's 2-metre repeater on Pebble at night to pass on the day's excitement or not. On one occasion Toni walked to the top of Bodie Peak to be able to speak directly to her mum. Eventually we got the phones and that communication continued.

We went through a heavy grieving period where Toni felt the guilt severely and how we should have dedicated more time to her mum in those last few months. I had my own grieving period but I tried not to revel in the misery that this death had brought and would try and focus on all the positive memories over the years.

We thought Caris would be devastated but she seemed so strong and people told her and Liam how brave they were. It was the little things that showed us how she felt, like the picture that she found of her and Granny that she mounted on in a frame and put by her bedside. It wasn't until years later that she was able to express her sorrow.

Fundraising
In a small community people are well aware of illness and whose got what. It generates a feeling sometimes that we aren't a very healthy community. Older members of our society often say that things were never this bad years ago. Cancer seems to be ripping through our community, but it may be that diagnosis is so much better these days and it just appears that way.

Serious illness in the Falklands is complicated and things like cancer means that you have to go to the UK for treatment. The Falkland Island Government pays for this but families and individuals sometimes struggle financially in these situations. There are a few organisations that fundraise and support these people with cash to help them cover extra costs.

With our family, like many others, having this brush with cancer we have tried to fundraise within our group to support these charities.

The first memorable effort was a head shave where we all went to Egg Harbour, an outside house belonging to Goose Green. There were three of us that were sponsored to have our heads shaved and with extra money raised if it was shaved off in a certain way. An example would be to leave a cross or a fringe. Toni was cutting and shaving the participants.

As the evening wore, on others were encouraged to have their hair shaved off for extravagant sums of money. With all the sponsorship and 'specials' we raised £1,000.

Derek and Trudi, my brother and sister-in-law came up with an idea to raise money with an annual fishing competition carried out in our farm's creek and by their cabin. The rules and regulations changed over time, but basically we would fish for a specified period and then it was prizes for specific categories. Most fish, biggest fish, biggest trout with a trout counting as double weight.

We would then have a big barbecue, a few beers and then a raffle and auction of donated items.

These events were epic, with the competitive spirit moving into other areas such as cheating at the weigh-ins (by doing things like filling your fish with stones), jumping gates with youngsters, swimming in the sea and much more.

Unfortunately, this fundraiser has stopped due to Derek and Trudi working solidly through the summer at Volunteer Point looking after the biggest king penguin colony in the Falklands.

A medical situation (part five)

I was driving wool into town in 2001 on the back of our ex-army four-tonner lorry. Climbing the hill after Swan Inlet the water pump failed, but as luck would have it Toni was following so we went back to town and I got a lift back to Sussex where I took another pump from one of the lorries that I kept for spares. I then got back to the lorry and fitted the water pump on to it. Unfortunately, it didn't work and it was leaking, but by this time I was running out of daylight and I was feeling ill so I started walking in the direction of town. Toni was in town shooting at the full-bore range, then came out and picked me up and took me into town. The next day we went back out and tied a tarpaulin on the bales on the back of the lorry, or rather Ted and the others did. Our Land Rover was playing up because one of the injector pipes was leaking. Ted and Shelia were on the track with us as we limped along. I felt awful and when we got to Sussex I went straight to bed without so much as a wash.

I rolled around and groaned once more. 'You make such a fuss when you're ill, I'm off to sleep upstairs,' said Toni. I hardly noticed and graced her departure with another groan.

The children had had flu at the school hostel laying them low. So low in fact that they had wanted to come home – something that was unheard of. I thought no wonder they hadn't bounced back with their customary energy if they had felt as rough as I now did.

Living on a farm at the end of a long season I didn't really blame Toni for wanting some uninterrupted sleep.

I'm not sure that she went early enough because she was still slightly gruff when she appeared the next morning. 'You really smell. You'll have to have a bath.' Then off she went to run it.

I felt as if I had the mother of all hangovers and had a pain in my right chest muscle. I bumbled through to the bath, throwing my night attire into the washing basket as I went and climbed in. Toni who was still there looked me up and down and said, 'I don't think you've got flu, you're bright red down one side.' I hadn't noticed but I was cherry red down my right side. I also looked a bit like Pamela Anderson with the amount of swelling on that same side.

The primary care for everyone outside Stanley is by telephone, where a doctor's slot is provided between 9.30 and 10am. I spoke to Barry Elsby and described my symptoms, still thinking that I had flu. It wasn't until much later that I realised that this phone call probably saved my life. Barry, a no-nonsense doctor who didn't hand out drugs without very good reason, prescribed me antibiotics. Each farm has a small medicine chest, which has many of the commonly used drugs in it, including penicillin. These drugs had code names to help the rural layman identify the drug rather than struggling with some of the more unpronounceable names.

I continued to get worse, starting to vomit and feeling awful. Toni went back on the phone and a plane was arranged to pick me up from San Carlos.

Sod's law had it that our 110 Land Rover, which we had dubbed the white elephant because it had a capacity for needing an endless supply of spares and mechanical attention, had a split injector pipe and now wouldn't go. Our nearest neighbours were able to help but only just. Ted was in the north of East Falklands picking up rams, but Shelia was able to come over in an old box-shaped Suzuki jeep. These jeeps were tough, rugged little work vehicles but rough, jerky machines to travel over tracks in.

Shelia greeted me with 'If I didn't know you better I would think you were dying.' These were words that were to haunt her over the next few weeks. Off we went with the Suzuki, pig rooting on every little ripple of the dirt road and camp.

Everyone pulls together in an emergency and as we arrived at the airstrip Sheila and Terence McPhee were there clearing geese from the airstrip and raising the windsock.

I felt grim, but not so ill that I couldn't get into the plane. Troyd Bowles was the pilot and because there was no one else on the plane I sat alongside him for the flight into Stanley. It was an uneventful flight apart from the air traffic control making Troyd (and me, because I had the ear phones on) aware that there were two Tornados in the air and in our vicinity. We did see them in the distance but I couldn't help wondering if a fast jet pilot and navigator would notice such an insignificant plane as an Islander as they flashed by.

Freddie Ford was at the airport as I got out and it was then that I realised that all was seriously not well because I was unable to walk in a straight line and swerved out to one side as I made for the airport building.

The ambulance took me to hospital and I was soon in bed. My memory becomes a bit patchy but I remember different people coming to see me. Turpin commented that they might as well take me to the tip, which was the usual banter you would expect, but at that moment in time it was pretty close to the bone. A locum doctor took charge and went through the usual procedures, like taking my temperature, blood pressure, took some blood but the thing that really excited them was looking at the ever-growing redness, which was all over the right side of my torso.

The hospital's digital camera was broken so Derek P. came up and took some pictures with his and sent them off to the UK to see if they knew what was wrong with me. My illness was obviously trying the collective knowledge and skills of the hospital and although I can't remember it there were three doctors at the bottom of my bed at one stage flicking through a collection of medical textbooks.

I started to be sick, even though I wasn't eating, and provided for this activity was a grotty cardboard thing. It wasn't something decent that you could really hurl into like a bucket. I used the loo, which wasn't that easy trailing my portable drip along with me. Things got from bad to worse and I found myself in intensive care behind the nurse's station. I also suffered the indignity of having a catheter inserted. The one thing that is really etched on my memory is when they decided to operate on me. The surgeon was Dutch and he came and spoke to me about the procedure. I had seen enough of *Holby City* and *Casualty* on TV to know that as a patient one should ask some intelligent questions. I REALLY wish I hadn't.

In a calm and friendly manner, the surgeon told me that they might have to remove the chest muscle on the right side and then when he saw or smelt my fear he went on to say that a plastic surgeon should be able to rebuild it at some stage.

Concerned?! I was bricking it.

The time came and I was wheeled to the operating theatre and had all these faces peering down on me as I disappeared into sleep. The last person I remember seeing was Mandy Bonner.

Funny old thing, but the first thing I thought about when I came round was how much of me had been fed to the hospital pigs (joke).

It is human nature to bemoan one's luck and I do my fair share, but luck was with me on this one because apart from a cut from about my breast bone to under my left arm I was still whole. They left it open because air was meant to help my condition. It was quite a wound and I couldn't see how it would heal without stitches.

It was at about this time that they said that I was being sent to the Hospital Britanico in Montevideo, Uruguay. In the Falklands this was the height of seriousness because I couldn't be dealt with here and so it was considered by some to be the last resort.

Toni had phoned the UK to tell my mother that I had been taken into hospital but not to worry. Now things had changed Toni phoned Sally to pass on the bad news and delegated the job of informing my mother.

Later Sally related the visit to Mum and how when she delivered the news she went rigid with fright and normally a huggy sort of a person, she couldn't be embraced

Heading to Montevideo

Although I didn't feel as if I was dying, the decision to fly me out made me consider the possibility. I think Toni and I had a pretty open relationship and discussed all topics. All that is, apart from death. I felt that I should tell Toni that if I did die I had had a great life and that she, Caris and Liam needed to know that and then to get on with the rest of their lives. Of course, this topic would have been better debated before any crisis and the talk of dying just frightened Toni.

During this time the most painful procedure was carried out on me, where the surgeon pushed a mile of pipe into the artery in my neck so that the drips would pour directly into my heart. It was explained to me that they needed me to be responsive for this procedure and that was why they hadn't used any painkillers. I was able to help them out with the responsive part.

I had to be lashed onto the stretcher, which could have come out of a medieval torture museum, to be carried on to the Search and Rescue helicopter that was going to fly me from the football pitch to Mount Pleasant Airport. I lay on some heavy leather straps that came around and plugged into a large drum-like object that then sat on my chest.

I hate being confined in small places and even the modern tapered sleeping bags make me uncomfortable, but it was all to cater for my safety and security.

Family and friends came to say goodbye, but I can only remember Toni, Caris and Liam, Derek and Trudi and Tony P. It just seemed to me that Caris and Liam in particular didn't seem to be unduly upset, just totally stunned.

Strapped to the stretcher I was moved out of the hospital and into the ambulance and driven down to the football pitch where I was manhandled into the bright yellow Search and Rescue helicopter. There were a few more people I knew and there were shouts of farewell just to help me on my way. Karl, Ted and Shelia's nephew, who knew me well, was one of the firemen who was in attendance. His boss told him not to come into the helicopter, but Karl defied him as he said I was his friend and he wanted to say goodbye in case he never saw me again. Caris recalls overhearing some cheerful soul suggesting that this was the last they would see of me and her thinking 'but that's my dad.' I had my own medical team including doctors and nurses. I began to know what a sheep feels like when he gets stuck on his back or perhaps like a tortoise completely and utterly helpless and at the mercy of others. Doctor Diggle had a machine that could vacuum up sick if I was to chunder while lying on my back. It seemed far simpler to just let me sit up.

In this entourage was also a military doctor who was able to tell me what was happening in the helicopter. I am sure he was being sympathetic and helpful, but in an ungrateful moment I felt patronised. Did he think just because I lived in the Falklands that my normal transport was a horse and drag sleigh? I knew the ruddy thing was going to make a noise when it took off and the motion was going to be whatever.

The vibration of the Sea King went right through me as we flew those twenty minutes to Mount Pleasant Airport. I felt like a child as I lay incapacitated on my back asking Doctor Diggle how much longer? The military doctor was able to answer in that age-old way, 'Not much longer.'

On landing we were taken to the medical centre and by this time I was feeling every tiny bump. In fact, any movement was cruel.

While I was being cared for another drama was unfolding. There were two doctors at the military base and the senior man was hoping to accompany me, but he couldn't leave without the other doctor being on the base. Far from being ready to cover, the other guy was relaxing, incommunicado, fishing near Swan Inlet.

The military doctor was unable to travel with the party, and he was not at all amused, but he did send his own team to complement the civilian one to keep a close eye on everything.

The aircrew must have got the manifold temperature just right because we were called forward to catch the plane. Once more, we were bundled into the ambulance and taken out to board the Hercules. It didn't take long before we were rumbling down the runway and taking to the skies and heading for Montevideo, Uruguay.

The Hercules is an awesome aircraft but no one could ever suggest that it was designed as a luxury airliner. The inside of the airframe had been changed to one which could hold stretchers, although I was the sole incumbent. So there I was lying on this purpose-built frame with drugs trickling into me through the pipe into my neck and monitors recording my pulse, blood pressure and whether I needed a gin and tonic.

Time dragged but I couldn't sleep and after a while my oxygen levels plummeted and so they clapped an oxygen mask on my face. There wasn't a safety brief, food, and no in-flight entertainment, just a concerted effort to get me to a modern hospital to save my life and all I could do was vomit my appreciation.

Toni had been allowed to sit in the jump seat in the cockpit for the journey, which was good as she is not the best at flying. She listened to the pilot inform the Argentinian authorities about our position and received nothing in return. As we came into Montevideo's airport the plane flew over a beach crowded by bikini-clad women, which seemed to brighten the aircrews' day, and they joked that they may have to stay the night in Uruguay.

We landed and the back ramp was lowered. I was still cast but I would have to do something to get out of the plane. Two porters arrived but they didn't seem to have a clue about what to do and to be totally frank they didn't look like anything I'd seen on any medical soap I'd been subjected to. I kid you not, these guys looked like close relations of the Blues Brothers, with heavy dark glasses and hair slicked back with an abundance of hair gel.

The restraining harness was removed but I needed to get up and so the local nurse offered me her arm. Lisa had done a great job of looking after my medical needs since leaving the hospital in Stanley, but she was a slight lass and I felt sure she would disappear over my shoulder if I tried to heave myself up because I was still on my back.

Working together on our family farm I knew that Toni had built up her strength wrestling with milk cows, rolling wool bales and pushing and shoving sheep at the drafting pen. I called Toni over to pull me up and I was soon on my feet. I turned round to lie on this trolley thing with all the monitoring stuff and drips etc, that the Blues Brothers had brought, and they wheeled me off the plane and down into another ambulance.

On the way to hospital
The ambulance left the airport and headed for Hospital Britanico. I felt okay, in fact a long way from death, but every bump that we went over vibrated right through me. The ambulance was a small vehicle with tiny wheels that made it feel at times as if we were driving down a cobbled street. The movement was getting to me and I began to beg in my mind for the

journey to end. I once again asked Doctor Diggle, who was in the ambulance with me, how long before we arrived at the hospital. I knew asking wouldn't make a blind bit of difference, but I still asked the question.

I was taken into intensive care and it was like being in a penguin rookery or in the houses of parliament when they are debating. There were interpreters, military, civilian, Uruguayan nurses, doctors, the Blues Brothers, the works. I felt like crap.

The medical staff started changing the kit from our Falkland stuff to their gear and then they hooked up a couple of more bags from a rack hanging from the ceiling. One looked like a plastic bag full of milk. All these lines went down into this manifold which delivered everything through my neck. I had an additional drip into the back of my hand. A nurse in a pure white uniform came and took some blood and another ordinary nurse put an automatic blood pressure band on the top part of my arm and this thing began to squeeze my arm every twenty minutes, day and night for most of my stay. It had a tight grip.

The next three days are slightly jumbled and confused as I hallucinated like a seasoned pop star. I imagined a man from the countryside driving into the town on a motor scooter with a pack of Alsatians to make a point to government about scrap metal. I imagined people shooting at them from the rooftops including the hospital roof. I thought someone had been shot in the hospital grounds and that an argument had broken out among the staff because some felt that they couldn't stay when their jobs were to save people and not to be a part of murder.

At one stage all the Uruguayans spoke perfect English.

I also clearly saw Uruguayan and RAF planes on exercise over the hospital and heard a vehicle with a loud speaker circling the hospital threatening to bomb it because there was someone from the 'Malvinas' in there. I even thought that they were holding a wedding in the hospital and that I was ruining it all because I was the only patient in the ICU.

I now know this to be my severe paranoia but at the time it was incredibly real. The weirdest illusion of all was that my vision broke up so that everything was made up of thousands of little bits of coloured spaghetti and this would break up and then come together in front of my eyes. Or the room would look as if it was built out of cream and the clock would just be enveloped by it and then reappear.

I also saw brightly coloured wooden fish – which were the ones you used to see on BFBS but in the most vivid colours imaginable. I also saw a purple donkey and a tiger with the richest orange between its black stripes. I don't know what they were pumping into me but the bloody stuff was working.

While all this was tumbling from my junkied mind they put in yet another drip, this time into my foot, and then took me down to theatre to make another incision. The nurses pushed me down the passage out through the doors and past Toni who was waiting outside. 'Derek's coming over and your sister Sally is flying down.' said Toni as I went by.

'Am I dying?' I asked. But of course, drugged up to my eyeballs, I knew that even if I were, no one would tell me.

They took me down and made a small incision at the bottom of a red area on my front and then the surgeon seemed to be satisfied and took me back to the ICU.

The thing that I remember most about being ill was how dry my tongue and mouth was. So dry that I felt that the end of my tongue was split and that it was too big for my mouth. The hospital gave me some disgusting muck to suck, which tasted of Friars' Balsam.

I lay a lot of the time having these strange hallucinations day and night. I longed for sleep but only snatched a few minutes at a time, even if I thought I'd been asleep for ages.

The routine was the same most days. The pretty nurses in the pure white uniforms would come and take my blood morning, midday and in the evening. They would arrive, take my arm, find a vein and take some blood and leave. It wasn't long before my arm was very sore. That and the automatic blood pressure band were getting the better of me. In the second and subsequent week I used to pull the band off once it had done its stuff and a nurse would come by to put it back on if they needed a reading.

The X-ray man would turn up once a day, usually after lunch, with his portable machine. He would put the plates behind me and on my chest, push the button and disappear.

I was in an air-conditioned ward which dried me out. I could only suck on ice cubes and even the fluid from these I could not keep down. It didn't help matters that I was still being constantly sick well into the second week.

More tremendous fun was just around the corner with an anaesthetist who came in and pushed two big, curved, hollow needles into the blood vessels in my groin. Attached to these needles were two coloured connectors, one blue and one red. This was in preparation for me to have dialysis, because at this stage my organs were shutting down. A doctor and a technician would then come round with the machine and join these connections to the machine. There was always a doctor on hand to supervise this procedure. They would inject a liquid into each connection with a syringe and then connect me to the machine. During this time Toni was never allowed in, even though it was the most boring operation watching the flow of blood going up, being scrubbed and returning to a grateful me. There was one jolly woman doctor who asked me about my farm and life and so I told it to her in sign language and animal noises. They seemed to enjoy this pantomime but I don't think I would have tried this in any other situation.

To a nurse what I have to say is pathetic, but I was intrigued at how they changed the bed while I was still in it and gave me a bed bath and even washed my hair on occasions. I didn't get out of bed for the best part of two weeks. A nurse even cut my hair one night.

It all depended on how busy the nurses were. I was there for three weeks and so I saw quite a few other patients come and go. At times it was frantic with nurses and doctors running to and fro and working hard to keep someone alive, but at other times there was nothing to do apart from watch over me.

After I had been there a few days one of the nurses scrubbed my oil stained hands with a soft brush. I found it very therapeutic as she spent hours gently rubbing and scrubbing. It was an act of kindness more than a nursing duty. As a naturally cold Brit I found these acts of warm humanity very moving.

Sally duly arrived and the three of them, Toni, Derek and Sally, took turns to sit at the bottom of the bed when they were allowed. I was very much in and out at that stage and I would see Toni, only for it to turn into Derek to Sally and back again. I would miss the arrivals and departures and think I was hallucinating again.

Even though my fluid intake was mostly through the drip I was peeing every 20 minutes, which was proving that my kidneys weren't working properly. By this stage my dignity had been hammered into submission because it seemed that if any passing doctor or nurse or passer-by wanted to have a look they would just whip back the sheet I lay under. In fact, at times I felt that most of the South American mainland had viewed my naked body. So each time I filled the 'violin' (urine bottle) I just passed it to whoever was there because I had totally overcome any vestige of shyness. Sally was a bit shocked the first time.

I wasn't well.

In the first week or so my back was so sore, but the nurses would turn me on to my side and rub oils into my back, which also prevented me getting bed sores. I also complained to Toni and Sally that I was feeling dried out by the air conditioning and could do with some rain in my face. Sally said to Toni that you could get water in an aerosol can, so off they went to see if they could find some. Wonder of wonders they did and Toni would give me a blast in the face, which was most invigorating. After a period in this air-conditioned room it was quite revitalising and even made me homesick for a few Falkland Island squalls. The first time the nurses saw this, Toni could understand enough Spanish to make out that they were saying 'Look at those mad English, spraying perfume on him.' She was able to reply, also in Spanish, 'No, it's water,' which had them examining it in wonder.

There were some lovely nurses and I don't just mean in the looks department. There was one little lady, Graciella, who was good looking, kind and noisy. You could always tell when she was on duty because she would come in and she would chat, chat, chat, laugh, titter, laugh. Her enthusiasm for life was infectious and lifted the mood in the ward. She would breeze into my room and do all the nurse things with a smile and with friendly good nature which lifted my spirits no end. There were times, however, in the middle of the night when I could have screamed, 'For Christ's sake shut up.'

Keeping me alive
The nutritionists would come up and try and tempt me with delicious foods prepared by the hospitals award-winning chefs. The menu was extensive but I didn't eat anything until the last few days and then it wasn't much. I was still being sick and all the food tasted of chemicals even when I tried it because of the amount that they were pouring into me. There were two lady nutritionists, one was a thin person that seemed to have an anti-food aura and then there was a more rounded woman who used to say in English, 'What would you like, fish, meat, salad?' and then after a pause, 'Whisky, rum, gin?'

Eventually I did have a few mouthfuls of food and, although it was obvious that it was cooked to perfection, I couldn't get the taste of chemicals out of my mouth and I had that taste for a while even after I had returned home.

My main diet was ice lollies which I would suck or, in the early days, Toni would feed me, teaspoonful by teaspoonful, but I was in such a pitiful state most of the ice had melted before

I could get it all down. I was also allowed to eat ice, which was called something like 'yellow' (*heilo*) and to reinforce my credentials as a Brit I called for 'yellow ice'. I suppose I must have got some benefit from them but nothing stayed down for very long. It was so boring at times that I would try and ask for a lolly every hour just to break the monotony. One of the nurses ate one of my ice lollies but I don't think she was meant to because as she started, another nurse came along and she just snaffled it down in one go. Ill or tip-top, there is no way that I could ever do that. It was a learning experience because I had never come across a grape-flavoured iced lolly before. They were disgusting even more than everything else I ate in the ICU.

You really have to be very ill yourself to understand serious illness. If I had heard some of the things that I experienced from somebody else, I would have thought what a drama queen. For the initial week to ten days I was so ill music was just an irritating noise. I was unable to write a postcard to the children. I struggled out 'Dear Caris and Dear Liam', signed my name at the bottom and that was it I was exhausted.

Later in my stay I did start to feel better and the nurses asked me if I wanted to sit in a chair. It was like being a kid and being offered a trip to the seaside, zoo or Disneyland. They had to tell me the day before the event so that I could cope with the excitement.

Next day the time to move to the chair arrived. I got ready to get out of bed and into the chair. 'No, wait for the porter to help you over,' said the duty nurse. I was adamant that I could do it but I was still plugged into the cocktail bar so I couldn't just show them. As it turned out that was a good thing because when I went to move from the bed to the chair my legs couldn't carry my weight and the porters had to help me. With help I was soon sitting in the chair and feeling cock-a-hoop ignoring my recent failings.

Bad stuff was just around the corner though. I was still being sick, but at least in Uruguay you could be sick into a stainless steel receptacle. The powers that be decided that they had to put an ultrasound endoscope down my throat to look at my heart. God in heaven that is one of the worst sensations I have ever had. The nurse painted some horrible tasting stuff in the back of my mouth to make my throat numb and then an ultrasound technician and two gorgeous looking Finnish doctors turned up.

'Just swallow,' said the technician bod. I gagged and retched and with much fuss managed to get the scope into my throat. Technician bod was in show-off mode with these two angel-like females studying his every move. The son of a bitch could have been sweeping a chimney as he charged this thing up and down my throat pushing this button and that switch on the visuals. As he was getting his message across in Spanish one of the Finnish doctors said in perfect English, 'Your heart is fine, you are okay.' Mr Ruddy Dyno-rod was too busy demonstrating all the bells and whistles to enlighten me. I had really wanted to see the image but I was unable to raise my head.

The next day Doctor Stanham, head of the saving-my-life effort Uruguay, came to see me to tell me that they were going to put the endoscope back down my throat and into my stomach, but this time with a camera on the end. The medical team were concerned that I was still being sick and were looking for a reason why. I couldn't believe it. Why hadn't they done it when they had it down my throat yesterday? Different technology. I know it was irrational but I was getting to the end of my reserves. So once more the technician came back with a new broom and swept my chimney. It was a little better the second time because he had no one to show off to.

I was just getting over this when the anaesthetist told me that he was going to have to change the feed into my neck to the other side because if he didn't I would be susceptible to an infection. It was cruel in Stanley and there was no change in the Hospital Britanico. He did elaborate and say that they don't anaesthetise because if they did they might end up pushing the tube out through the blood vessel's wall.

That very same day I was on dialysis and plugged into the machine. The flow of blood was slow and things don't seem to be working properly. Somehow the tubes in my groin were getting blocked. They decided to improve the flow by using the connection from my neck as well as one of the connections in the groin. I had been hanging around for ages and I needed a pee but I couldn't do it lying down and so they allowed me to sit up. As I was manoeuvring, all hell let loose. The piece in my groin came out and blood shot everywhere. There were a few shouts and the squeal of shoes on hard flooring and a nurse was administering direct pressure onto my groin to stop the bleeding. An oxygen mask was clapped on my face.

I had had three days of pain and with all the rest of it I had had enough. I began to cry like a big baby. Toni was called in, the first time ever during my dialysis, and I continued to blub and pull my oxygen mask off so I could complain more bitterly.

The staff carried on working on me as the anaesthetist pushed two more inserts into my left groin, plugs and all, and connected me once more to the blood scrubber. I apologised to the cleaner for all the mess as she cleaned my blood off the wall and floor and then began to collect myself.

These cleaners are very thorough in this hospital. They work on a shift system and would be constantly cleaning. Each shift would come on and start up at the door and work down to the other end with their mop and bucket and then back again. They would always seem to be at it and once that shift was done the next cleaner would be equally diligent. After I had squirted my blood around my cell I was given a transfusion with 'screened' blood. The nurses made a great fuss about the blood, so screened blood must be rare or expensive or both in Uruguay. It must have been special because it had to be replaced, which lead to a military plane coming back for me and flying me home to the Islands.

After weeks of lying helplessly and then a few hours in the chair, I eventually got to the stage where they would unplug me and I could go to the loo unaided. Once again this was an exciting milestone in my recovery. I did have a few issues after they took the catheter out because I was unable, as the Americans say, to go to the bathroom. I would be desperate but I couldn't pee. I had to have a little tablet under my tongue on a few occasions until I rediscovered the ability.

Then the day came when they unplugged me and Toni and Derek took me down to the café on the ground floor. I stumbled along with very little control or strength, with a stagger this way and a stagger the other. Going downhill was the hardest task. I just didn't feel like me. After my lolly at the cafe I did wonder if I would be strong enough to get back because my legs were so weak. Under my own steam, and with a little bit of directional muscle from

Toni and Derek, I managed to make it back.

Each day after this we would go down to this place but it didn't get much easier. I had done some serious moaning about the air conditioning so on one of these lolly runs I was invited by Toni and Derek to go outside and sit on the wall by the main entrance. It was hot as in HOT and very humid. I only sat there for a few minutes before I was sweltering. Needless to say, there was not much mention of the air conditioning after that.

Getting better

My room was opposite the nursing station and one day Keith Heathman rang me from the Falklands. My bed was pushed close to the door and the phone was handed over from the nurse's station with the lead as tight as a fence wire. We chatted away as the functions of the rest of the ICU continued. Doctors and nurses were ducking under or climbing over and generally finding the phone call a bit of an inconvenience. For me, it was one of the best tonics that I could have had. The technicians put a longer lead on and so, when I later spoke to Ted, the whole operation was less fraught.

I had two cuts, one on my side under my arm, which was about six inches long and had been carried out in Stanley, and a smaller cut on my stomach carried out in Montevideo. Both cuts had been left open to let the air into my flesh. Twice a day the nurses would pull a string of bandage out of these wounds and then push back clean ones. It was interesting how they made sure that any infection from one wouldn't be transported to the other. They would put on a pair of latex gloves to pull the wadding out of the big wound and then they would wash it with saline solution and then this would be cleaned away including the gloves, which were taken off in such a way that the fingers and hand of either hand didn't touch the outside of the gloves before starting to work on the second cut. Surprisingly it did not hurt but after watching for the first few times I was happy to look the other way.

I thought the cuts would never heal without stitches but gradually over weeks the sides of the wound just came together and perhaps with stitches the wounds might have been neater but I marvelled at the human body's ability to repair itself.

The Hercules was sent back up from the Falklands to get me and the doctor who had missed the first flight was there with the screened blood. The blood must have been an issue but when the doctor arrived with it no one seemed to be that interested. He sat there talking to me with his eyes flicking over to where the blood was sitting. He started to get a bit agitated but I knew most of the staff on duty couldn't speak English very well. This chap began to get quite worked up that the blood should be taken to the hospital's chilled blood bank and tried his hardest to put this over to the nurses.

He was right of course that the blood should be stored at the right temperature, and at this level they did seem to be rather blasé after the senior doctors had asked for the blood that I had consumed to be replaced. However, the doctor had brought it over and it was up to the hospital to look after the stuff now.

The nurses could see that it was the blood that was causing the grief and so after a while they just picked it up and put it in a room out of sight of the doctor. The doctor left after a while.

The Blues Brothers turned up from nowhere pushing a wheelchair. Not in the conventional way, but mimicking a dragster car with it high on its back wheels. These guys had style. I sat in the wheelchair while all the nurses came and kissed me goodbye and wished me well. A doctor came along and told me the Spanish had a saying for people like me and it meant that I had paid very little for this serious illness.

Heading home

Apparently the crew were keen to have a MacDonalds, there being no such establishment on the Islands. They were joking that they could sell sniffs of the napkins at 50p a go when they got back to Mount Pleasant Airport.

So off we went, like a poor man's Santa Pod, on the back wheels of the wheelchair along the corridor, down in the lift, along another corridor and then into the back of a van. I seemed to be in the van for ages with no activity at all. I began to feel like the Sunday roast, with sweat just raining from me. Eventually the gum-chewing Blues Brothers came and got me out and, although we couldn't communicate, I realised I was going back to the ICU. We roared along on the back wheels and made a grand entrance being welcomed back like the prodigal son. 'Richard, back so soon?' After all the sweating and welcome-back kissing I was feeling a tad dehydrated.

The Blues Brothers took me once more down to their van/ambulance and we travelled out to the airport. I couldn't see much, which was a shame because I had been in Uruguay for three weeks and seen very little of the country. I felt a bit like claiming that I'd visited the country when you have only landed at the airport on the way to somewhere else. We went to a side entrance where there was a boom barring the way and two disinterested Uruguayan squaddies.

The Falkland contingent gathered for our trip home and I couldn't stop smiling when I saw the plane sitting on the tarmac ready to fly us all home. I think it got even bigger as we sped down the runway and headed south. It had been a hard run for us all.

Somewhere over the South Atlantic I needed the inevitable. Another pee. The kidneys were still not 100 per cent. The military doctor made a big show of giving me some privacy but the one benefit of this whole episode was that I had overcome all my inhibitions to such an extent that I could have probably stood on top of a box and perfected my aim from a distance.

We flew over the squidding fleet off the north coast but I haven't a clue how close to the Islands they were. It was strange to see all those lights together knowing that they were in the middle of the sea. There were probably as many people there as there are in the whole of the Falklands.

Things went a bit downhill for Toni because the wind was from the north and this was creating a lot of turbulence. The Hercules began to move about a lot as we came in over the Wickham Heights. Toni went a funny colour as we came closer to the airport, which gave the crew and her brother a bit of a chuckle, but this all stopped as she started vomiting. Someone found a bucket and another conjured up a cold flannel to put on the back of her neck.

We taxied up the runway to the reception committee, which included an ambulance and the children. I came off the plane trying to walk as normally as possible. 'Where's Mum?'

asked Caris. Toni was finishing being sick before she staggered out looking, and at that moment probably feeling, worse than I did.

I sat in the front of the ambulance with Keith. I had had enough of lying on stretchers. Here I was home, which was a surprise to some, alive and kicking and a couple of stone lighter.

It was great to be back and over the next few days, although no one said that they didn't expect me to return directly, one doctor said how tough Falkland people are and how even patients you don't expect to recover sometimes prove you wrong.

Back in the King Edward VII Memorial Hospital I was put on to a ward that consisted of people from the fishing fleet. There wasn't another local to be seen. One of these guys had had an appendix operation. Another had been hit in the head by something hard while at sea and this had affected his gait. There was also a Brazilian from a visiting cruise ship who was ill. He had had a stroke at some stage, but from the way he was talking that was not what he was in for. It wasn't a problem but I did feel strange that I was in the Falklands but unable to talk to anyone. They monopolised the satellite TV to watch Spanish-speaking programmes, but that was something I didn't mind one jot.

That night the Korean fisherman got up and walked out with all his drips pulling out as he left. No one seemed to notice so eventually I went and informed a nurse. Three nurses were instantly dispatched and went charging down the corridor in hot pursuit. A while later they returned with the fugitive. Poor sod was completely disorientated, probably as a result of all the drugs he was consuming.

I felt a fraud lying next to these people who were really sick. I wasn't on medication, and I didn't have a temperature. The only thing pending was my wounds, which needed dressing every day. My arms were another reminder that I had been ill, being bloody sore after three weeks of giving blood and having my blood pressure taken. On the second day back I asked if I could go home. After a short conflab with colleagues, the doctor agreed, not to the farm but with family in Stanley.

Recuperation

I was over my illness, but boy was I weak. I couldn't walk very far at all before my legs felt like jelly. Sometimes I felt that I was close to my legs just folding under me. Because of this I was billeted with Derek and Trudi at their house in Eliza Cove Crescent, which hasn't got stairs. It was a wise move because I just couldn't have climbed the stairs at Tony's easily and I would definitely have had problems coming down. As it was, I still needed regular visits to the rest room, which in Derek and Trudi's home was no problem.

I had another weak moment when I seemed to be just overwhelmed with what had just passed. All the possibilities, now it was all over, kept spinning round in my head. I didn't want to chat to all those well-meaning folk who had welcomed me home. Of course I did, but I had to work at it.

My old chum, John, from the Council in the 1990s offered to take me on his meals on wheels delivery, which I thought would be fun. John came to the front gate and so I walked out of the door and down the two steps. But once again I had overestimated my recovery, because just the force of going down two steps at normal speed I thought I was going to keep going until I was down on my haunches.

I was soon fed up in Stanley. Derek and Trudi treated me like royalty but I wanted to get home. Unfortunately, my wounds were still a long way from being healed. I was going to the hospital daily to have them dressed. I pleaded with the doctors to let me go home and assured them of Toni's competence in dressing a few cuts, once again stating her qualifications after all the study time she had had on all the major medical dramas.

The nursing staff asked Toni if she thought she would be up to it. Of course, living on a farm for nearly twenty years had stood her in good stead and she was quite able to deal with most things including dressing wounds. Toni was subsequently invited to come and see the procedure.

As they took off the bandage, Toni gasps and said, 'Oh my god.'

'No,' said the nurse, 'You are meant to say, "wow that looks really good. It is healing nicely Richard."'

We left the hospital with a mountain of bandages and latex gloves, a lake of saline solution, and a cutlery drawer of plastic tongs.

Apart from the initial shock, Toni was the perfect nurse cleaning and dressing my wounds from that day on at Sussex. The doctors or a nurse checked me out any time that I was in Stanley.

I was so pleased to be back home that I forgot that I didn't have any power or stamina. I went to have a look at the shed, checking out the dogs as I went. I didn't rush and I didn't go into the shed. Walking back, I just ran out of steam and Toni had to get a vehicle to take me back to the house. I was like that for months, but slowly getting stronger all the time.

I was still a bit vulnerable because the veins in my arms were reacting to the many times they had been pricked by needles to take blood. The veins under my skin felt like biros or miniature pieces of alkathene, hard and alien. I thought I was having blood clots building up and that I was on the verge of having an embolism. I phoned Doctor Diggle who was able to bring me down and reassure me that nothing was wrong and that my veins would soon recover.

My wounds slowly came together and healed but that last little bit, when I wanted to join everyone in the swimming pool, seemed to take forever.

Toni likes to say that the reason I am still here is that her mum had her foot on the Pearly Gates and would not let me in as she had instructed me to look after her daughter.

Getting on with life

While I was recuperating Toni and I would drive round the farm. I could open the gates but little else. We went to check the fences and when we got to the fence between Pinza and the Low Pass we could see that it was lying down. Toni got out and walked back to where it needed standing up and gingerly, because it was an electric fence, stood it up. On the way back she could see why it had fallen – a tie down had lifted in a small valley. (A tie-down is a metal or wooden stake driven into the ground and the fence is tied to it when it has risen off the ground.) Without thinking, she got hold of the top wire to force the standard and tie-down back into the ground. Her arms were thrown up in the air with the shock and she was nearly thrown off her feet. It did look very comical and I was unable not to laugh.

We had the veterinary surgeon out later in the year, but still in my convalescing period, to have a look at a foal's leg which seemed to be growing twisted. We would go up into Shepherds Brook and go to the old lamb-marking pen with some horse nuts and usually after a few shouts the horses would turn up. Well, this day was very similar apart from a few were slower getting to the pens than the majority. I didn't want to put the food down in piles before they were all there because the slower horses wouldn't get their fair share. The horses were all jockeying around, pushing and shoving, unwilling to wait for the others and this old mare turned round and gave me both barrels in the stomach and sent me flying into the grass. I could have done without that experience and it is the first time ever with all the work that we did with horses that I got a full-bodied kick from a horse.

It was December, some nine months later, when I realised that I was better. We were gathering the mountain piece to get the wethers in for shearing. Ted and Shelia were helping us. We would start at the east end by Bodie Peak and then drive the sheep to the west. There are always a group of troublemakers in every flock and the wethers had a group that used to charge up into the rocks on the side of Bodie and try and give us the run around.

I could see this group winding its way up into the rocks and ultimately trying to get behind us. There is only so far you can go on a quad so I jumped off with my dogs and gave chase. My heart was pounding so loudly that I could hear the banging in my ears. I kept pushing on hoping that the Finnish goddess had been right when she said my heart was okay. I eventually was able to see them and put Bess out who got to the front and brought them back, passing everyone who was waiting under the rocks on the Snipe Camp side.

I lay on the grass for about 20 minutes absolutely knackered. As I was walking back to the quad it dawned on me what I had done. I did have times when I had thought I would never be able to do that kind of thing ever again. I drove over to the others and told them where I had been and said that I think I am over my illness or as good as I'll ever be.

To date I still have issues, but they are small to the extreme. If I am working on a vehicle or engine and get oil on my hands I find it difficult to carry on. I am a lot better, but even now once I notice it try as I might I can't carry on for too many minutes before I have to go and wash my hands.

I suppose the Uruguayan doctor was right – I had paid a small price indeed. To emphasise this point, I looked up necrotising fasciitis on the internet and found out that most people die and the ones like me who survive usually lose limbs or are badly scarred for life.

11. THE FALKLANDS: MOVING ON

The land reform programme

The land reform programme was driven and lead predominantly by the Falkland Island Government over such a short time frame – between 1980 and 1990. I think that people always saw the family unit using dogs and horses, burning peat and having small, economical generators that powered the lights and maybe a TV and video player if you were ultra-modern.

I believe it was the new wealth that the country got from fishing that boosted wages which in turn transformed the standard of living in the Falkland Islands. People wanted modern houses with central heating and double and triple-glazed windows. Oil-fired stoves replaced the peat and many people could afford modern vehicles.

This happened mainly in Stanley where government wages improved and the private sector had to go with them to retain quality employees. Many farm workers of that period moved into town to enjoy the good times.

In camp, the wages reflected the value of wool which plummeted at the beginning of the 1990s. Government stepped in with direct subsidies and other schemes including mortgage relief for the many new farmers that had large mortgages hanging over their heads, and they also funded a replacement fencing programme. Unfortunately, there was never the political will to rectify the problems that government unwittingly contributed to, by addressing the issue of the many farms that were too small.

People in camp didn't want to be society's paupers and many wanted improved dwellings and nice vehicles, but other costs started to rear their heads with telephones and oil-fired stoves. Farming practices also changed dramatically over the following few years, with the horse being phased out in most places and the motorbike, three-wheeler and quads coming in. All these improvements had financial implications for farmers.

Robin Goodwin was the first farm in our area to amalgamate with a neighbour, when he bought out Geoff and Marilyn Butler who owned Waimea, or what was once called the Third Corral section. The principle was sound but the execution was difficult because the Butlers wanted something for their efforts and the price tag was high, compared to the original price, but equally something is worth what someone is prepared to pay. The downside of Waimea was that it was a large area of marginal ground, which had historically been used as wether ground, with only the Rincon being deemed reasonable land for the more vulnerable stock such as ewes, lambs and hoggets. Unfortunately for Rob and Mandy, very shortly after they doubled the size of their farm, the wool prices collapsed and remained low for many years.

Gerald Findlay was the next farm of the original seven to give up on health grounds. This farm would have been ideal for us to expand into at the right price, but it never came on the open market, with Gerald making a deal with his old boss and fellow San Carlos section holders Pat and Isobel Short.

The next farm to go was Ron and Iris who decided enough was enough and they left to go back and work at Goose Green. The story goes that Sheila and Terence McPhee were saying how they would like a farm at a function at the Goose Green club and so Ron said well you can have mine. We were sort of in the frame for this farm, but the McPhees were ready with the dosh and Ron seemed to think that by selling to us he was passing us the poison chalice. In some ways it would have quadrupled our workload and limited any development outside wool, but it would have given us a viable farm with the potential to run a combined 7,000 sheep.

Pat was the next to sell up and his daughter Michelle and son-in-law, Adrian Minnell took over Blue Beach and Maryfield. This arrangement lasted a few years when Maryfield was sold once more in a private arrangement. Of course, from Toni and my perspective, it would have been good to split the farm between the Wreck and us and raised both farms' numbers, but yet again it wasn't to be and in any case the price, which included the infrastructure, wasn't worth the extra grazing. So into the re-named Head of the Bay came our good friends Ted and Shelia Jones with their children Mark and Deena.

Robin and Mandy, who were first to see the need to expand, eventually went to town for family reasons and then decided to sell pieces of their farm off to different people including the San Carlos river bank. They retained the Third Corral Rincon and some of the settlement in the valley where Geoff built Waimea.

In 1989/90 FIC sold up 99 per cent of its land interests to the Falkland Island Government. FIG paid a lot more money than it was worth as a business, but the majority consensus was that they were paying a political price for what amounted to a third of the Islands' sheep and a huge area of the Falkland Islands in relative terms.

We had made a number of tentative enquiries to the FIC about the possibilities of buying Cantera, which was next door. On one occasion the FIC told us that the land to the south of Shepherds Brook was theirs, even though the boundary fence was 100 metres to the south in places, although I can't remember the detail. One of the directors said it was a gnat's cock to the company to which we responded by saying it was only a gnat's cock to them but a part of the farm that would make a difference to us.

A year or so before the sale to government, FIC put a number of camp houses with a small amount of land up for sale including Cantera. We put an offer in for the house and all of the land known as Cantera, but subsequently found that the offer that had secured the house was more than we had offered for everything. We had been shackled by farm economics. We knew it was a long shot but we felt that it was pointless to whinge about our dilemma and it was up to us to find a way to help ourselves. We said good luck to the successful purchasers, Angela and Jimmy Moffatt and their three children Kelly, Jay and Sean. It wasn't really the house that we wanted, it was the extra land that we desperately needed at a price to make our farm viable. The Moffatt's went on to invest more money and time into Cantera house than we could and would have done.

While the negotiations between FIC and FIG were going on one of the Falkland Island Company bigwigs came down to the Islands which gave me the opportunity to write a begging letter to Dr Muirhouse, followed by some demeaning grovelling in a further attempt to buy Cantera when he stayed at the Blue Beach Lodge in San Carlos. I wish I had known beforehand it was going to fail, because then I would have only half-heartedly grovelled. Reasonably enough, although a bit of a choker, they didn't want to jeopardise the sale by hiving a bit off to us. He felt that the best chance for us was to buy from FIG because they were talking of buying to sell pieces off at a later date. I, however, had a feeling that this was our best chance, which is why I put in so much effort. It was no consolation to find out, over time, how right I was.

Falkland Land Holdings

Falkland Land Holdings was created and Robin Lee, part owner of the largest private farm Port Howard, took the reins of the four farms. Fitzroy, Goose Green, Walker Creek and North Arm, plus the 200,000 sheep that that entailed. FLH was given £1M working capital and they had no mortgage repayments. The government in the 1990s absorbed the loan so it was no longer a debt to the organisation.

I wrote my first letter to Robin, which initiated our serious campaign to get more land and to secure our faming future. More begging letters followed, bowing and scraping to Robin, councillors and to government's chief executive, but to no avail. We got a shedload of sympathy and I even saw an Executive council minute supporting our need but nothing came of it.

Many other people, remembering the initial idea of buying to later sell off, also approached FLH for land but it was a bad time for government to support further subdivision and putting more people in a vulnerable position with wool prices lower than they had been for years. The new general manager was from a large private farm and his drive was to revitalise FLH to the system that he had been successful with at Port Howard.

My view was different and that a part of FLH could have been used to address the problems of non-viable units that FIG had created. In the early 1990s it was still early days for many farmers and some might have been persuaded to move from a non-viable unit to a viable farm created from FLH. The farms that they left could then be shared out with neighbours. In my view this approach would have been a far cheaper and longer-lasting solution than perpetual subsidies and the reduction of effort on some farms due to people looking for opportunities in other places.

Natural forces have been cited, which some would see as routing out bad farmers, but I thought it wouldn't necessarily be the farms that were badly run that went under, it would be the farms that were a certain size or had a high percentage of marginal ground. Today this is not the financial issue it once was because other opportunities have come along which have helped farmers earn more money. There are, however, longer-term issues about farm development with people making money off-farm, but that will be the issue for farmers and politicians in future years.

We carried on our campaign to secure more land from FLH, but our pleas once again fell on deaf ears, even when it was quite clear that few locals wanted to work under the FLH system. The government's estate started recruiting workers from overseas on work permits rather than considering the needs of a large chunk of the farming sector.

Struggling at Sussex

After I spent three weeks in intensive care, where I was able to spend many hours pondering our future in camp, it didn't matter how I looked at it – we were financially finished at Sussex. Not that Toni and I couldn't have lived off the beach if we had had too, but we had the responsibilities of Caris and Liam who needed to have the same kind of things as their peers, within reason. Of course, Toni and I had discussed many times running up the white flag and going to town to get paid a reasonable wage for a modest amount of effort, but our emotional ties with Sussex always won the day.

We had played the leaving card over our campaign to buy more land and it wasn't ever an empty threat. It was a certainty. It really depended on how long we could hold on. We had been hanging on by our fingernails for a number of years and here we were having reached the very point of leaving our home of 17 years with all the memories of our farms and the homes development.

Bob Reid, the then Director of the Agriculture Department, had been really helpful and sympathetic to Toni once I became ill and helped our neighbours in supporting the farm while we were away. He had often supported the argument that we were too small, but this had never manifested itself into strong support on the FLH board.

Coming back to the Falklands I made it clear that the time had come, and that we couldn't carry on fighting a losing battle. Bob moved from passive support to throwing his weight behind our efforts to secure land. There were a few conditions, which we had to comply with, and one of these was to join a mentoring-type system through the Falkland Island Development Corporation where you came under the wing of another farmer. We resented this because at the time we were one of the heaviest stocked farms on the East Falklands and we performed near the top of the industry for micron and wool weight – the very thing that some people think would make us viable. We felt we didn't need mentoring, we knew what was wrong and that was the size of Sussex. We had to conform to survive and this to us was the last throw of the dice, and so we went along with it but not without some serious complaining. No one gave us any benefit of the doubt, even though we had been farming for nearly twenty years and had performed per sheep and per hectare better than most.

One of the other ridiculous things was the notion that as a breeding unit we would sell 100 per cent of our wether lambs. I argued as long as possible that there was just no way, but we had to do the sums. In fact, Richard Baker the Head of the Development Corporation got quite annoyed with my so-called negativity.

Even with Bob Reid's support there was still a lot of jockeying for land. One of the suggestions made was that we could buy land going east under Mount Usbourne, and yet again the most optimistic scenario was suggested as to how this land performed. Once again our knowledge of this area wasn't acknowledged at all with all the sway going with the management of FLH. The managing director and the Goose Green farm manager by this time were both Australians with neither having been in the Islands for any length of time.

Fortunately, Brook Hardcastle was on this development scheme and he was able to confirm, as a previous and long-standing general manager of this area, what we had been saying for months and that was that the top part of Camilla Creek had historically been used as a summer camp.

The government's chief executive at the time, Michael Blanch, Richard Baker the director of FIDC and the director of the Agricultural Department Bob Reid came out to the farm and we struck a deal. We had to perform in the top 20 per cent of farms with wool micron and weights. I wanted to just outperform the previous owners, which would have been better for us, but there was no room to negotiate. We then had to pay a ridiculous rent for four years during our probation, which we only accepted once we had secured that this sum would be taken off the purchase price if we met the criteria and bought the land. Presumably if we hadn't performed we would have lost everything, but we were fairly confident, probably too confident in hindsight, and we had one foot in the door. I hated the principle of paying silly money but there were areas of negotiation where we just couldn't prevail.

Landholdings Management were not keen. They had done everything in their power to frustrate the process. They couldn't or wouldn't provide any stock and the toughest thing for us was that they wouldn't hand the land over until May. The lack of sheep was a serious business but we were allocated money by government to buy stock which again did rankle because FLH, a government enterprise and farming organisation of 200,000 sheep could have found 1 per cent of their total to get us going. So FLH would have killed thousands of cull sheep that year, but instead of giving us a few we were given government money to buy sheep from other farms. This money and the generosity of some farms made it possible to stock Cantera.

The May handover was the hardest bit to overcome. People are not going to keep sheep that they no longer want eating grass for around three months and also sheep that move from farm to farm in the Falklands usually prosper a lot better if they move as soon as possible before the weather breaks. We had nowhere where we could hold 2,000 sheep either, being two-thirds again of what we ran on Sussex.

As luck would have it we were able to buy some young sheep from Pete and Melanie Guilding at Port Louis who were reducing numbers, and Shane Clarke was prepared to take them to Sussex in his lorry using the stock crate belonging to FIDC.

Cap in hand I went back to the general manager of Goose Green and asked if we could have Terra Motas, which is a part of Cantera, which could hold the young sheep until the handover. We were initially told that it was difficult because Goose Green needed it. So I explained to Greg Bradfield, the new general manager of FLH, who had taken over from Colin Houghton, and to his boss i.e. the government's chief executive, that Terra Motas had only been used for six weeks annually for the last ten years or more. Goose Green fenced this point off solely for the ewes of Cantera to have a dedicated tupping paddock while the rams were out. With this reasoning it seemed rather dog in a manger to want to hang on to it, as historically it was never used until after FLH's proposed hand over date anyway. Some sense prevailed and we were allowed to use Terra Motas, which is across the creek, opposite our house.

We still had a lot more sheep to go. We had bought some young and age culls from Hew Grierson and Sue Smith from Blue Beach, and Stephen and Ella Poole at Race Point Farm Port San Carlos had given us all their cull ewes and all we had to do was to take them away.

Stephen and Ella weren't going to keep ewes hanging around for the best part of three months and even if they had they would have become just skin and bone. I had to think of something quickly because it was pointless getting more land if we couldn't stock it.

I went and asked Bob Anderson, the manager of Goose Green, whether we could put more sheep in the Cantera Horse paddock. He told me that the fence was flat in a few places and wouldn't be sheep proof but he didn't say no we couldn't use it but equally he didn't say yes either.

Next day we were at the Cantera Horse Paddock fence repairing and strengthening it. We also replaced 300–400 yards starting 50 metres from the beach, which was ropey. It took us most of the day to pull the old down and build the new plus all the repair work and then we rounded all FLH sheep up and put them out into Cantera.

So all we had to do was to collect up the sheep from different farms and put them into the Cantera Horse Paddock.

Hew had arranged to help us drive all the sheep from the San Carlos River that we were getting from the Poole's. So we spent a day with Hew at Blue Beach going through the age culls and picking the best. Race Point was further away than Blue Beach and so Hew then put his and Sue's sheep in a paddock for us to pick up when we came through with the other sheep from Stephen and Ella.

We stayed the night with Stephen and Ella and then drove the sheep from Port San Carlos down to the river the next morning. There wasn't a bridge over the San Carlos River then, although there is one now.

We arrived at the river which on the Land Rover track is about 20 metres across and, although it had been one of the driest years on record, the last few days there had been a change and it wasn't ideal conditions but still doable.

We had some dog power with ours, Stephen's and Hew's but the sheep just did not want to cross. We were there trying for hours when Stephen carried a ewe out to a reef out in the main channel. This ewe had been in the water a couple of times and had got cold so she just stood there not trying to get back or to go across. Once some of the other sheep saw one of their own halfway, a number of them walked out. The dogs, encouraged by some movement in the right direction, found new vigour and the sheep went passed the stranded one and headed for the opposite bank. It was really a sight to behold, as the sheep went across Indian style one in front of the other. They went across in a straight line at first when the sheep were able to touch the bottom of the river, but then there was a huge bow in the line, as they were lifted off their feet for about five metres before regaining their feet as they reached the far side. I regret that we didn't have a camera to record this feat of hundreds of sheep crossing the San Carlos River in this way.

We lost three or four, which was remarkable really considering the size of the river and the amount of water. It was the weaker sheep that perished and would probably have done on the journey back to Cantera anyway.

Hew, Toni and I collected up the sheep and slowly headed for Blue Beach coming into a race and in to the farm from the north. We mixed these sheep with the ones we had selected from Hew ready for the drive back to Sussex.

The next day there were a few more to drive, but because of a number of factors there were stronger and weaker sheep. Young and old and the ones that had had a good hike already. The ewes that hadn't raised a lamb were also stronger and in better condition than the ones that had. Every time we came to any gradient the weaker sheep would weave to and fro to get up the hill while the stronger sheep took a more direct path. It was a case of holding the front of the flock with the dogs and coaxing the elderly mothers along at a sedate pace controlling the spread of sheep with the dogs at the same time.

We took them along the track through Kingsford Valley Farm and then into the Head of the Bay ground as we came up to the foot of Sussex Mountain. We progressed east but climbing a little at the same time. At the top of the mountain we went through the boundary between Head of the Bay and Sussex using the wire gate north of the old San Carlos track and Gin Rock gate.

The last really notable climb was going out of Hells Kitchen valley on the road where the flock spread over a large area. Hew stayed in the valley having a snack while I dogged the sheep trying to keep them in a manageable flock. It was slow going from there until we put them into the Cantera Horse Park, their new home. This was a big and arduous job jobbed. It should have been the end of the story but our dealings with FLH had never been easy and they were to feature prominently in the continuing saga.

The sheep were in Cantera Horse Paddock and I thought it wise to inform the general manager what I had done. As luck would have it, when I visited the office in Stanley the general manager was there with the manager from Goose Green. I told them what I had done and I then said when they gathered their sheep for tallying that our sheep would have an end fork and if any had got out we would like them back. I had even helpfully drawn a picture of an end fork, which is our sheep's earmark, on a piece of paper to help them identify them.

Imagine our surprise when my Goose Green informant told me that they had gathered Cantera and that our sheep were now at Goose Green. I got on the phone to Bob Anderson and he was ready for me and ripped into me. I had come to the end of my tether and so I didn't pull any punches when I told him that there was no way that it was going to be the general manager's or his 'way' because my actions were based on need and not the spoiling tactics that they were engaged in. We did have a frank exchange of views.

The general manager then spoke to me and said that I would have to go and get the sheep from Goose Green, which I refused to do because I had informed Bob and him where our sheep were and he had ignored me. He then denied that I had told him and said that his staff couldn't remember me telling them where our sheep were. I told him in the bluntest of terms that it was their problem and that they could drive the sheep back.

To cut a long story short we went up and helped them draft and count our sheep. They weren't all there so to give Bob his due he counted off the missing number from FLH sheep and made up the deficit. Brian Hewitt then drove the sheep back to Cantera with us in attendance, although without our dogs. We were supposed to put them back into the Cantera Horse Paddock, but when we arrived at the gate into Cantera I opened it and Brian drove the sheep through. I shut the gate once they were through with all of us including Brian on the Goose Green side of the gate. We had a yarn as the sheep spread and then Brian left. It was at this time that I suddenly felt that not only had we won the battle but we had also won the war against FLH. There were, however the odd skirmish still to come.

Fighting our corner

The lease was another area of friction where we found it impossible to find common ground and we seemed to have few, if any allies, even when things appeared to be ridiculous. We should have taken legal advice but because the government's legal department was handling it we believed that they would be impartial. More by luck than judgement, Toni was sitting in the Land Rover as we were waiting for Bob when we sorted the sheep in Goose Green, and she went through the lease one more time before we signed it. It said that they would negotiate the price which one would expect, but then went on to say however that the price had to be over £64,000. We refused to sign but the sheep were in situ so they took that part out.

We were beginning to think more long term and the fact that some people in FLH were never going to think the sale was justified. As insurance, we took pictures of fence lines and all areas of camp so we could defend ourselves against any accusations of overgrazing or any other nonsense. FLH did the same. One of the clauses that they insisted on putting in the lease was for us not to plant any noxious weed in Cantera. As one of two farms that were seriously affected by an introduced plant we would be the last people to plant more or encourage its propagation. A member of the Coutts family brought it to the Islands to create a shelter for sheep many years ago. For some reason, calafate really enjoys the ground at Sussex and has covered about seven square kilometres between Head of the Bay Farm and here. It probably affects us more because it is in all our paddocks that we use to work the sheep during shearing.

A while into our lease the FLH management wanted to come and inspect Cantera because supposedly someone had reported that it was being eaten out. We said no, and that the lease stipulated that they had to have a good reason to do this. They said they would come with the Agricultural Department but again we said no. They were then going to prove by pictures that we were causing damage and enforce an inspection. What had happened was that Bob Anderson, for whatever reason, had put some maiden ewes into Cantera just before we started to lease it and these young sheep had pulled back in the direction of their old grazing ground. This made the fence line stand out suggesting overgrazing. The whole thing backfired, much to our delight, because FLH couldn't find their pictures.

The lease ran its course and we erected all the subdivision fencing in Cantera with the help of Gilberto, who built the fence running to the north of the road and the fence running north to south beginning at the Sussex boundary west of the old clay track over to the Cantera Horse Paddock. Toni and I built the first fence, east and west cutting Cantera in two. Liam and I built the fences around the reseeds. We also built pens where all the fences came together to make things slightly easier when rotating and lamb marking and generally managing stock.

Malcolm Ashworth, who endeavoured to show us that sleep was a luxury enjoyed by others, carried out the reseed work.

The Agricultural Department did the number crunching and found that we were in the performance category outlined in the lease. So now it was carry on paying out every gain that the extra piece of land gave us in rent, or try and buy at a realistic price taking farm economics into account. Being old campaigners we had a feeling that we were in for another lively fight. We weren't disappointed.

Because we were dealing with government we thought at this stage we would be treated fairly but FLH's valuation was £96,000. This was a piece of ground with no stock, sheep or otherwise, no buildings or other structural assets and surrounded by fences that were past their best. The Cantera Horse Paddock fence needed replacing imminently.

For people like us who had paid £60,000 for Sussex, with 3,000 sheep, 90 cattle, horses, a house and a seventh share of the materials and stores of the donor farm it was nonsensical, especially as we had spent the whole of the 1990s, along with the majority of farms, being bailed out by government with grants and the most telling help, which was mortgage relief. It was obvious that farm values were too high.

It was pointless to pay that kind of money because it would have put us right back into the position that we had fought so hard to overcome – a farm that couldn't pay its way. It was a time to hold our nerve and stand up to the figures that were being presented which, if true, would have made Sussex a gold mine and Cantera an extravagance we didn't need. Eventually, after a lot of research like digging up FIDC farm valuation papers and seeking advice from a previous economist, we came to an agreement. I think we pushed it as far as we could but it was irritating that no one on the government side had any connection to the realities of the economies of a small family farm and the figures quoted for 100 per cent lambs and £5 per head for all their cast ewes had not been realised by any farms even with reseeds and crops. Some farms with these recourses or with lightly stocked farms might be able to work to a high percentage of these targets but never 100 per cent.

I always try to understand why someone has acted in such a way when it is so far removed from how I think. I can understand the resentment of people who live and have even lived on these farms and don't want to see the whole diluted, but I fail to understand how the opinions of two people with first-hand knowledge are dismissed so easily. I think it is because the knowledge base is so small in the Islands. If you challenge the Agricultural Department, the government officer goes to the Agricultural Department to find the information you are challenging. In a bigger society, there are many independent sources of information and ways of challenging government.

We were strongly advised by a lawyer working for FIG to take our deeds to an independent lawyer, which renewed my faith in people and further dented my confidence in being fairly treated by some areas of government. Our independent lawyer had a surprise for us and it wasn't a spontaneous party at the Globe Bar. FLH still wanted access to our water assets which meant that they could give anyone permission to fish in the ponds, brooks and sea anywhere in Cantera. They also wanted us to be totally responsible for the boundary fences, even though it is traditionally a fifty/fifty share of labour and materials. They were just trying it on with one more throw of the dice, one more twist of the knife. We wouldn't accept these conditions and the senior management of FLH knew it was all over and agreed to common practice. We had Cantera but we had earned the right and now we had to forget about the struggle and start to pay it off.

12. THE RACE FOR CARIS' PASSPORT!

In about 2003, Caris was part of the school team that won the International Newspaper Day competition and was one of the children that was chosen to represent the Falkland Islands Community School in London when they picked up their prize.

Caris' passport just happened to be at Sussex and two days before her flight the heavens opened and deposited a foot of snow on most of the Falklands. With the wind whipping it up there were some large snow drifts scattered here and there.

In the good old days, with not a road anywhere, one could drive around most drifts and find a track to get home. With the roads it was different and because many had big ditches either side you were forced to stay on the road in many places. With snow on the road and filling these ditches it was difficult to know where it was wise to leave the roads.

We had little choice but to try and take Caris' passport to her.

In Sussex there are many valleys where the snow can build up and fill them, making sections of the road impassable, but on this trip luck was with us and we charged what was there in some of the valleys, sneaked through the gate in the valley of Hells Kitchen and using the wire gate, beside the iron swinging gate on the road which we normally used for stock, at the head of the creek.

This is where the good fortune ended because although we got over Shepherds Brook we were unable to get through the boundary gate between Sussex and Cantera. There was a huge drift stretching right across the gateway and being on an uphill run it was hard to imagine a successful outcome if we charged it. We reverted back to the old clay track by going back a few hundred yards and heading up to the wire gate in the fence line.

From there to nearly at the Darwin Road it was plain sailing, with the terrain being exposed and mostly flat the snow hadn't accumulated anywhere to any extent.

This was not the case when we arrived at the last gate into the Goose Green Horse Paddock. The roadway was in a small cutting which was full right up to the gate and there wasn't a wire gate for stock, as there had been before, to give us scope to creep by. We drove back 20 or 30 metres and drove through the ditch and up onto the bank and drove up to the fence. We then undid the fence from the standards and laid it on the ground and drove the Land Rover over.

For some reason the snow hadn't drifted as badly on the San Carlos road running sort of west to east, but the Darwin road running more north to south seemed to have picked up hundreds of drifts.

There was so much snow it was hard to tell where the edge of the road was and, because on a lot of it the ditches are big with severe inclines, it was a case of slowly feeling our way along. But occasionally it was obvious that you had to bypass some of the bigger and medium multiple drifts.

All the time you are leaving the road you are wondering what to do if you get stuck in ditch by the side of the road.

We carried along like this, trying to charge the smaller stuff and only being forced off when it was obvious that charging was futile. We seemed to be doing reasonably well until just before the High Hill Gate where the road goes into a hollow and there was quite a bit of snow. It is also on a climb.

It looked as if it may be possible to punch our way through but there was just a touch too much snow and with a climb as well we could not maintain the momentum. So we ended up on top of a little bit of snow and had some serious digging to get on with.

We were there for an hour or so digging the snow away, digging under the vehicle to allow the tyres to find the firm because charging the drift with the Land Rover had compacted the snow and the vehicle's forward motion had pushed it up on top of the drift.

We were both beginning to wonder if we could carry on just because of the time involved, but after another 75 to 100 metres we went over the cattle grid and there was the government grader which had been working as a snow plough pushing the snow from the road.

It was a good feeling to know that apart from an act of god we would be able to deliver Caris' passport to her and she would be off to the UK representing her school and the Falkland Islands.

A medical situation (part six)

Tony P., Toni's father, was a likeable guy, generous to a fault and a hard worker spending many hours at work in the government printing office. He had spent all his working life printing documents for government. His more recent responsibilities included printing the *Penguin News* to a very tight deadline.

It is a fact that Tony had great willpower and this was demonstrated when he gave up smoking when he had been used to consuming 40 to 60 cigarettes a day.

Heather and Tony booked themselves into an acupuncture clinic to try and help them give up smoking. Tony was worried that he might not be able to give up, even with this help, so gave up beforehand to see if he could and never smoked again. The twist to the story is that the appointment they had was cancelled because they had temporarily run out of needles. Tony's trial run to see if he would be able to give up worked but Heather was never able to overcome her addiction.

In his late fifties, Tony's health began to deteriorate. During a visit from the chiropodist the health department were alerted to the fact that Tony's circulation wasn't what it should be and the blood supply to his feet was very poor. He was subsequently diagnosed as a diabetic. His circulation became critical and Tony had a few toes removed. Eventually he was medevaced out of the Islands and off to Britain to have a synthetic vein put into his leg. Toni went along with Tony to give him support.

Before Tony left, Toni and I went to see the surgeon to get a feel of how serious things were and how long Toni might be with her father. The facts were quite shocking and deeply upsetting because his veins were furred up in every part of his body and his liver wasn't in great shape either.

So off they went to Southampton General with a weak supply of optimism.

This was the start of five months of me holding the fort at Sussex while Toni gave Tony P. serious back up, and I mean serious.

It was a long time, but I thought if they could stabilise Tony and get him back into reasonable health it would be worth all the upheaval.

Ever since my father's stroke in Yorkshire and our experiences in North Allerton Hospital my opinion of the NHS had been pretty low. Toni's experiences didn't improve this view, in fact, far from it because many of the stories sounded more like the rabid reporting from the tabloids. It was a thing of that time that waiting lists were long and satisfaction with the service was low.

The week would start with nurses recounting their weekend activities to their colleagues. Attending to their nursing duties weren't looked at as such a high priority. Even later in the week no one seemed to be bursting a blood vessel to address the patients' needs.

Most of the people in Tony's ward were senior or had chronic illness and needed that extra care. Toni was able to give her father that extra care, but there were many others that needed more and did not get it.

There was an elderly gent who couldn't feed himself and the orderlies who were serving the food were non-English speakers who would just plonk the food down and let him get on with it. Back at the nursing station they were discussing the boyfriend's newest tattoo or willie piercing. Toni felt sorry for the elderly gent and helped him eat. A couple of days later he decided that he didn't want any more medication. No one seemed to be that bothered in trying to cheer the poor sod up, discussing hope or even moving away from tattoos and on to medical related topics.

On one particular day a few Islanders came to visit Tony. After the visit Toni went down to the entrance to say thanks and goodbye. When she returned the man who had decided not to take any more medication was dead. Toni waited a while but eventually she went to the nurse's station and told them that this patient had passed away. The nurses arrived and drew the curtains around the dead man and later he was removed from the ward.

Even though Tony had a synthetic vein put into his leg to help circulation it wasn't enough and having already lost toes in the Falklands he now had to lose all his toes and a couple of inches of his foot on one leg. This was a great shocker for us all, even though we knew that things weren't great from the beginning. Even so we tried to focus on the greater good and for Granddad to return to the Falklands.

It was five months of hell for all of us, but particularly for Toni although she did have a bolthole, which gave her a huge amount of support. She lodged with Pat and Mally Lee, Falkland Islanders who live in Southampton, and they treated her like a member of the family, lifting her spirits when she was down and just being there for her during some pretty tough times.

What do you say when you are only visiting someone in hospital and very little else? Toni and I were in daily email contact, which allowed me to keep her up to date with the gossip of the Falklands and she in turn told me whom the best nurse of the day was. Toni joined the library, which gave her two hours free internet access daily.

Toni found it hard to keep Tony amused visiting him for many hours each day. Tony loved playing crib, so Toni started scouring the city of Southampton to find a cribbage set. This act alone kept Toni busy for days. For those that don't know, cribbage is a card game, which has a wooden board with two rows of holes where you record your scores by moving a peg. One row on one side of the board is for one player and the row on the other side is for the other. Toni couldn't play the game but she can now due to the hours of playing.

Tony didn't enjoy the hospital food and so he would ask Toni to pick up a Chinese meal for him in the evenings. Tony got so used to this routine that if Toni was late arriving with the food he would get a little grumpy. Even at 8,000 miles away I felt that Tony didn't appreciate the efforts of his daughter, but then it was an ordeal for him just lying in bed hour upon hour, week after week, month after month collecting bedsores. I did often wonder who else in the family could have given this patient, reliable, attentive care and I couldn't think of anyone else. Even on reflection I realised how difficult it was for Tony, but I still couldn't have hacked the ingratitude on the spur of the moment and would probably have mentioned it on an off day.

I eventually went over and we planned to slip away to Crete for Toni to recharge her batteries and to have some family quality time. Being in Europe, we were still in range for a quick flight back to the UK. We had arranged for Toni and the young adults to undertake a diving course, which everyone was looking forward to.

Days before the off, things at the Southampton General took a turn for the worse and it really looked grim for Tony. The forecast for him to live was gloomy and the prospects for survival pretty remote.

We all sat around feeling pretty fed up with Tony's predicament and our plans in tatters. Toni announced that she couldn't go and that we should still go and make the most of it, considering we had been looking forward to it for ages. It seemed an impossibility to be able to go and have an enjoyable holiday, especially knowing that Toni wasn't there. But go we did and make the most of it we also did.

My sister lent me her mobile phone and any ring had me fearing the worst, but Tony P. hung on tenaciously. Toni and I exchanged a number of calls and it sounded so dire I really couldn't see how he would get better. Tony was a tough old bastard and he proved it once again.

Caris and Liam did their PADI course and I went on their first dive from a boat. The instructor took us to a spot where he must take many of his dive clients. He opened a bag of food and fish just appeared from everywhere. One fairly big fish swam out of the depths for his share, much to our excitement. Later, in a way that typifies Falkland Islanders, we called him Mr Taverna. When Mr Taverna appeared, I estimated that he must have been around three-feet long, Caris and Liam were making knife and fork gestures.

Liam caught an ear infection at the end of his course, which put the mockers on passing out which was disappointing, but he had still completed 90 per cent of the agenda. Luckily, staying with my sister, a native of 30 years, she was able to take us to the local ear, nose and throat clinic and get Liam some antibiotics. This is the work that Toni excels at, but I was able to muddle through as a poor substitute. I couldn't rise to the challenge and try as I might I was incapable of putting a positive spin on Liam not being able to eat ice cream for the rest of his holiday.

There were moments of guilt when we would be stuffing our faces with Greek food, mostly courtesy of Yiannis who is an extremely good cook, but we tried to put a brave face on it and get on with it.

We have sneaked a few holidays in Crete over the years and all but this one with Toni. There is something warm and (extended) family-orientated about Greek culture. At the table it is all about helping yourself to the many dishes that come to the table using your hands, much more than you would in the UK. Yiannis would find something to his liking and cut pieces off and share them around the table for everyone to appreciate. Living in the Falklands on a farm we are used to eating bits of an animal that more discerning folk may pass by, such as heart, tripe, brain fritters etc., but our experience was widened in Crete. We were enjoying liver in gravy but some of it didn't have the texture of liver. It was spongy and not as dense.

On further investigation we found that we were eating lungs, which in the thick livery gravy had momentarily fooled us.

I think one of the greatest things that continues to impress me was the household's ability to manufacture their own wine in quantities that kept them going over a full year.

The Gallos would buy in grapes and put them in a rectangular wooden structure, being about four foot by two foot and about a foot high. A hose was attached to one corner down into big wooden barrels in the cellar.

We were there one year when the grapes were put into this contraption and we jumped up and down on the grapes and the juice went down the pipe into the cellar. The most amazing thing is that they don't add anything like one would do in the UK or the Falklands. Not sugar, nor any airlock. It certainly is nothing like the paraphernalia involved in wine making as it is at home. Six weeks later you can drink it.

We returned to UK to find that Tony, against all the odds had managed not to die. I returned to the Falklands and a while later father and daughter returned home and our lives returned to normal. Tony was in a bit of a state, with a number of bedsores and his foot hadn't completely healed, the former due to the care and attention that he hadn't received from the NHS.

Tony's diet

On my second term on Council I became even closer to Tony, staying with him during my trips to town. At times he only seemed to tolerate me disturbing his quiet life, but his kindness shone through. He was very house-proud, getting up in the morning to start a routine of opening the curtains with his walking stick and saying something welcoming like 'Are you still here?' He would then go into the kitchen and draw the curtains, moving on to worry the mats into their rightful place with his stick, then readjusting the cushions on his chair that sat between the oil-fired burner and the kitchen units and the sink on the south wall.

Then the breakfast ritual would start. A whole tin of prunes would go into his bowl topped with a sugar substitute of blizzard proportions. If his prunes weren't covered in a snowdrift of Canderel of at least half an inch in the shallow areas, it was clear he must have run short.

In fact, Tony's diet couldn't have helped his health because he seemed to like everything that is bad for you. He liked a roast of meat with so much fat on it suggested that the sheep donating it was close to a heart attack anyway before its demise, let alone anyone that would plough through this heart-stopping fat.

When Tony lived with us on the farm he would cast his eyes over the mutton and feel their tails. If the tail wasn't three inches across he thought the animal was emaciated.

Tony liked heart and offal and had a particular fondness for brains, and all this soused with a liberal sprinkling of salt and swamped with Lea & Perrins sauce. Members of the family tried to tactfully point out the benefits of a balanced diet but this only made him grumpy. In a way, it was a cop out that we didn't stick to our guns but equally we didn't want perpetual confrontation.

My mother and father

It is a funny situation to be living so far away from your parents, and when I came to the Falklands it was all about seeing the world and seeking adventure. How my folk felt seemed irrelevant although I can't even remember consciously thinking that way. I was so busy doing my own thing, that how they felt didn't occur to me. Staying in the Falklands forever hadn't either. I suppose it is stating the obvious, but as time has gone on my folk have become older and more vulnerable. There is not much you can do in an emergency when you live 8,000 miles away with only two flights a week back to the UK.

Father's stroke had been incredibly cruel because it had taken away his ability to read and write, the two things he loved to do the most. His quality of life remained high, however, and he was able to be fairly independent living with Mother. They went on a couple of holidays, including one to Russia. It did get tough for Mum because Father would get frustrated with his predicament. He would say things that were hurtful like wishing he were dead, which I am sure he would never have said if he had been himself.

Six years after Father's stroke the phone went during the night. Father had been taken ill. He had had a heart attack and was in hospital in Chelmsford, but not St Liam's (the name we jokingly gave to St John's hospital after Liam was born there). Always the optimist, I saw him bouncing back and thought I would wait a few days to see what was what before charging off to the northern hemisphere.

The Pettersson clan however were pessimistic and told me to get going and so I packed a suitcase and left. I didn't have any problem getting a flight, which was asked for at very short notice, as it was treated as a compassionate case. Dad had always been pragmatic about his demise and told me not to waste money flying back to his funeral, but people's deaths of course are as much about those that are left behind.

Of all the luck as I flew home I caught a blasted cold and couldn't go to see Father for a few days. My elder sister, Caris J., was in the country having flown over from Greece so there were still enough people to be at his bedside.

When I did get in to see Dad he seemed weak, but much the same as before struggling for some of his words but looking as if recovery was a possibility. Our daughter Caris, and Zoe, my sister's daughter, came up from university. Plus all the members of my younger sister's family were able to pop in.

At this time Mother and Father lived in Maylandsea in Essex, next to miles and miles of tidal creeks.

Even though it was a traumatic episode it was a family time where we had all gravitated to support Mum and it gave us all quality time with one another. My sister Caris and I lived with my mother. Mum found the whole thing of travelling to and from the hospital and the visit itself exhausting and so she would go to bed to rest in the afternoon while Caris and I would go for a walk along the creek side, a little way from the house. It was very enjoyable to walk together chatting about all things.

Caris had a habit of buying jam doughnuts and leaving them in the cupboard. Mother had a habit of telling us how she didn't like them because they were sweet and sickly and bad for her diet. Funny old thing, because on our return from our walk we would be ready for a drink and put the kettle on and seek out the doughnuts only to find at least one unaccounted for.

After a while, Father moved towards the door leading out of the ward and we were told this was good news because it meant that he was improving and the people closest to the doors found the next step was to go home. It looked really good, but it didn't last long. Something happened during one of the nights and he was taken back closer to the nursing station which was a backwards step. Although we were never officially informed, we assumed that he had had another heart attack. Basically, his heart had lost its capacity to function properly. We spent a number of days hoping that his heart would stabilise, but Father's contributions got fewer and fewer until they were zero. I remember him waking up after his move back into the bowels of the ward and seeming surprised that he was still alive. His last request was a great one. He wanted to drink some beer. In we came to the hospital with a couple of bottles for father to sup. The nurses allowing us to ply their patient with beer, told us that the game was up.

I have given North Allerton and Southampton General the thumbs down, but this Essex hospital was excellent and its staff bent over backwards to be sympathetic and helpful.

The days came when the doctors wanted to meet with us to review Dad's situation. Basically and tragically Dad wasn't going to recover and he was being kept alive with drugs, which they asked if they could stop administering. Alive really is the wrong term because Dad lay there sleeping.

It wasn't until the early hours of the following morning that Father past away with Mother, Caris and I by his side. Sally had only just left.

Dad had always been a chronic asthmatic and many doctors had predicted a short life. He had proved them all wrong achieving his three score years and ten plus some. It was a sad time but it was timely in as much as that he was worn out after a full and active life.

My sister Caris and I went to arrange the funeral. They told us that the firm's speciality was the director walking in front of the hearse as it left the church. We thought that Father would think that this was a bit ostentatious and said we would prefer that he didn't. We then had a form-filling frenzy and the deed was done.

The funeral was held in a small local church a few miles from Maylandsea. The director did his speciality anyway, but I could see Dad seeing the funny side of all this pomp, especially as they had asked us whether they should do it and been instructed not to. I thought it was funny so I hope he did.

Depressing in its formality and finality we followed the hearse to the crematorium and sat there duty-bound as the coffin disappeared behind the curtain. We went back to the house to have nibbles and a drink and I needed one by that time. It was a funny time to find out that Uncle John, my father's brother, was a Norwich and Ipswich fan. I thought you were either one or the other. Cousin Pip is a Sheffield Wednesday fan, which is just like supporting Gillingham (my team) with a big stadium.

I stayed around for a few more days which I hoped would be good for Mum, although it wasn't through choice it was due to being unable to get a flight home straight away. I admit to the odd whinge about the military air bridge but there have to be rules and when it came to a compassionate flight up, I was slotted straight in.

Caris and I had many more walks around the Blackwater and Mother consumed more of the sugary doughnuts that she doesn't really like as we came to the end of an important chapter of our family's life.

13. COUNCIL 2005 TO 2009

Overseas trips

In 2005 I was voted back on Council. The Stanley Councillors were Andrea Clausen, Richard Cockwell, Richard Davies, Janet Robertson and Mike Summers. The camp members were Ian Hansen, Mike Rendell and me. I knew everyone by name but I didn't really know Richard Davies, Mike Rendell or Janet Robertson. This was soon to change. I had worked with Mike Summers for a spell when I was on before.

Virtually straight away there seemed to be a genuine good feel to the group and although we were sorely tested over our term the good-natured camaraderie prevailed. We had our disagreements and we had our agreements, but it never felt to me as if anyone held a grudge or that anyone was trying to score points from one another. I never felt, even when we were giving each other a hard time, that any of us would hold it against another or wait for an opportunity to put the boot in. There was, in general, an all for one and one for all unspoken ethos.

The set up was fairly similar to the last time, although the level of accountability was much higher and the direct hands-on of Councillors' work, through the government, was reflected by weekly meetings with the Government's Chief Executive.

One of my first overseas trips was to New York and the United Nations doing the Committee of 24 for the second time with Dr Richard Davies. He flew LAN via Chile and I went via the UK as I took the opportunity to visit the two main colleges that students from the Falklands attend in the UK as part of my portfolio responsibilities.

So it all kicked off in New York back to the oldie-worldie Beekman Towers to rest our bones. The maintenance crew still hadn't improved on the work poor Eric had started with the air conditioning and it was still like living in an aircraft hangar.

It was really the same process as years ago, apart from the bilaterals that were all done in the UN. In fact, the majority was done in a backroom overlooking the east river. It was a great place to work and the view and activity was so good I had to have my back to the window to be able to give the job my full attention.

We decided to have a plan where Richard would get things going with a situation report and when we were going as a community and at some appropriate place in the proceedings, I would ask them straight out whether they would support us with an intervention by their mission at the committee.

The day of delivering our petitions arrived and we stood before the Committee of 24, but this time there wasn't the huge party of Argentines. We spoke and then the Argentinian petitioners had their moment. I was saddened to see one of Lucas Bridges' descendants,

Delores Reynolds, supporting the Argentine cause. Not surprising that she felt the way she did, but implying that the original Bridges family thought this way seemed to contradict the book that I had read.

Lucas Bridges wrote a fascinating book about his life, *Uttermost Part of The Earth*, which started with his father who was part of a mission effort to Christianise the natives of Tierra Del Fuego, that was based on Keppel Island in the Falklands. His father moved over to the continent to continue this work and he eventually set up a home at Harberton in the south of South America and tried to help the Indians survive. It is interesting that the book documents how the menfolk went back to the UK to find brides and how the next generation went back to the UK for their education. Today's Argentine generation interprets this behaviour as somehow supporting the notion that the Falklands was and is Argentine. This book also documents the time, very late in the 1800s, when the Argentines ran up their flag in that part of their own country.

My colleague Richard, was a really easy guy to talk to and work with. We talked a lot about developing this side of things in this current Council and how best to do it. We felt that members should specialise in areas, rather than to see things like the UN as a perk to be apportioned fairly throughout the individual Councillors. We thought that one member, taking a different colleague each year, would help one person build up relationships with the many individuals from the varying missions.

The only problem with this system is that some might feel that they don't get their fair share of the overseas responsibilities, but to Richard and me it made sense to maximise the effect of this mission for the greater good of the Falklands.

Richard and I did a small amount of touristy stuff, visiting the South Street Seaport Museum that has shown an interest in our Falkland ship wrecks over the years.

Recently Councillors had been adding Washington to the UN itinerary and visiting the State Department and talking with the Americans who deal with the southern cone, which includes Argentina.

We travelled down to Washington on a small turbo prop, having sat in the departure lounge looking at the rain tumbling down in buckets. It didn't seem to postpone anything and we were soon lifting off and climbing through the cloud.

If the Beekman Tower had a historic aspect, the Mayflower Hotel in Washington was one of the best hotels I have stayed in. There were so many pillows on the bed you had to fire several off before you could find the duvet and clamber in. In most hotels these days you are asked to only leave towels on the floor that need to be washed, thus saving hot water and detergent (and the hotels profit) and the environment. I could have left a polite note mentioning the extravagance of having to wash so many pillow cases and thus putting more pressure on the environment, but I didn't.

The next day, after a deep sleep in a mountain of bed linen, we travelled to the British Embassy for a brief and then on to the American State Department. The Americans seemed to be genuinely interested in our country and what we were doing developing our constitution, how our fisheries management was developing and what was happening with hydrocarbons.

These were busy people but we talked easily for over an hour. Richard and I didn't high five when we left, but we were really pleased with how we seemed to connect with our American brethren.

Just before I had left for New York, Tony Heathman had asked me to take some money to give to some military folk that he met in the Falklands who were now working at the mission in Washington. He wanted them to get him a camera and send it to him. The whole process seemed rather involved to me. Why didn't he just go on the internet? Knowing Tony there must have been a scheme to get the camera without paying freight or saving money in some way. It was no big deal so I said I would take the money.

It got really complicated at the beginning where someone had picked the money up from Nyree (Tony and Ailsa's daughter) and then given it to a third party who gave it to me. An envelope with $350 dollars was duly handed over. The wad of dollars was huge. It was so big that I had a job squeezing it into my jacket pocket. I felt like a secret agent with this huge bulge like a pistol and holster under my jacket. Actually what I really felt like was a potential mugging target with a huge wad of money in my pocket. I should have had a message written on my forehead. Mug. Please rob me.

Later I was to learn that there had been a cock up at the Heathman management level. Instead of getting the envelope with $350 in large denominations, I got the other envelope that happened to have the same amount, but was mostly in ones and other low-value notes. These were the tips that they had accrued during the tourist season.

So there I was going through Chile and America giving the entire underworld in these countries the message that I was an easy target. Perhaps it was so obvious that all the crooks thought it was a sting operation.

When I got to Washington I phoned these friends of the Heathman's from a phone booth outside a restaurant. It took me a few goes to conquer this bloody contraption. Anyway I eventually get through and the lady knew exactly where I was and would come directly. We waited for absolutely ages before we had to go. No sign of Tony's contacts.

I had been giving the tip money some exercise in an attempt to reduce its size, replacing stacks of ones with tens and twenties. I carried on trying to contact these people, but my attempt seemed to be doomed to failure. I managed to speak to the lady of the house from the airport as my final attempt to hand over the dosh, but her husband wasn't home and she didn't like driving in the rush hour.

Richard D. was a great companion and very thoughtful and intelligent. As a doctor he is a man that looks as if he has the weight of the world's problems on his shoulders and one nearly feels guilty adding to them by bringing some mild malady to his surgery.

There are some fantastic places to visit in Washington. We chose to go to the Natural History Museum, but it was so vast one would have to have a life membership to do the place justice.

Richard travelled back via LAN and I flew back to the UK and home via the air bridge.

I went to Belfast to do a Commonwealth Parliamentary Association regional meeting with veteran Councillor Richard Cockwell. It was a great time to see Northern Island, just after the end of the troubles and the start of the power-sharing agreement. The mood in the parliament was buoyant. There seemed to be so much going on, particularly in building terms everywhere.

Richard C. had been the mainstay of the Falkland CPA movement for many years and we carried on with this system with another Councillor joining him each time to learn the ropes.

Richard C. was a great people person and another great communicator. The first day as we checked in he would be dishing out sincere handshakes, warm smiles and compliments. The number of handshakes and cheek kisses he administered on the first day would have calloused the hands and dried up the saliva glands of a lesser man. He seemed to know everyone. People just liked this larger than life character from the Falklands. I felt rather insignificant at first with 'Your Richard's colleague, aren't you?' 'Yes, we know Richard very well. We have all been coming for many years.'

We went to the dry dock where the *Titanic* was finished and the story went how her sister ship had been damaged colliding with a British war ship, so they took the *Titanic* out of the dock to repair the damaged vessel. This led to the *Titanic* being launched later than was intended and consequently her maiden voyage coincided with the iceberg season.

Another memorable part of our tour was seeing the murals that graced the walls of buildings as a reminder of the divisions in the community.

Richard found the social events a little too much, especially the ones where you stand around for hours. He would tell me he wasn't coming but he would be networking with some friends of the Falklands. He would meet up for a meal and have some wine and update them on what was happening in the South Atlantic.

The smaller regional CPAs were very useful and you were able to feel like part of a supportive family. The workshops and debates seemed relevant and people appeared to be really interested in your country's welfare. The plenary sessions were something else and that feeling for me of being one big family became rather tenuous, although it was an opportunity to 'network' with many friendly folk from countries like Australia, New Zealand, Canada and the Norfolk Islands to name a few.

India with Toni

Toni and I took a two-week holiday and tagged it on to our trip to India where I was attending a Commonwealth Parliamentarian Association plenary. We bought a round-the-world ticket and went via New Zealand and Australia, catching up with some camp teachers of old in New Zealand and doing the touristy stuff in Australia including diving on the barrier reef.

Early on the first morning in New Zealand we got a phone call from home saying that Toni's father was ill and it was a great concern that all the following updates were of a slow decline. Eventually Tony was flown to Santiago in Chile. We were considering whether Toni should fly home but Tony was adamant that she should carry on to India.

We flew on to India from Australia via Hong Kong and were met by CPA people at the airport. They interrupted the flow of people coming from the plane. Toni got a bouquet of flowers and I got a garland around my neck. We also were the only ones in the VIP lounge, but then it was 2am. They then asked us about our visas. We were told in the Falklands that they would sort it on arrival, as we do not have an embassy here, but it threw them into disarray with lots of animated chatting on the phone and people coming in and out to look at us. They were also struggling to find our luggage which made us slightly apprehensive about the outcome with our visas. The people were very friendly and asked us if we would like to 'take tea' every few minutes but after leaving at ridiculous o'clock and arriving at an equally impossible time we were all tea'd out. Fortunately, they found a low-tech solution and someone wrote '15 days gratis' in biro into our passports. Sorted, as they say. A country of hundreds of millions and they fall back on to some basic common sense. I was deeply impressed.

I have never seen myself as that important, but our security was very impressive. We got in an estate car with armed escorts in behind the back seats and then we had a car in front and a car behind. We then made our way to the Taj Hotel.

The scenes that we saw take some telling from anyone that hasn't visited India or doesn't understand real poverty. We drove along and there were a few people just drifting about, even at 2 or 3 o'clock in the morning. But others seemed to have just gone to sleep where they were overcome by tiredness. I noticed a few tuc-tucs (motorised rickshaws) with the driver's legs hanging out of one side. As we went round a roundabout there were people sleeping on it, like segments of a cake with a smaller circle of people above that and a smaller one above that.

We arrived at the hotel and were ushered to our rooms by our chaperons that included two very pretty Indian girls. They asked us numerous questions and eventually asked for Toni's contribution which one has to pay if your spouse accompanies you. We were all in and collapsed into bed to catch up on a few zzzs.

My compadre, Cockers, wasn't allowed to board a British Airways plane at Heathrow and had to spend a day getting his visa in London. The Council Secretary phoned from the office in Stanley in a panic to see where we were. God knows what would have happened if Cathay Pacific had refused to let us board in Sydney.

While Richard Cockwell was getting a visa, we had several days to make friends and see some of India. We didn't get very far on the first day, because our minder said that it was too dangerous to go down into Imodium City (Delhi). I was okay with that for the first few days because we did need time to collect our thoughts and unwind after our lightning tour of the southern colonies.

Everyone in India that has a job, regardless of the position, guards it jealously. We didn't realise that on our first foray to the pool. We arrived and put our towels on the loungers around the pool before the pool man could intervene, but he did come over and encourage us to sign the book to say that we were at the pool and then later to sign out to say that we had left. No problem. The next time we came near the pool he was ready for us and made a grand gesture of asking us where we wanted to put our towels and then taking them from us to throw extravagantly onto our chosen lounger. This kind of dedication was new to me but made Toni uncomfortable because she found it difficult to cope with this level of subservience.

In the main reception area there was a grand piano where in the evening for a number of hours a pianist and a violinist would play live music until quite late. To me it created an unbeatable atmosphere. During the day however and into the evening you could 'take tea'. You would sit down and usually another attractive Indian lady would come and take your order. When she came back to serve the tea it was like a ceremony. The woman had on long white gloves and wherever possible she would hold one hand and forearm up behind her back while she poured tea with the other. It was really quite special in a simple kind of way.

Even in the loos the team were extremely attentive, to a worrying degree, from the minute you opened the door to enter to them holding the door open for you to leave. In you would go and they would stand back in a kind of attentive, respectful but congratulatory manner. On completion as you turned to the hand basins they would turn the taps on and squeeze the soap into your hands and then quickly pass you the towel as needed. The door was then held open for your departure. No one said 'missing you already' but you felt that they would be waiting attentively for your next visit.

It doesn't take much to understand that they rely on tips to make their wages a living reward for their endeavours.

The people working the rooms didn't miss a trick either and made sure they introduced themselves. Our cleaner was forward-thinking enough to come to tell us of his dedication over the period of our stay, but also to thoughtfully let us know that he would be absent on the day of our departure.

Spending a few hours by the pool we were able to see the gardening staff in action mowing the lawn. They had a decent-sized manual lawn mower which one person pushed and steered while two others were attached to the front by light rope to give it a bit more power. They made short work of the grass area around the pool and projected a positive green image for the hotel to boot. Tree bush work was also labour intensive with two people pulling dead and decaying leaves and bits from the bushes and dropping them on the ground for another team to come round and pick the bits up and cart away.

The people that I admired most of all were the individuals outside the hotel, supporting the door, i.e. opening the doors for arriving and departing taxis. A lot of these regal individuals stood out in the blazing sun in some of the most exotic and warm-looking uniforms you could imagine, looking more appropriate for Mongolia or inside the Arctic Circle.

We were soon bored with studying the people who seemed to work at least 14-hour days. We needed to see India other than the day of culture that had been planned for us. A forceful lady appeared on the scene. She was from the Norfolk Islands and her name was Vicky. 'You don't ask them darling, you tell them you are going.' So with that Vicky, Toni and I, plus our minder, went into downtown Imodium.

The traffic was just unbelievable. It was worse than South America, but at a slower pace. There didn't seem to be any rules and your taxi driver would join an intersection with some kind of faith that you wouldn't hit another vehicle. It was mayhem with all types of vehicles, bikes, tuc-tucs, lorries, coaches, buses and cars fighting for their piece of tarmac.

I don't think I have ever been more frightened in a vehicle. This was the start of our trips to different venues to buy souvenirs and things. There was a serious side, however, demonstrating the reality of the danger and the value of human life. On one of these trips a dead person had been thrown up onto a pile of rubbish by the side of the road after being knocked down by a bus.

We went to a street which contained state-sponsored stores where merchandise from all over India is sold. The prices seemed to be very good and we went back time and time again. Toni bought a silver elephant and a chain in one shop and they remembered us every time we appeared in the neighbourhood, let alone the shop. So did I and made a better effort to control our spending by skirting the whole area whenever possible. Buying stuff was a complex task. First you indicated you wanted to buy something and they gave you a bit of paper. This happened for each item you wanted and then you were ready to pay. As you made your way to the cashier you could imagine these changing hands between areas of responsibilities and floors as they too made their way to the cashier. So you paid one person who gave you a receipt as another person wrapped it and someone else handed it to you. I bought myself a pair of hand-made slippers for about three pounds on my first outing. The bloody things were nearly worn out by the time they had made it to the till.

Richard C. eventually arrived and caused a commotion because he reckoned he saw some elephants on the way in from the airport. Some of the more unkind individuals suggested, quite unfairly, that Richard had partaken in too much hospitality in BA business class and that perhaps he had seen pink elephants.

One evening we went to look at some carpets. The attention the sellers give you is intensive. If they think you are serious they will give you some tea and then they are into their performance. They bring these hand-tied silk carpets in and then flick them out across the floor. They ask you to admire the colours that change when viewed from different directions. Vicky bought a really expensive carpet and this got the others to see potential in the rest of us and carpets were being thrown about in every direction. Richard Cockwell was backed into a small part of the shop and I could hear him saying how nice they were but he didn't want one. I suggested that he might buy one for Jackson (his basset hound) but he didn't weaken. They didn't try very hard with us, they knew tight bastards when they saw them.

Toni went on to better things with her friend from Gibraltar who was actually born in India. We found out that haggling is expected and is all a bit of a game. At one shop they went to they went through many items with one assistant bringing the merchandise and showing it to them while another member of staff was folding and putting away. Toni hadn't got into the swing of things at this time, because she felt sorry for all this effort for scant reward at times, but it wasn't long before she was playing hardball and getting some good bargains. In one shop we were offered some stuff and we were only slightly interested but the shopkeeper must have thought we were good for a sale and was actually offering us the same merchandise for a third of the price in the doorway of the premises as we left.

We had kept in touch with home and Chile via our mobile using Vodaphone but here in India getting a sim card was a process in itself.

I went to the man in the hotel that could fix everything and asked to buy a sim card for the mobile phone. It was incredibly difficult but I had to persevere so that we were able to keep in instant touch rather than rely on emails. The form was to be filled out in triplicate (it could have been more) and a copy of your passport and a separate picture was required. Eventually I got my sim card and put £30 credit on it. We gave that line some work phoning Chile, phoning the Falklands, phoning the UK and on our departure we were still trying to use the credit we had. Because of the number of people in India the phone tariffs were very cheap.

The big CPAs are massive and it is hard to get debate and interaction between the different parties. I found that it was only certain countries that you could knock up a decent rapport with. Australians, New Zealanders, Canadians and the smaller countries were the easiest to chat with and find something in common.

Our day of culture arrived and we went on a day's trip to the Taj Mahal. We got on a train in Delhi and slowly trundled to Agra. Some of the sights along the railway track were depressing in their awfulness, with poverty as clear as day and the piles of refuse and the feeling of utter neglect. Men would be using the railway lines as their toilet squatting unashamedly as the train passed by with a bottle of water instead of loo roll. The train hardly got out of a crawl. Perhaps it was because there were so many people on the track. When we got to Agra we were put in coaches, which took us close to the tour destiny, but the last few miles we had to travel in electric buses, which don't cause any pollution or damage to the Taj Mahal.

Seeing is believing. Pictures show it to be an amazing place but actually visiting is something really memorable. To think that the whole site was shut to accommodate the guests of the CPA.

It was a special day for us all and going back to Delhi, a huge red sun gradually sank beneath the trees and houses that were along the track. No picture that we took does the sun justice.

Meals were lavish to the extreme but most of us were incredibly careful not to eat uncooked stuff or washed fruit and salads.

I think it was on the second day of the meetings. We went for our supper as always and had our fill and then had a few drinks with our antipodean friends and then went to bed. Early the next morning I woke up to sharp pains in my stomach and I knew I had the dreaded Delhi Belly.

I took an Imodium tablet and felt a lot better that night. Vicky came to my rescue by bringing a few things to my attention. 'Look at them, darling, some of the people serving the food are pretty grubby.' She wasn't wrong and close inspection did highlight a few that looked as if they had rolled to work. I had been so absorbed with all the fresh fruit and different food that I hadn't looked much further. Even though I was careful and usually I don't have gut problems I got struck down again before we left. Toni got it once but I was the lucky one because she got it on the way home on the plane.

Eventually it was time to wind our way home and join the masses trying to get themselves and their luggage through all the airport controls and onto the plane back to London. On this part of the leg we were on British Airways and one that I have always seen as a solid and efficient carrier.

I know this doesn't sound reasonable but I don't like British Airways anymore because they skimp on the lavatory paper. They buy the cheapest flimsiest rubbish that their bursars can find. To me they might as well hang up squares of newspaper on string.

My colleague Richard has a very long back and so he upgrades when at all possible to business class. And why not, he is not in his first spring of youth either. Fortunately, he was sitting not that far away and so he was able to look back from all his business class comfort with the three-ply toilet paper and see us in steerage class discomfort, all in the name of austerity for FIG.

Toni was feeling a lot better on our arrival at Heathrow. We all met at the luggage carousel and Richard was able to say his flight had been marvellous; the service had been super and the food good, for that type of thing. It felt rather churlish to bring up any flaws that we might have discovered in the planes comfort facilities.

We made our way back to Southend to stay with my sister Sally. Not the most stimulating town I've ever been to, but it did have one blessing and that is we were able to travel without our ever-present supply of Imodium. You didn't have to barter and you weren't on a 24/7 elephant watch. God knows when the last elephant was seen in Southend, although I am sure there is someone in the area that could tell you.

Tony

I had to hurry back to the Falklands and carry on with the farm and Council responsibilities and Toni planned to have a couple of weeks in Brighton with the young adults before heading back. The idea was to stop off and lend support to Derek who was with Tony P. in Clinica Alemana in Santiago.

Things were not going that well in Chile and it was obvious that Derek was getting swamped with all the pressures and trauma of Tony's treatment and so Toni followed me south within days and headed for Santiago.

It was all pretty depressing and although the staff's professionalism couldn't be criticised, there were operational differences that Toni found alien to what she had witnessed elsewhere. Tony P. was restrained at all times in his hospital bed and it was also an emotional battering to see and hear the ventilator chugging in and out relentlessly.

In those situations, if there's hope there's a reason for optimism but the hope was very sparse with Tony not responding at all day after day after day. It is true to say that at no time did the Chilean doctors or nurses give up.

After nearly three weeks Tony was getting worse and the proposals that were being suggested were a bridge too far with very little prospect of success.

Eventually Derek and Toni came back to the Falklands with Tony in a coffin, one of the last bodies to be flown back to the Islands from Chile. (Although there was a period of time when bodies didn't return, this practice has started again.)

It was a tough time for us all. Caris and Liam were in the UK and we encouraged them not to come home but to write personal tributes to their grandfather which I read out in church.

Once more I thought of the good times over the years, especially when he came and lived with us for a while and he showed us that although he had been a townie all his life he was a bit of a gaucho at heart and could do all the camp jobs. He had worked at the butchery during the war and so knew how to skin a sheep and, although I had moved on from the Great Island days, Tony thought he could show me a few pointers.

There wasn't anywhere to kill in the early days and so I usually killed outside at the palinkey which was a tall frame where you hung beef up, but this day for my lesson I set up a small block and tackle in the cowshed. I can't remember the detail of what happened, but in such close confines a huge great wether got charging around and it ended up with Tony and I wrestling it in an undignified way to the ground. There were times when the mutton was on top, but fortunately we prevailed. Because it was such a fiasco we ended up covered in dust and grime, laughing at our predicament.

So here we were in Christ Church Cathedral where different folk had contributed to the celebration of Tony's life – a top student, badminton player and a footballer that held the record number of goals in a season. Tony was a government employee for all his working years. The church was full. Although I tried to remember all the good times I couldn't help feeling robbed. Heather and Tony were both so young.

To Gibraltar

Toni accompanied Richard Cockwell and me to Gibraltar. She had had a tough time with her father dying and so we thought a break, which would include time in the UK with the kids, would be beneficial. On route to Gibraltar we stayed at the hotel at Gatwick Airport and Toni thought it was one of the most comfortable beds she had ever slept in.

Landing in Gibraltar is quite novel because the runway is built out into the sea on one side and meets the sea at the other end. The strip is right on the border so you cross it to go to Spain and immediately on the other side is customs.

The funniest part of it all was that Gibraltar is only one-third of the size of our farm and yet over 35,000 people live there, compared to two at Port Sussex.

Being a regional CPA there was a lot more dialogue through all the countries and we discussed the environment and green issues which were right up our street. With our three wind turbines (at that time), waste heat recovery from our power station heating the hospital and the swimming pool plus other initiatives like the glass imploders which makes usable aggregate from bottles, we were able to offer a lot of input.

We had our day of culture looking for dolphins in the bay, one of Gibraltar's tourist highlights after the apes. In many ways I was dreading it because Toni is not a good sailor. But messing about in boats for me is a pleasure and I don't mind rough seas.

We all piled on the boat, went out into the bay and around we went again… and again… and again. As we were spinning round the wind got up and the sea became a little choppy. A few people had sat at the front in anticipation of seeing the dolphins first and as it began to get rough and water began to come over the bow a number of people got drenched. We spent hours circling but didn't even get a glimpse. Richard had had the right idea. He had been doing these things for over a decade. He was off happily 'networking' with like-minded people.

The positives didn't involve dolphins, we didn't even see a stuffed one. But Toni had had an excellent time and wasn't sick and didn't even feel sick. I was delighted for her and gobsmacked at the same time.

I was surprised at how much there is to see on Gibraltar. There are many miles of tunnels within the rock and all the different cannons from the different eras.

We went to look at the caves and the stalagmites and stalactites. One of the places where it opens up underground was huge. Lots of people were taking photos. I do hope they are better than the rubbishy efforts I took. The areas were so big the flash was just overwhelmed.

Outside there was the all-important shop to sell decent pictures of the caves and sweets, drinks and ice cream. One poor bloke was still thinking of his underground experience and so wasn't alert enough when one of the apes snatched his ice cream out of his hand. With his prize the primate leapt up onto a nearby fence. This ape had either studied how to eat ice creams from people or he had had one before because instead of ripping into it, he casually unwrapped it and ate it looking at his victim as much as to say, 'try getting it back.' They were all pretty bold and you had to keep an eye on them at all times.

This boldness is their undoing, because human food isn't good for them but it is easier to get than their natural diet that they have to win from their environment. Consequently, the life span of these apes is far shorter than it should be and that is why people are discouraged from feeding them deliberately or otherwise.

On the last day of our Gibraltar experience we managed to cross the airstrip and enter Spain. There is traffic control on the runway that stops traffic when a plane is coming in. The whole runway is treated like a huge railway crossing. There are barriers, lights and claxons. We were stopped as this happened. The plane lands and parks, the barriers go up and the traffic streams across in either direction. We went through customs and into Spain. The customs officer seemed less than disinterested. Coming back, the customs official didn't even raise his head.

We met a fellow CPA delegate returning from Spain. 'It's a dump,' he said. 'A waste of time,' he added as he disappeared back to Gibraltar.

We must be easily pleased because we found it quite interesting. We found a shop to put our pictures from our camera onto disk and then we had a coffee and a snack. Following that we went to a market where everything was so cheap. I am sure most Falkland Islanders would weep if they saw how cheap and good the quality of the fruit was here. Toni bought a large amount of cherries for the euro equivalent of very little.

I found the whole experience rather good. Walking back, we saw a group of young Spanish girls showing off to some young men by writing graffiti on a white wall.

It wasn't long before we were winging our way back to the UK, with a quick stop at Brighton to see the brats, as we waited for a plane back to the Falklands.

A bi-election

Unbelievably and totally unfairly in my opinion, Richard Davies had to resign and fight for his seat at a bi-election. He had been badly advised, but this doesn't constitute a reasonable excuse, so he had to battle for his political life at what must be the most difficult time; mid-term. His crime was to stand in, for a short period of time, as the senior medical officer, a position whose incumbent is banned from taking political office.

Personally, I think we should have come clean with the electorate and explained that it was a genuine mistake caused by bad advice which hadn't led to any mismanagement or inappropriate decisions in Council or the Medical Department and moved on. This was not the legal advice and there wasn't the appetite to play it as I suggested, so Richard was made to fall on his sword.

I think Richard gave us a humanitarian angle that was seriously diluted when he left and, contrary to what I heard many people say at the time, he had a great understanding of the workings of ordinary people in the community and was a great defender of their position and needs.

This was the third time that I had been involved in a bi-election and to the polls we went. Richard Davies, John Birmingham, Roger Edwards and Jamie Peck fought for the seat. Every candidate slagged off the Council's performance apart from Richard, who defended with all the loose ends from work in progress. He was in for a hiding to nothing. Richard was out and back came John Birmingham who had been elected in during another bi-election way back in the 1990s when he first entered politics.

John had returned for twenty months of work with seven people he had just given a verbal working over. The first thing he did was to apologise but to say that he didn't agree with some of the stuff we were doing. He also went on to say, and there is a lot of truth in what he said, that he would never have got in if he hadn't been critical in some way. With hindsight, John may feel that he got tainted with the malcontent that was attached to this Council/Assembly when we eventually went to the polls.

I had the dubious pleasure of being the number two on the Municipal Services and so I led that portfolio along with my own once Richard resigned, and I carried on doubling up until John was elected. Never a dull moment but I always had Janet and Andrea to fall back on in my own portfolio.

The UN

This brings me nicely back to the UN and the third visit of that council. Richard Davies had been given the lead role after we returned and discussed our views about developing our approach by having one Councillor (Assembly member) going every year of the four years of the Assembly and taking another Councillor along to learn the ropes. The idea was that the lead Councillor would build up a better rapport with the people he met each year. You would know who was fully briefed from previous meetings and people that were new and also who was worth that extra push and so on.

Richard had gone with Ian Hansen on the second year and so I suggested that now with

Richard gone perhaps Ian and I should split the two remaining years working at the UN to maintain the continuity with him going again and me also a year later. Ian didn't support the idea and said how he felt uncomfortable meeting and dealing with the Argentines. So I grabbed the baton of continuity, but this wasn't without a lot of discussion.

Janet Robertson and I were given the task of going to the UN and carrying on the good work. I had worked a lot with Janet because she was second on my portfolio and she also led the Immigration Working Group, of which I was a member. I was also third on the Health and Medical Services, her portfolio, and so sat on that Committee when her Vice Chair was not available for any reason. We worked well together but didn't see eye to eye on every issue, which was quite healthy.

Janet was another big character, with a mass of curly red hair that gave her a striking appearance. In my opinion she was one our best Members of this Legislative Assembly and a good foil for the other strong members of our group. She was not satisfied with the first idea and would challenge us all to look at things in different ways. Janet was very serious at work but light hearted, down to earth and good company during the periods of downtime. If I was to criticise Janet in any way it is in her timekeeping, which isn't one of my strengths either. If I saw Janet's car outside a meeting I was attending, I knew it had either broken down the last time she was there or I was very late.

So the day came to leave the Islands and as I was coming in from camp I left a bit earlier, to cover the possibility of breakdown or getting a puncture as there is less chance that someone will pass, at that very instant, to get you to the airport on time. We didn't break down or have a puncture, so we arrived at the airport at the start of check-in and began one of the many long waits that you have in travel especially at airports.

LAN has a good reputation for reliability and flying into the Falklands and that is saying something. Having said that, they do have a lot of practice because conditions in the south of their own country can be challenging at times. Even us locals give them praise for their service and we don't give that easily.

I had been sitting there half a lifetime before Janet arrived, judging her entrance to the last few seconds, to be processed.

You begin to know that something is not right when the airport staff start whispering/murmuring to one another and then there is an announcement that LAN are having bother, due to fog, getting into Punta. They need to get to Punta to pick up life rafts for the flight over water to the Falklands.

Eventually the news is not good. Today is the day that rarely happens. LAN is delayed.

We went home and had another go two days later. This was not good for Janet and I as the loss of days seriously affected our efforts in New York.

Eventually we got the plane out. Toni was delivering me to Mount Pleasant Airport and we were able to give our neighbours Terence and Sheila a lift with us. Janet's mother and father were also on the flight. Ann was flying out to get a hip replacement privately because she couldn't tolerate the pain any longer and couldn't wait for our Medical Department to arrive at this conclusion sometime, unknown, in the future.

The flight over to Punta Arenas is a short hop and then you decant, go through immigration and then you are back into the plane and off to Santiago. This leg is a few hours and not so casual. One also arrives late into Santiago.

So not at all daunted by the hour, Janet suggested that we look for something to eat. Off we went into town and as typical Falkland Islanders looked for something outside. It is not that warm outside at that time of night and to be honest not that warm in June during the day either, but there is no doubt it is a lot warmer than the Falklands. The waiters coaxed us in to the warm. We had something with the obligatory bottle of red wine.

Not wanting to give other people too many attributes, in fear of overshadowing mine, I have to admit that Janet had another awesome skill for travelling in South and North America, and that was her ability to speak Spanish.

The next night we are on the flight to JFK. It was a long and gruelling flight and with the plane packed we were shoulder to shoulder. It was a good payday for LAN but not for creature comforts for the cattle class customer.

We arrived in the USA tired and drained, looking forward to a long hot shower and brush up in our hotel rooms before the commencement of work.

We arrived at the geriatric Beekman Towers only to find out that our pre-booked rooms had been sold to others. I gave a token gesture of disappointment but Janet was ready for an all-in fight. Fortunately, I was able to persuade her not to expend her remaining energy on something we couldn't change.

They did say brightly that we could take advantage of the showers in the fitness suite. They were barely adequate and it was as close to showering and changing in a broom cupboard as you can get.

So it was shower, teeth, what remains of my hair, into one's best and then down to meet up with our minder, Mark ORiley, all within less than one and a half hours of leaving the airport.

We had a hectic day in the UN, in a room overlooking the water. There was hardly time to draw breath as a continuous stream of ambassadors and mission heads came to hear our points of view. On a couple of occasions we quickly went down to a lounge. At times when we had double-booked, Janet and I would do one each, one in the lounge and one in the room.

We gave it everything. There was no time to relax and collect ourselves and at the end of the day we were exhausted. There was no time to go back to the hotel and prepare for the evening's reception. We left the UN and went straight to the British Deputy Ambassador's apartment, had a quick brush up in the bathrooms and then straight out and into meeting the invited guests.

Janet and I worked the floor, meeting all the people present, probably doing 85 per cent each. Everyone seemed very interested and sympathetic to our position but this wasn't reflected later during the debate on our right to self-determination.

We were totally shattered by the time we got back to the Beekman Towers Hotel, having arrived after an overnight flight, cramming two day's bilaterals into one and then doing an evening stint. We retired to the rooftop bar and a few revitalizing G &Ts to toast a job well done against all the odds.

Being an old campaigner when it came to delivering our petition to the Committee of 24, I warned Janet of the united front of South America and how it had hit me on my first visit. We delivered our petitions as a couple of Argentine photographers clicked away down below us.

The Argentine petitioners spent most of their time emphasising their credibility as responsible members of their community before starting the 'Malvinas belong to the Argentine' stuff. One was a teacher whose very distant relative was supposedly the first Argentine Governor of the Falklands. The other was a scientist in agriculture whose family had gone to Argentina from the Falklands generations ago.

Then it was on to the South American solidarity and then countries whose representatives we had met. As each country spoke I wrote comments in the margin. I didn't detect any support for us from many of the missions whose people we had met at the UK's Deputy Ambassador's residence, which we both found bitterly disappointing.

We did have some countries support our right of having self-determination, but again a small number compared to the verbal encouragement that we had received during those many bilaterals.

So a few postcards and one or two small gifts and we were back to our hotel to pick up our belongings and off to catch a train to Washington. Ian and Richard had had some problems with the planes the year before so now we had a train journey to look forward to.

Train travel to Washington

To me, who has done a reasonable amount of train travel in my time including the London underground, I found New York Pennsylvania Railway Station very confusing. The list of times of arrivals and departures was broken down and there didn't seem to be any fall-back position. We ended up asking someone where our train was and what time was it leaving.

We were told that the train was just about to leave, so we tore down some steps and leapt aboard and grabbed some seats. In our rush we had chosen a quite carriage. No loud talking, no mobiles. It copied a sort of library atmosphere. I thought we could cope with the no mobiles but the quiet talking over a few hours, I had my doubts.

So off we went, Mark (from the FCO) always remembering to whisper and Janet and I occasionally forgetting. Janet and I were still working although the big event was behind us. We were answering some questions that a journalist had asked us by email. In the first hour Mark asked us if we would like some tea and we forgot and said in voices that cut right through the carriage – 'Yes please.' Mark's voice was very soft anyway so it was easy to forget that he was in fact whispering.

Later in the journey it was dark outside and we had finished the work and it was difficult to settle down and read. I suggested a Sam Adams all round. I wanted one and so did Janet but Mark didn't. Fair enough, so off Janet and I went to the buffet car.

I don't know if it was down to tiredness or relief that the main job had been done, but the beer made us a little light-headed. Janet asked the very good question of why was it that the British invented many sports and then went on to be rubbish at them. A sweeping statement yes, but with an element of truth never the less. I demanded to know why synchronised swimming was an Olympic sport and had some British cretin invented that.

So whilst debating this intellectually challenging subject, Janet saw the funny side of things and we both began to laugh. Janet began to snort and guffaw as she breathed in and out, failing abysmally to fit this noise into the etiquette of a quiet carriage. It was a release of tension in some ways but genuinely funny as well, although I can't remember Mark laughing. The Americans probably tolerated these quaint Brits travelling on what was probably some kind of commuter service.

Arriving late at the Mayflower once again, we went and got bar meals washed down with another Sam Adams for Janet and I. Mark had orange juice. If he felt that we were a bit exuberant or a bit over the top, he didn't mention it.

Washington

So once more we went back to the State Department. This time with Janet's knowledge of Argentina, we really got a discussion going. The desk officers from the American Embassy in Buenos Aires were there, one that was on the point of handing over and one that was going. We must have talked for even longer than last year with Richard. It was really interesting listening to their perspective and I think they were interested in what we had to say. We did ask them if they thought the American stance towards us would alter when there was a change in government. They answered to the negatory.

The main effort was behind us and so we had a bit of time to kill. We got tickets for the on-and-off buses that ply their trade around the capital. The idea of these buses is simple – you buy a ticket and then you can get on or off at any point. If you see something you like you just leave the bus and equally once you have seen enough you hop back on to the next point of interest. We travelled down to the Native American Museum and spent many hours browsing looking at the different cultures. It did occur to me that the particular Indians whose staple food was acorns would have welcomed the white invaders ashore inviting them to slaughter them, as they walked ashore, to stop them eating any more acorns.

It was a fascinating few hours but I was disappointed that the Indians of Tierra del Fuego didn't get much of a mention.

I had a very ethnic buffalo steak and beans with a large coffee to wash it down. Janet went outside for a cigarette.

Janet thought it would be nice to have a go in a pedalo down on a lake so, in pursuit of that dream, she lay down under the shade of a tree while I went on a trek that Shackleton would have been proud of, in tropical temperatures, to find said lake and boats.
I went back for Janet and we strolled down to the lake and hired a pedalo. We bombed about a bit and covered most of the shoreline and then posed for pictures (not for our constituents). In fact, it was a fun, relaxing jaunt to blow away the cobwebs of the past week.

As we were heading back to the shore an angry black cloud approached and the wind sprung up from zero to at least 20 knots in minutes. As we walked out of the area, after getting our deposit back, the boat keepers were calling the boats in.

The rain started to lash down, but at least it was still warm.

We ambled up to where we hoped to catch a bus and waited ages. On the advert it said one every ten or fifteen minutes. Obviously a lot less if it starts to rain. This bus was the last of the day and did the mopping up operation of those who were left. It also only went as far as the depot.

Miami

It was goodbye to Washington and we were winging our way to Miami. There aren't that many flights in and out of the Falklands and you have nearly a week when you can't get home via Chile.

With the new container service to the Falklands, Miami was the gateway to American goods and so Janet was going to make the most of it by dropping in on the way back and buying some new furniture. I decided to go along for the trip and offer my limited expertise rather than sit around in Santiago.

Miami to me was a huge eye-opener, starting off from the premise that the USA is the most powerful country in the world.

The first night we wandered from our hotel over to the nearest touristy place with bars, restaurants and shops that spread down to the sea. The walk over was not without interest and we were approached by a number of weirdoes asking for money. Fortunately, they didn't get upset when we said we didn't have any, although one followed us for a while which was disconcerting. Later we were advised not to do that kind of thing, so in future we caught a taxi. It just seemed like tempting fate to go against local knowledge.

The next day we were off to do some serious furniture shopping. 'Whoopee do,' Janet had done a bit of research and had some names of large furniture stores that she wanted to visit. We get a taxi outside the hotel. 'Can you take us to the Golden Furniture Collection?'

'Where's that?'

'It is meant to be the biggest furniture store in Miami, do you know it?'

'What street is it on?'

I felt like saying, 'Well you're the ruddy taxi driver,' but we kept our cool and Janet rummaged into her bag and came up with the avenue and street and we were off on our Miami furniture adventure.

Our taxi driver's name was Omar Flores and he was from Nicaragua. Like many of the drivers that drove us during this shopping spree, probably destined to be one of the first millionaire cab drivers. Miami is enormous and spread over a huge distance there weren't that many high-rise things away from the hotel area.

During the whole trip, Janet, as a Spanish speaker, would whisper that the people behind us on the plane were Argentine, or the people at the next table in a restaurant and at other locations. Even in New York she identified some of our western neighbours.

Good old Omar dropped us off and recognising the goose that lays the golden egg, helpfully said he would work in the vicinity until we were ready to move on.

This shop wasn't the biggest that we visited during our stay but it was still large. The furniture consisted largely of the gaudiest stuff ever imaginable. There were only a few pieces that I would want in my house. I didn't really know what Janet wanted at first but, once armed with the knowledge, there didn't seem to be much there that we were looking for so eventually we asked for some assistance. Most of the people that we dealt with struggled with English as a first language and try as Janet might in English the chap at the first shop was in this category. Janet switched effortlessly to Spanish and the man's eyes lit up with recognition. 'Are you an Argentine?' he asked. Of course from what had gone before I nearly split my sides laughing.

Our Nicaraguan friend was just a phone call away and turned up promptly to give us the chance to be robbed blind for the next leg. This time Janet thought she knew where the place was and Omar thought it was somewhere else. Although Janet was new to Miami, Omar didn't fill me with confidence but as Janet was picking up the tab we tried her address. Nothing. We then tried Omar. Ditto. So with the meter ticking away he belatedly contacted his firm who were able to point us in the right direction.

Even Janet was running out of topics to chat to Omar about, but we were in his cab so long we got on to the merits of Nicaraguan food. 'Oh it is very good,' said Omar.

'Like what?' we asked. '

Meat, onion, rice.'

'Okay, so what is your favourite Nicaraguan dish?'

'The one my mother make,' said Omar, followed by a long pause.

'Which is?' we encouraged.

'Meat, onion and rice.'

'What kind of meat?'

'Any meat with onion and rice.'

With that topic exhausted we moved on to household economics and how Omar saved for luxuries. Omar's tactics were simple in that he saved as much as he could afford each week. His present aim was to save for a large plasma TV screen.

Janet was not finding the stuff she wanted so we asked Omar if he had any suggestions of where we should go to buy furniture that doesn't dazzle you with its shiny veneer. Off we went and he took us to where 'everyone' goes, and drops us of.

'Just phone me when you need to move on.'

It didn't take long to see that the product quality was high and so were the prices. We carried on down the street and to be fair there was some really nice stuff, but far outside a normal budget. It was soon time to call our Nicaraguan taxi driver.

'Tomorrow I will take you to the place where ordinary folk buy their furniture.' As he dropped us off he handed us his card and looked forward to driving us tomorrow.

We had had a longish but unproductive day and Janet felt that she had singlehandedly bought Omar's plasma TV. I even dreamt that night of the Flores family all sitting back, showing their laughter lines, while watching a brand new, gigantic, plasma screen.

That evening we went back to the place by the sea and had a meal in a semi-deserted Nicaraguan restaurant. Contrary to Omar's recommendation and superlative build up of the food from his country of birth, the food wasn't much more than 'meat, onions, and rice' made edible with a couple of bottles of red wine that I, for one, felt that we had deserved.

Next day we did find a big furniture store, but without the help of Omar, who had burnt his bridges in Janet's eyes (the final straw being the last night's meal). Again the furniture was 90 per cent shite and 10 per cent maybe. We tried out the sort of stuff we thought the Robertson-Pompert mob might like. Chairs and sofas where the backs reclined and bits come out to support your feet. The two seat sofas were called love seats. This was a quaint American label that I had never come across before. These two seaters could rock independently. The theory maybe that if you were in a grump with your partner you could rock forward as they were rocking back, and when things were going well you could rock in unison.

I took a number of shots of Janet posing on all of the possibilities so that the Stanley members, Joost, Sorrel and Sophie could participate in the choice. When we arrived we were swamped with overly helpful reps all jockeying for our business, but Janet soon made it clear that we needed our space. It was quite amusing browsing around, especially when we found a dressing table in the colours of a zebra. Another positive was armchairs that moved to help you onto your feet. The poshest examples you could adjust the speed but not to a level where it threw you across the room, unfortunately.

We came back the next day with the choices being made. I didn't realise shopping could be so much fun and I suppose not having to live with the decisions made it easier for me, but by this time I do believe I had reached saturation point.

The next task on another day was to buy household stuff like sheets and there just wasn't the opportunity to have any banter, so I left Janet to it and I went to see if I could buy a washing machine for the Stevens' household.

We were in a huge mall like a three-legged starfish, that coincidently the taxi driver of the day hadn't heard of, within which I soon found a store selling the stuff I was after.

To me a salesman earns his commission by selling his product and being helpful, i.e. it's the most reliable, value for money, etc. Doing something that stops you moving on to a different brand or another store. I found the model that I wanted but it was 110Volts and the load weights were in imperial not metric. I asked my attentive sales person if he could convert to kilograms.

'No.'

'Do you have a calculator so that I can?'

'No.'

'Could your store supply a 240 volt model?'

'No.'

I knew that this company did make 240-volt equipment because I had seen other 240-volt models in Chile. I didn't ask him whether he thought he was worth his commission, or not, because I already knew and I had a feeling that he wouldn't know the answer. We did sort of talk things through and he either thought I was an idiot or he was one, because he went on to say this manufacturer had the whole of the United States to supply so they weren't interested in other markets. I was staggered at such ignorance. It must be a rare manufacturer that isn't interested in more trade and greater profits. This sales person wasn't a salesman at all. He just wanted someone to walk in, select something, hand over the money and for him to do the paper work. No wonder other countries are so competitive. Can you imagine this from a Japanese, Chinese or Indian sales person?

Another form of ignorance was ours. We went shopping in another massive shopping mall that another taxi driver had never heard of. Once again, being grid squares, we had to provide the street and avenue details and as if by magic we drove straight there.

We went shopping and I bought a Wii. I must be paranoid because once I had bought it I felt, once again, like a potential mugging victim. I invested in a green canvas bag that I hoped made the Wii look more like a bag of vegetables.

It was fairly late before we decided enough was enough and we felt sufficiently shopped out. As we had invested heavily in the taxi firms we thought we should try public transport for a value for money ride. We caught a bus that was heading back towards downtown Miami. This bus went everywhere, criss-crossing its way towards our hotel. We were reading the notices on the bus and realised there were three languages, not just Spanish and English. A very helpful youth told us it was Creole, which is also spoken in this part of the world.

There is absolutely no doubt that we stuck out like sore thumbs being definitely non-local and dressed unlike any of the other folk using the bus. I suppose we must have done a couple of hours and had to change buses and we did get some questioning looks from the people and the bus staff. Eventually some caring soul of a bus driver persuaded us to get off the bus at a fuel station for our own safety saying it was unwise to carry on in this location at that time of night.

What a kind and considerate man. Off we went to the fuel station and asked the cashiers if they would order us a taxi. A chap picked up the phone and rang a firm but didn't know the address of his place of work and neither did the others. One was wise enough to tell the chap to look at the bottom of a till receipt.

We got ourselves a coffee from a sophisticated machine that could give you any kind, strength or breed and waited.

At this stage of an eventful journey one would have thought that that would be it but no, we get into a taxi whose driver was another character and whose birthplace happened to be Nigeria. I sat behind the driver and Janet sat the opposite side so that when the driver turned round to speak or looked in the mirror his attentions focused on Janet. He helpfully told us of his life being in the wilderness before he met Jesus and how his life was made up of the dark time that was before Jesus and the light that was after. He had been bought to Jesus when a member of his family burst into flames for no apparent reason. Then half way through the story of his family member burning, he asked Janet if she believed in god. As a so-called politician with usually a comment and answer about anything she stumbled along with an unconvincing 'maybe' that sounded like a definite no.

All the time this sincere discussion was carrying on I was trying to catch Janet's eye and make her snort and guffaw as she had on the train during our journey to Washington. She was equally determined not to as she was trying not to break down.

This was more evidence that one or both of us were serious weirdo magnets although nothing too serious.

Small world it is because, on the day that we left, we bumped into Andrew Newman who was attending a conference in his capacity as Director of Civil Aviation. We did the usual catching up, like Islanders do when they meet, and then eventually went our separate ways.

The flight back to Santiago wasn't too bad, with a few spare seats so we were able to spread out and travel in relative comfort.

Santiago seemed a little tame, compared to and after Miami and a city where the taxi drivers seemed to know where things were without the name of the avenue and street number and a sat nav.

Back home... and then back to the UN again

When we got back to the Falklands I did something for the *Penguin News* and Janet did something on the local radio. I tried to portray two dedicated Falkland politicians working hard for the greater good of the Islands and performing under very trying circumstances.

The following week in the *Penguin News* a letter appeared suggesting that video conferencing would be a lot more efficient and cost effective.

In the real world the Argentines put a lot of effort into lobbying their case. The foreign minister of a big, influential country of 40 million people in a lot of instances probably does this over lunch. We, on the other hand, are unknown representatives of a minute country who meet people in half-hour slots over coffee and biscuits. To downgrade to a situation where we would be talking on a poor conferencing link when we are already working at a disadvantage can only be false economy.

Circumstances had Janet and myself going for her second and my fourth time overall. I would like to think it was our colleague's recognition of our efforts the previous year.

We got off to a brilliant start with the plane leaving on time. There was a downside, which was my brother-in-law and his lovely wife Trudi were on the same flight. I/we had arranged to meet up for lunch as long as he promised not to be rude to Janet or give me a hard time.

The next day in Santiago we had a game of spot the Falkland Islander. It was the middle of winter for the Chileans and they dressed appropriately with coats done up to the top button, two or three turns of a scarf and hats pulled down passed the ears. In among these local inhabitants were pale-looking individuals wearing short-sleeved shirts and some were even in shorts. Yes, you've got it. It was the visitors from the southern isles.

Derek recommended a lunch venue that turned out to be pretty good. In this place as many as eight people could sit around the large tables with a hot plate on one side. The chef came over to our table and with a certain amount of showmanship cooked our meal. The performance got off to a pathetic start with chef using the slice and things as drumsticks, but from that point it got better and better and was quite entertaining. He flicked the eggs up with the slice breaking them on the edge as they came down. Not hard enough to split them in two but just the same as you would if cracking them on the side of a frying pan. As the food was flying through the air and spinning on the hob we ordered cocktails and started to drink them. I am not really a cocktail person so perhaps my choice was suspect, but I found mine was not nice and would have been more suited to lighter fuel or fuelling a high-performance engine. I did however have a second just to make sure it was totally foul.

Janet went off to shop while the rest of us retired to Derek and Trudi's hotel where we picked out a red wine and had a few glasses. Janet had promised to return in an hour and to my surprise she was bang on time. Well, it was Liberation Day so a small celebration wasn't out of order. I am pleased however that Janet and I had to leave prematurely to catch the plane to New York. The office kept one of our hotel rooms so we were able to shower and freshen up for the journey. We also decided to discuss further and higher-education funding for the umpteenth time. Neither of us could see the other's view or were prepared to compromise a jot. We got a taxi to the airport and had a silent coffee and silent wait for the plane to JFK.

The queues weren't as hectic as I had thought and it didn't take long to get through the passport control, pick up our luggage and head for our hotel. We had decided to try the Millennium Hotel on the UN Plaza. Things were going so smoothly up until this point. But it was all going to go pear-shaped.

We checked in only to find that there was just one room and that they didn't have a spare while we sorted out the confusion. So apart from panic mode we tried to ring the Falklands, but then it was a public holiday so we couldn't raise the secretary at Gilbert House. We couldn't raise anyone. Janet's sister, a number of friends of her's and mine... Surely they couldn't all be out.

So we phoned Toni in the UK and got her to phone the Falklands and find the secretary.

Soon the secretary was on the phone, even though it was her day off saying that she would try and sort it out. We sat around for bloody ages waiting for something to happen, knowing that she would be beavering away to try and get it sorted. I can't emphasis enough that this delay was the last thing we wanted after the long overnight flight. It was becoming a bit deja vu.

The secretary phoned back to tell us it was sorted and just go to the front desk. So back we went and this time they were all smiles. I did however ask why, when we had asked about another room, there wasn't one spare and yet now one had miraculously been found. Apparently this was a booking issue and nothing to do with reception. Oh, right!

My room was okay but my expensive internet connection was crap. I phoned the reception that night and the following day and they kept saying that someone would sort it. Eventually I asked if I could speak to the manager and that resulted in a cable arriving at the door. It wasn't what I needed. I finally traced the fault myself to an extension lead, so I swapped it with the one on the TV and was suddenly online. The cheeky bastards tried to charge me for my internet connection during my stay but they took it off the bill when I complained.

With Toni in the UK, farm sitters in Stanley or Sussex and Caris in New York somewhere, it was important that I had comms.

We eventually got down to doing the bilaterals in a far better shape than the year before. Our meetings were held once again in the lounge or our room overlooking the water.

You are learning all the time. One of the lessons that one learns is to make sure you understand someone's intentions. During the last meeting we had, we seemed to be engaging really well, the ambassador and his second-in-command were asking questions and even volunteering parts of the conversation that he had with the Argentines, and a joke against their foreign minister. I didn't ask if they were going to make an intervention because it seemed a certainty. It appeared rather unnecessary when one of our Foreign Office minders asked his Excellency if he would be at the Committee of 24 meeting the next day. No, regrettably he was very busy with something else. We had given it our all, even overrunning our half-hour slot. I was flabbergasted.

The Committee of 24 was much the same as previous years apart from the Argentine petitioners seemed pretty feeble. One of Lucus Bridges's descendants, Delores Reynolds, was back trying to suggest, once more, that the original Bridges family saw the Falklands as part of Argentina. We obviously read different books.

The other petitioner who was related and named after a so-called Argentine governor was abysmal. He foresaw a day when a visiting Argentine would catch the eye of a Falkland Islander at the Tourist Jetty Centre and that would be the start of a monumental understanding. I wished I had bought my sudoku.

Then it was time to listen to the South American solidarity. I thought it was time for a coffee, but of course there were our supporters yet to come and we didn't want to miss them.

We felt a little disappointed even if we knew from experience that the support we got face-to-face was never mirrored at the meeting, but for all that effort it would have been nice to get greater recognition.

The meeting was adjourned before the end, but we had to go to catch our train. This time we could have travelled on the quiet carriage without breaking any rules. Mark was really quiet, but then he always was compared to his wards.

The Washington trip was going to be an upgrade on the previous year, meeting a Special Assistant to the President and Senior Director for Western Hemisphere Affairs in the Dwight Eisenhower Executive Office Building, one Daniel A. Restrepo. Because it was a first and a bit out of the blue that we should be meeting with such a senior member of the United States government, we phoned Mike Summers, whose responsibilities include foreign affairs, to see if he had anything to add.

We went in and met this important member of Obama's staff. 'I'm Dan,' was the self-effacing welcome. We really went through the same stuff about the Falklands and our development and our concerns and our desire to have self-determination. Dan seemed to be interested in the Falklands and asked us a number of questions. We overran our allotted time, which is always a healthy sign.

We then went back to our usual routine and went to the State Department to meet our usual contacts.

One night we were out in Washington having a pub meal. I think we had already had one Sam Adams and the table service was a little slow so Janet went to order another. I was sitting outside and I could hear all this cackling from Janet and she was saying, 'No, I don't mind, it's a huge compliment, thank you.' The proprietor had only asked Janet for ID to check she was 21 and old enough to buy alcohol.

Our touristy stuff was in a serious vein this year and we visited the Washington Memorial and the Vietnam Memorial. I found the latter quite moving, seeing all those names of the dead. I suppose that Vietnam was very current in my youth. Not that I fought there but the news was full of it. The peace marches and the protest songs and the college I attended had American teachers who were draft dodgers. Draft dodging was a huge issue and I remember trying to get my head around all those men that went and died and those that survived and how I would feel if I had gone and returned to know that others had managed to get out of it through foul means.

I can't help feeling, as I do with our own war, that it is always awful to realise the sacrifice of those young lives. Vietnam eventually seemed so pointless. What will we be saying in thirty or forty years' time about Iraq and Afghanistan??

Back we went to New York, meeting up with Caris, who was there to meet up with a girl she had befriended during a trip to Thailand whilst at university, and using the time before flying south. One of the first trips we did after meeting up with Caris was to walk across Brooklyn Bridge, which was quite a feat of engineering when it was built but rather insignificant in this day and age. We went to Liberty Island but it wasn't as frenetic and as vital as last time with Toni in the 1990s, although there was a guy there with a snake on our return. On the Island you can no longer go up inside the Statue of Liberty but you could go up onto the plinth. The Statue has been closed since the Twin Towers attacks but they are thinking about opening it again.

We were in a hotel called the Novatel. I had been phoning them for days to see if it was all right to have Caris share my room. You would get an answerphone to try another number that also had a message. Each message was in three languages and took forever but I still didn't get through to a human being to ask my question. When we all shipped up to the hotel I was bracing myself for another battle, but it was a non-issue and Caris had a pull out bed to sleep on.

Just as in Santiago it was spot the Falkland Islander, in New York it was spot the non-local. It was tropical last year when we had attended and it had been the same when Richard Davies and I had been here. Both times it was over thirty degrees and sweltering. Not this year. This year it was cold and chucking it down every day that we were in the city. You could leave in the dry, thinking perhaps it's clearing at last and then the heavens would open and it would just bucket it down in torrents. The local New Yorkers were like the gunslingers of the Wild West, but instead of a colt 45, it was an umbrella they were drawing out in a fraction of a second. As the first drops hit, the umbrellas would be heaved out in one fell swoop and in most cases it seemed as if they came from nowhere. The visitors like us got a soaking on more than one occasion, although our minders were armed with them.

The day I put Caris on a train at Penn Station, New York, to go back to her friends, was to demonstrate my non-local status. At first, walking back to my hotel, there were a couple of drops and then light rain and then in less than a block it was belting down and I was soaked. I could have rung out my clothes on arriving back at my hotel.

JFK beckoned and it was a stinker of a flight. Starting at JFK, then on to Ecuador, Santiago and then a few hours later on to Punta Arenas. The first leg was packed shoulder to shoulder and the entertainment screens on our part of the plane weren't working. We landed in Ecuador and the people that were travelling on to Santiago were kept on the plane.

There were seven of us. I took some pictures of the airport out of the window. We just stood around stretching our legs as the cleaners went through the plane.

No one joined the plane so there were just seven of us flying on to Santiago. There must have been the least number of passengers on a commercial flight that I had ever been on by some margin. We just chose a row of seats and relaxed. It is at times like these that I wish I could sleep, but try as I might I couldn't.

We arrived at Santiago, picked up our luggage and went through customs. That was the plan, but we stood by the carousel watching the other handful get their stuff and mine didn't materialise. Thank heavens for my Spanish-speaking companion who got the message across. A few quick phone calls and 'I'm sorry your bag was offloaded in Ecuador.' They said it would be with me in Punta Arenas tomorrow night.

In the meantime, while getting a few pesos and having a cup of coffee, I realised I hadn't got my camera any more.

After the flight down to Santiago with hardly any one else on board, I was saying that I couldn't see many people on this three o clock flight to Punta on a Friday. WRONG. It was chockers. I didn't see any spare seats.

So down to Punta we went and on landing Janet spoke to someone about the camera and then we headed for our hotel. I was completely shattered and went straight to my room for some zzzs. Janet, the insomniac, went for a coffee.

Three hours later and bleary eyed we were off to meet the Administrator of the Magellanic University. Of course I only had the clothes I had flown in, so I felt a little stale even though I had showered thoroughly. We had a good look around at the facilities and saw what was available.

We wanted to go to the new shopping mall so the administrator took us there where we had a coffee and a further chat and then we went our separate ways.

It had been a long haul from leaving New York but being our last night we ended it on a high.

Janet knows Punta reasonably well and so suggested we walk down towards the dock to a restaurant she knew. We had a drink at the bar before we left to fortify ourselves against the winter weather. The place in question looked deserted but it was still early evening so we wandered on until we found somewhere that looked open. I think it was the toughest steak I have ever paid for. When we ordered the salad the waiter shouted through a door to the chef asking if he had this ingredient or that. The wine was the get-out-of-jail card and made all the other frailties acceptable.

We walked back to the Hotel Cabo de Hornos, but it was still quite early so we had a couple of Chilean gin and tonics. Chilean spirits don't seem to have a measure. They put some ice in a tall glass and glugged the gin in.

In the morning, after breakfast, I asked Janet to ask reception if my case had turned up. They looked a little puzzled and explained that they had delivered it to my room last night. Not only had I not seen it the previous night, I hadn't seen it that morning either. I just put it down to the couple of gigantic Chilean G&Ts I'd had the night before.

Many people in the Falklands see these trips as jollies and you do get downtime, but only because the weekly flights make it impossible to fly to a tighter schedule. But the work and travel commitments can be very tough.

Education and immigration

While I am writing about the Legislative Assembly I would like to record two issues. One is the restructuring of the schools and the work that we did in developing the Immigration Ordinance.

My portfolio was Education and I was chair of the Education Board. Janet was the Vice Chair and Andrea was the third Councillor/assembly member. We were to remain on this board throughout the term although Andrea was to become the Executive Member on the board. The difference being that generally she wasn't meant to speak but could take the rational of any debate to Exco, so that they would have some understanding of the Committee's thought processes and recommendations etc.

It was quickly apparent, at the start of our four years, that there was some bad behaviour issues in the Community School and our Director at the time was advising us that our best option was to set up a separate unit to deal with the unruly element. The costs were eye-watering and the needs were great at a time when money was very tight. There would have to be a building to support two classes, two teachers, one of each sex. Before these proposals came to anything our director, Sylvia Cole, came to the end of her contract and left and the headmaster of the Community School stood in until her successor came down to the Islands.

Barbara Booth came down as our new Director and it was the start of a new regime. She spoke to parents and staff, visited all the schools. She asked Councillors and other senior managers for their thoughts.

Due to poor timing that was nothing to do with Barbara, an internal enquiry ruled that the Head of the Community School and recent Acting Director was found culpable of not following Education Department policy when excluding a pupil. The Chief Executive posted the ruling to the head of the Community School as he was leaving the Islands on business.

The headmaster had been going through a difficult time in his personal life with his wife dying and this for him was the final straw and he walked out of the school taking his grievances to the Government Secretary, who was acting Chief Executive, when the man himself was absent, and the Director of Human Resources was also involved. They promptly took it to the Governor and the proverbial hit the fan.

Barbara had only been here a few weeks and she and I were summoned to Government House to stand before the Governor, Howard Pearce. There was no discussion and he had nailed his colours to a particular mast and started berating us for our failings. In fact, it was an internal enquiry that had been conducted by a senior director under the Chief Executive's instruction. I felt that he wasn't seeing the issue in a balanced way and argued that we needed to deal with it 'in-house.'

I wrote a press statement only to find that Sir had written one. I tried to reach him but he was visiting a mountain site with the Commander British Forces. As he came off the helicopter I managed to get him on the phone where we had a frank exchange of views. He saw it as his domain and I saw it as the Education Department's and mine and I told him so. 'Are you telling me what to do?' he bellowed down the phone. I said, 'No. I wouldn't be so impertinent Sir, but I can hardly preach about self-determination and self-governing in our local affairs at places like the UN if the Governor acts in a way that contradicts this.'

Howard and I got on a lot better after this and he assured me he would help in any capacity to solve this issue outside his responsibilities as Governor. I did run my press statement by Howard and I did deliver all the points I needed to. I also included a small piece of no consequence to appease him but the press release was from the Falkland Island Education Department.

So the dust was in the air when the Councillors and Barbara looked at all the issues, especially the increasing amount of bad behaviour in the schools and also structure for local teachers with ambition to have some kind of career pathway. Like all governments we had to do it within an incredibly tight budget.

Barbara came back with a restructuring programme that monitored quality of teaching and learning and gave responsibility posts to teachers, bringing a structure where teachers could work their way up the ladder of pay and responsibility.

These were proposals with a period of consultation where Barbara and Janet and I would visit the schools and discuss.

It was like a bomb going off with massive collateral damage. Some staff were openly hostile and they accused us of having already made the decisions and that the consultations were pointless.

The hostility at the Community School was unbelievable, with some classroom teachers thinking they knew better than the Director. No one likes change, and we knew that there would be opposition, but the anger was strong and raw from a group of teachers that wanted things to be done their way. There were things that were wrong but it was as if even the smallest hint of criticism, in any area, administered a blow throughout the whole staff. Even individuals that were praised for their endeavours felt slighted by the collective hurt.

The meeting with the Infant and Junior School was also a very rough ride but they did participate with ideas of their own about creating spare capacity within the school that they thought was paramount.

We had several more meetings at each school. The Chief Executive joined us during one of these meetings at the Community School. On one particular occasion a member of staff was offensive and rude to the Director in a manner that would have been unacceptable from a child. I was surprised, not by the opposition, but by the manner of a lot of the input. Basically I was shocked that such highly respected professionals should react in such a manner. The staff at the Infant and Junior School, after their initial grump, embraced the concepts and recognised the approach we were trying to deliver.

Janet and I both put a lot of effort into the consultation process and we were quick to concede, on our part, that we could have tried to manage it better but some of the suggestions of workshops had me visualising us all holding hands in vast circles, burning joss sticks forever more. Even with an endless process of non-confrontational workshops, eventually you have to arrive at decisions that some people aren't happy with. With the seriousness of the problems that we had, we also had to start addressing them with some speed.

Since the Fishing Industry has been established, Councillors have invested in numerous extensions at the Infant and Junior School and a brand new designer building for the Community School. It is something that the community is very proud of. Hopefully our legacy will be one of providing a structure that maintains standards of education for years to come. Now the systems are in place to plot every child through their school life, picking up their failings and helping them or recognising their special skills and developing them. It also helps the schools to maintain standards in teaching, a process that is commonplace in most other countries.

On the morning of one of the regular Education Board meetings I knew I was going down with something. I felt really sick. It was rather an important meeting and although I had great faith in Janet and Andrea, I felt that I wanted to add my views on certain subjects. Rough as I felt, I could suppress the urge to vomit with positive thinking until the meeting was over.

It wasn't until I had left the room at least twice that I realised I had to throw in the towel and go back to my Stanley lodgings. I asked Janet to chair and left.

In hindsight I should have phoned Toni to come and get me, but I felt so grim that I thought a dose of fresh air would help to clear my head. My lodgings were on Davis Street and the Education Department worked out of offices down on Ross Road at the front of town on the seafront. Stanley is built on the side of a hill and Davis Street is at the top.

By the time I had reached Davis Street I had about 300 yards to go and I was feeling rougher than a bear's arse. I began to speed up, even though this was making me feel worse. I began to think that I wasn't going to make it or that despite positive thinking it was going to be close.

I swayed into the hedge at the house opposite where I was staying, dropped my briefcase on the pavement and was sick. I was straightening myself out when a young lad walked by shaking his head. It did occur to me that he may have thought I was staggering back from some kind of Councillors' drinking festivity rather than the victim of some potent virus.

The Immigration Working Group was set up to modernise and bring systems into place to control immigration into the Islands. It was the hardest brain-numbing process that I was involved in. Trying to construct a fair and equitable points system and then have mandatory areas like a medical and police record checks. We were trying to deliver a system to minimise risk to the Falklands, that weeded out the serious criminal and the individual that might cost us tens of thousands if they had to be medevaced to Santiago or even need expensive drugs to live in the Islands.

The group was made up of Janet Robertson as the lead, Dr Andrea Clausen and I as the Councillors and then the Government Secretary and his secretary, the Immigrations Officer and a member of his staff. We often had the Senior Crown Council and also called in the Senior Medical Office and others when needed.

We spent hours thrashing out the detail. One small issue was an English test and whether one was needed for all applicants. How detailed should it be, considering that we have a handful of Chileans that have been here for years and have been active members of the community but whose English is pretty poor.

Historically, many people have come to the Islands with very little and become, over time, successful members of the community. We were looking at a minimum wage below which point someone wouldn't be able to proceed along to a permanent resident permit and on to status holder. The thought behind this was that we would discourage people that might become a drain on society. Should there be a maximum age for people entering the Islands? The medical advice is that before the age of five and after 65 are the times of greatest cost.

We argued to a standstill on these and many other issues in the group and then we would present our thoughts to all Councillors and have the same arguments over again.

I can remember Bill Luxton chairing a similar group in the 1990s and many others have taken it on but with no visible progress. Roger Edwards and Jan Cheek had been the champions in the previous Council.

I have no doubt that if it hadn't been for the fighting spirit of Andrea and Janet, who wouldn't take no for an answer, we would have gone the same way as all the others. I played my part but it was more in the areas of tempering extremism. Where Andrea might have thought a degree in English was appropriate for the English test for immigrants for whom it wasn't their first language, I would be content with them showing commitment to work and to our society and being able to ask for two beers in the Globe. Obviously the issue was a serious one and it is difficult to integrate into a society if you can't speak the language and there is a fear that people from different countries would form micro-societies within ours, a situation that has led to difficulties in other communities.

We were very optimistic at the start with our leader Janet saying forcefully that the work would be completed in the year. I had my doubts about that but I felt from day one that we would achieve something. To complicate matters, the portfolio system was changed at just after the mid-way point and Mike Rendell took the lead in bringing all our work to some conclusion. I didn't realise how close it was going to be, to get anything done at all, by the close of our four-year term. We got much of our work through on the last Assembly meeting of our innings.

I don't think any of us involved thought that this was the finished article, but more a strong foundation with solid reasoning which could be adjusted with the experience of time.

In highlighting a few of the workings of government it will give a flavour and overview of what went on in general.

Driving on the roads

There are other bits to record, like the many hours that I spent on the unsurfaced roads driving into Stanley. In the summer the roads are usually good where the maintenance crews are out grading and rolling the surface and keeping the roads in good shape. Trips of under an hour and a half were the norm. The greatest trial would be the summer winds that tug at your vehicle and move it about on the road. The worst wind is one that comes from the north and picks up speed as it comes off the mountain. During extremely high winds from the north a Land Rover, which isn't very aerodynamic, will move its own width across the road. In dry conditions any vehicle leaves a huge cloud of dust behind. A large lorry will make it look as if a huge desert sand storm is on its way.

The winter is completely different and it is like driving sitting in a pipe because after a few miles, from clean, the side windows are covered in clay. Conditions generally deteriorate as the maintenance crews can't grade the sticky surface and it starts to become potholed. Depending on the winter, one can expect at least one or two months of driving on a heavily cratered surface. It does get boring and the tendency is to go faster than the 40mph speed limit to get the journey done.

When Toni's father died we inherited his top-of-the-range Mitsubishi Shogun. Unlike the Land Rover that handles okay but is no speed king, the Shogun had independent suspension, a fuel-injected 3.3 turbo diesel engine and was incredibly smooth to drive. 40mph in the Land Rover feels like 40mph. 60–70mph in the Shogun feels like the Land Rover's 40mph.

I think most people drive on the Falklands' dirt roads as much by feel as by watching the speedo or rev counter. The main focus is driving on the loose gravel and clay roads. The first time I took the Shogun home, even though I was constantly checking my speed, I knew that I severely broke the 40mph speed limit. I also left a blanket of dust trailing miles behind me and hanging over the East Falklands on what was a nice calm day. It was perfect conditions in every respect for driving in the Falklands.

I got home, put the kettle on and I was sorting out my briefcase and my overnight bag when there was a knock on the door. I could see through the window that it was the Royal Falkland Island Police. I instantly thought that they must have been on the road doing speed checks and not only was I speeding but I was going so fast I must have shot past before they had a chance to step into the road and stop me and I'd probably bathed them in dust for good measure.

I could imagine the *Penguin News* headlines already. 'Councillor done for speeding. Chased for miles by our brave boys in blue.'

What can you do in circumstances like this? I decided to brazen it out.

'Hello, come in. You are lucky. I am just making a cuppa. Do you want one?'

To cut a long story short they were on the first patrol in our area for about 15 years and thought they would pop in. We had a nice relaxing hot drink and a friendly chat, mostly about dogs and then they were off to the next location.

Leaving the Assembly

Sadly, like all good things, the Assembly ran its course and on the November 5 2009 an election had all eight of us unceremoniously booted out. In fact, it was only six of us that stood again but I am sure it would have been all if the other two had stood. Yet again it was nine if you think that Richard Davies had been removed by the voting power of the Stanley constituents.

There were many accusations about us not listening and not coming up with the goods, but we were unable to do what people wanted, and what we would have liked for everyone including ourselves, because of the financial circumstances

Ironically, two big projects that affected everyone in camp were seriously delayed because of the consultation that went on. In the case of the enhanced television there was much debate on whether the private sector provider should be given a) a monopoly, or b) the monopoly if they could deliver certain programmes that were provided by BFBS.

We had to make some tough but correct decisions over our four years that annoyed people. We were unable to maintain budgets and had to continuously look for savings. We lost £10million from a £45million revenue through the illex squid not showing up and the world recession affecting our investments, so we had little choice.

Two of us consistently argued to spread the flow of information coming out of Gilbert House but the majority view was that Exco Councillors should, with their executive authority, be the mouthpiece of our Assembly. I am not totally convinced however that a greater participation would have negated, or made the decisions more palatable, that we were forced to make.

Probably the other nail in the coffin was how the government review was handled. It did try and address many issues in one major hit but the general public focused on the redundancies of two popular government officials. Even during the elections candidates were rubbishing the review but demanding the very things it was designed to deliver, like career paths for locals and for government to perform better.

For camp, the absence of TV and radio for six months and the problems associated with the new telecommunications in camp did not help the camp Councillors. One has to ask oneself if another group of Councillors could have done a better job dealing with the non-commercial BFBS, the private sector concerns and the officers dealing with the project and the all-encompassing pressure to save money at all times.

Regardless of all these problems, even when cash was scarce, we invested heavily in camp and its future. Something that hasn't been equalled in the past, in times of plenty, and it is unlikely to be equalled in the future unless oil is developed.

We did bite the bullet on revamping the telecommunications, something that had been obsolete for years in camp relying on secondhand spares and the goodwill of an overseas company who were repairing equipment out of contract.

We did introduce the ferry after many years of wanting one. We did initiate a modern reliable TV set-up which didn't rely on isolated repeaters on top of, at times, inaccessible mountain tops.

Time, however, was not on our side and many of these new things did not bed in quickly.

To me it was an enjoyable four years working through the problems with like-minded people, looking into and planning for the future and not just reacting as things occur.

It felt like a being part of a band of brothers. Working with Richard Davies in New York and enjoying his dedication and his relaxed style. Richard Cockwell's gigantic capacity to make friends and pass on the Falklands' message to many people. His work at the CPA will take some beating. My portfolio and the support Janet gave as my deputy. Not always agreeing, apart from always having the passion for achieving quality and accountable education. Andrea, as well, who brought determination to challenge and support us, even after the portfolio change. The UN trips with Janet were also memorable for overcoming adversity, companionship and a sense of humour.

I didn't feel sorry for myself, even though I felt that I had achieved so much, but I am sorry that Andrea and Janet didn't get re-elected because they were top players in our Assembly and represented, to me, a future of forward-thinking politicians with vision, not relying on rhetoric or jingoistic hang-ups from our past.

Probably the one person that deserved even more pity was the Government's Chief Executive, who was maligned from start to finish, although well paid for this burden. During the election a number of candidates, who were subsequently elected, called for his head. The last government and their work had been heavily criticised but none of the past politicians had to face up to their critics and work with them. The CE did.

I think you have to be a Councillor/MLA before you realise that for most committed members how totally consuming it is and how it affects friends and family.

Certainly on my first tour the criticism that I got hurt Toni to some degree, but occasionally the whole family was affected. When we were camping with family and friends down in Lafonia we approached North Arm to find a message nailed to the gate saying 'Stevens not welcome'. Of course, the children could read and they kept asking why we weren't welcome. I did my best to explain that it wasn't us it was really me, and the reasons for that but it wasn't pleasant.

In our situation Toni had to do more for me to be able to spend a considerable amount of time away from the farm. The period spent in Stanley had increased dramatically since my first four years in the 1990s. The management style on the farm had increased the workload at least ten fold with rotational grazing on the three different flocks each being moved once a week. One big cervical AI programme didn't fall on the right dates and although I was in the thick of it for the synchronising, was absent for the actual AI which included lifting 600 sheep out of the pens and onto the floor for the procedure. Luckily for us, Pauline Sackett, Iain Thom and Derek Goodwin came to help Toni. Compare this even to the 1990s when we rotated our young sheep between two camps, and some years we eye locked (clipped the wool from around the eyes of the sheep to enable them to see better), but apart from that we did very little with the stock.

A family crisis hit us in the last year of my last term which took Toni overseas for six months which made it increasingly difficult for me with me covering my Assembly duties including the UN, visiting the West and East Falklands to discuss the future of the hostel with interested parties, and running the farm, constantly moving sheep. My tongue was hanging out at times, but I did manage to cope.

We were indebted to our friends who stepped into the breach to support our needs like the AI programme and on one other occasion when our neighbour Ted, who came over to the house in the worst weather for about ten years, over the mountain, through a foot of snow on his quad, to make sure everything was all right because our house/farm sitters couldn't make it out from Stanley.

Today, with full-time politicians, it is hard to see a strong way forward for camp MLAs. The minute you are voted in from camp you basically become a townie, whereas living in town you just change jobs. I hope others can see the importance of politicians from outside Stanley and allow them to do their office hours at home. Obviously there will still be a commitment to work in town but to a lesser extent with camp MLAs still having a life in camp. I have always supported full time Members of Legislative Assembly to match the full-time administration, but it takes the recognition of all members to see the importance of maintaining this strong home link.